W9-BJV-385

Claiming the Heritage

Claiming the Heritage

AFRICAN-AMERICAN
WOMEN NOVELISTS AND HISTORY

by

Missy Dehn Kubitschek

University Press of Mississippi
Jackson & London

94 93 92 91   4 3 2 1

The paper in this book meets the guidelines for permanence and durability of the Committee on Production Guidelines for Book Longevity of the Council on Library Resources.

Portions of Chapters 1, 3, and 4 appeared earlier, in somewhat different form, as " 'Tuh de horizon and Back': The Female Quest in Hurston's *Their Eyes Were Watching God*," *Black American Literature Forum* 17 (1983): 18–22; and "Paule Marshall's Women on Quest," *Black American Literature Forum* 21 (1987): 41–60.

Excerpts from *Linden Hills* by Gloria Naylor. Copyright © 1985 by Gloria Naylor. Reprinted by permission of Houghton Mifflin Co.

Excerpts from *Their Eyes Were Watching God* by Zora Neale Hurston. Copyright © 1937 by Harper & Row, Publishers, Inc. Copyright renewed 1965 by John Hurston and Joel Hurston. Foreword copyright © 1978 by the Board of Trustees of the University of Illinois. Reprinted by permission of Harper & Row, Publishers, Inc.

From *Corregidora* by Gayl Jones. Copyright © 1975 by Gayl Jones. Reprinted by permission of Random House, Inc.

Excerpts from *Quicksand and Passing* by Nella Larsen, edited by Deborah E. McDowell. Copyright © 1986 by Rutgers, The State University, reprinted by permission of Rutgers University Press.

Excerpts from *Beloved* by Toni Morrison. Copyright © 1981 by Toni Morrison. Reprinted by permission of Toni Morrison.

Excerpts from *Tar Baby* by Toni Morrison. Copyright © 1987 by Toni Morrison. Reprinted by permission of Toni Morrison.

Excerpts from *Meridian* by Alice Walker. Copyright © 1977 by Alice Walker. Reprinted by permission of Harcourt, Brace, Jovanovich, Inc.

Excerpts from *Praisesong for the Widow* by Paule Marshall. Copyright © 1983 by Paule Marshall. Reprinted by permission of Putnam Publishing Group, Inc.

Library of Congress Cataloging-in-Publication Data

Kubitschek, Missy Dehn.
    Claiming the heritage : African-American women's novels and history / by Missy Dehn Kubitschek.
    p. cm.
    Includes bibliographical references and index.
    ISBN 0-87805-456-1. — ISBN 0-87805-475-8 (pbk.)
    1. American fiction—Afro-American authors—History and criticism.
    2. Women and literature—United States—History—20th century.
    3. American fiction—Women authors—History and criticism.
    4. American fiction—20th century—History and criticism.
    5. Historical fiction, American—History and criticism. 6. Afro-American women—Intellectual life. 7. Slavery and slaves in literature. 8. Afro-Americans in literature. 9. Family in literature. I. Title.
PS374.N4K83 1991
813'.54099287—dc20   90-44984
                                                                    CIP

British Library Cataloguing-in-Publication data available

Dedicated to my parents,
George Henry Dehn and Maxine Brenner Dehn,
who began my education,
and to the entire class of Black Studies/English 225,
University of Nebraska–Omaha, Spring 1986,
who continued it.

CONTENTS

A Personal Preface

We need to theorize whiteness. That's next. How would you start?
—feminist academic, 1989, Cornell University

From what critical stance do you write, and how do you interrogate it?
—MLA job interviewer, 1989

Well, so what would you call a woman, I-mean-a-person, who thinks, well, like you do?
—white male sophomore, Eastern New Mexico University, 1979

Where did you get your degree, what did you write your dissertation on, why did you choose this book, and how do you know anything about Afro-American culture?
—opening day of class sequence, University of Nebraska-Omaha, Spring 1986.

THE ACADEMY INQUIRES after abstractions; students ask about my personal history. The rapid-fire sequence above came from Black Studies/English 225 (a sophomore-level, non-major course in the black short story). The talk from that integrated class resounds in my memory. People were honest; we said awful things to one another and revealed awful things about ourselves, sometimes accidentally. Through all the anger and confusion, we kept talking. As a class, we never agreed on the interpretation of a single story. Nevertheless, we became a quarrelsome interpretive community savoring our disagreements and celebrating our discoveries, which inevitably involved race, class, gender, and desire.

One short example. The men in the class could not understand the plot action of Carl Ruthven Offord's "So Peaceful in the Country." In this story, a white male employer unwittingly frightens his black maid, who fears sexual assault. Because Offord doesn't specify the sexual fear, the men concluded that the woman "just went crazy." The women, on the other hand, couldn't believe that the men didn't understand. During our discussion, I emphasized, first, women's vulnerability to assault and, second, the privileged position that allows men to remain unaware. After class, a black male student from Chicago told me that I was wrong. He described the dangers in his neighborhood, the necessity for him to be continually aware of physical threat. He was right. My "men" statement had assumed "men of middle class" as well as the relative safety of men in the homogeneous environments of the rural area where I grew up. (You can take the girl out of the country. . . .) Our next discussion incorporated his insights. Like me, many of the men, including the objecting student, had increased their awareness of others' experiences. The women's anger and our concrete descriptions had made our positions more real. The exchange of our stories in response to the literary text had enriched all of us. And it renewed my belief in teaching.

Any participant in the revitalizing critique of the literary canon has a personal story of coming to her or his individual awareness; students in my black studies and women's studies classes demand to hear that story. And their interest in personal experience isn't quite accidental. As Patricia Hill Collins points out in "The Social Construction of Black Feminist Thought," African-American culture as a whole and women's culture share important beliefs about legitimate authority that emphasize personal experience. First citing the numerous betrayals that have created profound suspicion of traditional "objective" expertise, Collins then compares the epistemological vision of feminist scholarship such as Carol Gilligan's *In a Different Voice* and *Women's Ways of Knowing,* by Mary Belenky et al., with that of African-American culture:

> The convergence of Afrocentric and feminist values in the ethic-of-care dimension of an alternative epistemology seems particularly acute. While white women may have access to a women's tradition valuing emotion and expressiveness, few white social institutions except the family validate this way of knowing. In contrast, Black women have long had the support of the Black church. . . . While Black men share in this Afrocentric tradition, they must resolve the contradictions that distinguish abstract, unemotional, Western masculinity from an Afrocentric ethic of caring. The differences among race/gender groups thus hinge on differences in their access to institutional supports valuing one type of knowing over another. (768)

Collins indicates a convergence of values between three groups: white women, black women, and black men. Two of these groups—white women and black men—experience definite conflict from competing value systems, however, while black women receive some institutional support for this ethic of care. Collins implies not only that individuals' growth into an ethic is mediated by race and gender but that their experience while acting on these values continues to differ. Convergence of values does not equal identical experience—people come to these values by separate experiential paths, and they act on them in different ways.

Collins suggests that the special role of black academic feminists—and, I would argue, ideally of all feminists—rests on their continued contact with and respect for the "ordinary knowledge" of their communities, which the scholars rearticulate. Black feminists in Collins's scheme are not passive, exact "translators" of experience into language for the inarticulate. Rather, they are facilitators; for example, through quotations, nonacademic community members often speak for themselves in her article. As she observes, "The goal here is not one of integrating Black female 'folk culture' into the substantiated body of academic knowledge, for that substantiated knowledge is, in many ways, antithetical to the best interests of Black women. Rather, the process is one of rearticulating a preexisting Black women's standpoint and recentering the language of existing academic discourse to accommodate these knowledge claims" (772).

Recentering or de-centering what Collins identifies as the Eurocentric, masculinist academy requires the sustained voicing of widely divergent experiences. Dedicated to an impossible objectivity, this academy discounts personal experiences as subjective bias or sheer irrelevance. To reshape the academy, we must delve into even apparent agreements such as the ethic-of-care: repeatedly telling our different stories helps to guard against a new consensus that reinscribes the old obliteration of difference.

Collins's article is a pioneering effort to delineate, if not common ground, then agreement on what to call the land sometimes shared by women's culture and Afrocentric culture. It is difficult to believe that scholars in these fields can construct mutually enabling perspectives—something different from the early white feminist appropriation of African-American experience by cheap comparisons of sexism and slavery. I would not believe that it could happen if I hadn't seen an analogous process in a classroom. Distant and visionary as that view of the academy is, it would be an almost microscopic part of a truly pluralistic, democratic United States.

The vision of such a United States inspires John Callahan's fine critical book *In the African-American Grain*. His first chapter, "Who You For?" explores his experience as an Irish-American growing up in New Haven, Connecticut; he traces the development of his own voice, along with his concern for literary voices, in his social context. My admiration for "Who You For?" led me to consider voicing my own simultaneously social and psychic travels as a prelude to this study of African-American women's novels. Laryngitis followed immediately. Callahan's story is studded with public events, especially sports events: his urban, male experience seemed "more typical" to me, more useful than my own. The events that shaped me took place in the rural Midwest, in private domains—the beauty shop, the graduate student office. The feeling was no less powerful for my awareness of intellectual systems—feminism's pronouncement that "the personal is the political," the cultural materialists' work, much of African-American literature—that deconstruct my assumed dichotomy between public and private spheres.

Callahan grew up with the consciousness of being both an outsider to the WASP power structure and a member of an identifiable tribe. Growing up with some understanding of at least class structure and racism, I considered myself, as a middle-class white, to be part of the power structure. Not until graduate school did I wonder why, if I really belonged, I was always so troubled by feelings of isolation. Some of Callahan's insights grew from his Irish immigrant grandfather's stories. None of my grandparents told stories. I'll never know for sure, but maybe their collective silence was unconsciously designed to do what it did: it led me to consider myself a natural part of the power structure, not a weld. That mixed metaphor itself is telling. My grandparents unconsciously knew that institutions were constructed, not natural. The ideology of a classless America with a self-reliant meritocracy remained so strong, however, that they believed in that too. They knew my position represented a weld, but they wanted me to think of it as a natural outgrowth of our tribe's talent and work.

Lacking Callahan's ancestral voices, I was surprised to discover the origins of our tribe. I was about ten when my father mentioned for the first time that my maternal grandparents were Jewish, English Jews who in the face of American anti-Semitism had dropped their Jewish identities with their bags on arrival in Chicago during the teens. Gramps, named Isadore John Clarence Cecil Brenner, became a manageable and ethnically unidentifiable Jack Brenner. My grandmother Minnie, whom we called Nanny, converted to Christian Science. The only traces of cultural Judaism consisted of chopped liver pâté and a version of matzah-ball soup for such holidays as Christmas.

Working class in perspective and experience, Minnie and Jack had been trained in a Jewish orphanage in London, she as a boarder. Jack had learned carpentry; Minnie, sewing. She flatly refused to talk about her childhood. About the orphanage, she said only, "They taught you to work." Only when she became too senile to hide the truth did she reveal that her mother had been a rabbi's daughter on some unnamed shtetl in what is now the Soviet Union. To avoid marrying the older man whom her father had chosen for her, she had run away to London with her own choice. When my great-grandmother's story emerged, I was a Victorianist reading George Eliot's *Daniel Deronda*. Suddenly Deronda's mother's denunciation of Judaic patriarchy seemed less separable, considerably more integral to the novel. And my conception of my family had fundamentally changed: first, we had seemed English, then a homogeneous group of settled Anglo-Jews. Now we were a conglomeration of peripatetic scrabblers including an independent great-grandmother.

My paternal grandparents were almost equally silent on family origins. Their German heritage was evident in their surnames, Schneider for my grandmother, Dehn for my grandfather. Grandma spoke of her childhood and her siblings with obvious affection; all else was a blank. Grandpa rarely talked to us children except to issue orders, occasionally to tease. He was so stern and remote that I couldn't imagine that he had ever been a child. Again, my father revealed the history. Both his parents were raised in a tiny German-speaking community in rural Illinois. His father had not been fluent in English when it was time for school. I never heard my grandfather speak German or show any knowledge of it. He reacted to my school activities with interest and pleasure only once, and that was when I took German in college. Grandma said she just couldn't remember any German words.

I speculate that the humiliation of not knowing English in first grade was succeeded by the humiliation of knowing German during World War I when German-Americans' patriotism was suspect. My grandfather served in the armed services but was never sent overseas. With World War II, the American suspicion of Germanic evil became a certainty. On the home front, my grandfather sold war bonds; in Europe, my father was fighting in the U.S. Navy. My paternal grandparents simply shed their knowledge of things German just as the maternal side had buried the Jewish heritage, with shame.

After these Dehn grandparents died in their late eighties, I went through their house to choose keepsakes. It was a house totally devoid of history, almost of personal taste. Building it in 1953, they threw away all the old things and replaced them with brand new furnishings to testify to Grandpa's success as a banker. In this house that bore no imprint of ethnicity, one drawer held a very old, beautifully illustrated child's book—in German.

All of my grandparents were kind to me. Writing now, though, I am painfully aware that I didn't know them and now can never know them directly. Gramps never became a U.S. citizen. How did he feel when the Axis powers attacked Great Britain? How did the Brenners feel when anti-Semitism became more virulent in Europe, when the Holocaust occurred? What did their voices sound like before they edited their accents? By the time I knew them, neither Gramps nor Nanny had a discernible British accent, except for Nanny's "bahth" and the incorrigible "aluminium." Similar questions arise for my Dehn grandparents. When I was about twelve, they introduced us to a German card game, called either *politische* or *klepper,* which we played at every family gathering for the next fifteen years. What allowed that particular piece of heritage to emerge then? What did it mean to them to see their grandchildren enjoy it? To understand my grandparents, I must become like John

Washington in David Bradley's *The Chaneysville Incident*. A professional historian intent on discovering what happened to his father, Washington finds that the known facts are not sufficient to reconstruct an objectively authoritative story. Instead, he must respond to tribal voices in the wind to hear and construct a sustaining narrative of his ancestors. My grandparents' silence forbade questions: their silence, as they perceived it, for my speech. To keep faith, I must say on.

If my family's origins were somewhat unclear but ultimately unimportant, our current status was satisfactory. All my grandparents had eighth-grade educations. Grandpa Dehn parlayed his extraordinary business acumen into power, eventually becoming president of a bank in Effingham, a town of 10,000 within a few miles of our village, Shumway (population 150). Once married, his wife never worked outside of her home. My dad practiced law. My mother was the only one in her family able to stay home to rear children. We were middle class. The Brenners lived 200 miles away, in Chicago, and we visited on holidays; the Dehns lived three miles from us, and we shared Sunday dinner every week. Despite their working class status, the Brenners preserved one English institution, the char. For more than thirty years, once a week a black woman named Zilla Scott cleaned their apartment. My two sets of grandparents understood that, although their positions in the social structure were different, they could both rejoice in being white.

My parents disagreed. So did the times. In the sixties, in small-town central Illinois, there were almost no blacks. Framed by segregated Chicago 200 miles to the north and plantation Cairo to the south, whites in central Illinois had very little contact with racial minorities. Racial attitudes consisted largely of traditional, nearly hereditary stereotypes, unmodified by contact with real people. Self-described moderate Democrats, my parents seemed radical to me because of the conservative context.

My first attempt to exercise my own voice involved a racial issue. It was 1962. I was twelve and without my mother (Maxine) in that crucial locus of 1950s and 1960s womanhood, the beauty parlor. An adult customer suddenly began spewing racial hatred and epithets. I was startled that a grownup could think that way. News reports had told me that not everybody agreed with my parents, but I had thought that those people lived in the South. My parents' friends didn't say these things. I stammered out that the customer was wrong, her statements untrue. Without ever directly addressing me, she excoriated disrespectful children. Even more confusingly, one of the young beauticians mouthed to me silently, "I agree with you." The older woman's diatribe confused me. Maybe I had been completely out of line. On the way home, I asked my mother. When she cried, I knew I'd done something awful. Then she said a brave thing: that she probably wouldn't have spoken up, but it was all right that I had. She was crying, she said, because things would be hard for me if I had to talk. Many different kinds of silence muffled my heritages—were my heritages—but Maxine did not make women's silence my portion. The importance of my mother to the development of my voice prepared me to see the theme highlighted in many African-American women's novels. Conversely, feeling my mother's support so crucial, I noticed the mother's absence in many novels showing an isolated heroine unable to sustain herself.

This small-town context made me understand "politics" mostly as talk, not action. When one's village has no representatives of an oppressed group, when voicing an unpopular opinion causes bar fights, talk seems not just sufficient but brave. I knew that my father had been among the first to integrate his naval gun crew during World War II, but I didn't seem to have such opportunities. Questioning the frame, becoming aware that the absence itself is evidence of racism, demands a higher level of social consciousness than I had.

My awareness of gender and race developed very slowly, often stalling out. It's hard to give urban folks an adequate idea of the intellectual and social isolation of small-town America in the 1950s and 1960s. Shumway's very limited population turnover depended mostly on birth and death. Everybody knew everybody else, their parents, what their grandparents had done—and when. We were out of range of an FM radio station. The interstates didn't come through Effingham until after my consciousness was largely formed. My mother took me to the Art Institute in Chicago once, but I don't remember seeing an art book until, at fifteen, I visited the Illinois College bookstore. My elementary school had two grades in the same room, and not as part of any progressive scheme. There were fifteen in my grade, the baby boom, but only nine coming up behind us. By eighth grade, I was correcting my teachers' grammar in exam questions.

Smart girls in rural areas had two options. We could disguise our intelligence and hope for dates or choose intellectual development and forego social life. Without any conscious articulation, I opted for intellect though the resulting nickname, "Dehn the brain," wounded me with its appalling rhyme and synecdoche. Books offered escape from constant ridicule, and I read deeply, in what became a kind of mental community for me, the second-rate Victorian writers like Bulwer-Lytton available in local libraries. These people knew what was important, I felt; they would have valued me, if we'd only had the good luck to live in the same century and place. Rapidly I became the kind of intellectual snob that smart girls were presumed to be. When my essay attributed a heroic couplet to "A. Pope" and my teacher, knowing that I was being reared a Catholic, queried "Which one?" my arrogance and desperation increased. In my early twenties, I finally learned that intellect and education couldn't protect me from emotional catastrophes. Discovering that cheap novels accurately depicted my feelings was both a comedown and an awakening. I belonged in the world after all.

During high school, I'd decided that escape from Shumway would involve education. In a real school, smart girls would be popular. In 1966, Phillips Exeter Academy's summer school gave me a taste of acceptance. I didn't know that it was their first coed summer school, and the racial mix gave me an entirely false idea about the usual makeup of educational institutions. Living in a dormitory there provided my first prolonged contact with people who weren't white. A black girl from Pine Bluff, Arkansas, and I became friends. With the arrogance of white privilege, I didn't think about race at all; we just liked each other. At the end of the six-week session, we confronted leaving one another.

The difficulty of leavetaking was six parts racial relations to one part adolescent self-dramatization. I suggested visiting one another. No, her parents would not allow her to go to people they didn't know. But my parents would call hers. Then I remembered my grandparents' racism. Well, we just wouldn't visit them, I thought. Finally, with careful patience, she told me that her parents wouldn't let her come because they'd be worried about her safety. Suddenly I understood that the problem was Grandpa writ large, that his power extended beyond his house and that, indeed, he could not be trusted. Sadly, I recognized that my parents could not guarantee my friend's safety. I could visit her, though. It was her turn to be sad. Hesitatingly, with intensity, she said, "My brother. He hates white people." Valued to its close, the relationship ended with the summer. We didn't discuss corresponding. Belatedly aware of social disapproval, I didn't see how we could sustain the friendship. Where are you now, Karen Fawcett?

Carleton College offered community, but nothing in the institutional structure stimulated any awareness of race or gender. Looking back, I can't see how someone in school from 1968 to 1972 could have heard so little of the women's movement, for example, although my major department had only two women. Perhaps developing the retarded social aspects of my personality just took up all my time. Racial awareness receded. Contemplating black pride, I wondered aloud why blacks were proud of their color when I was not. My urban, white boyfriend stared in disbelief, then snapped, "You don't have to be. You're white. Everything around you is proud FOR you." Social structures simply didn't exist in my perspective. Because I didn't take any course specifically designated as American literature, it may be unfair to note that on graduation in 1972, I'd read only one book by a black writer. Ironically and predictably, it was *Invisible Man*.

Graduate school at the University of Illinois had institutionally much the same effect as Carleton, not much impact on my political consciousness. During those seven years, however, issues of gender and race became progressively more important to my development. First, my Grandmother Dehn changed her mind about race, an event that changed my mind about identity. As Grandpa's diminishing mental powers made him less a force, Grandma was thrown more on her own resources. Despite her isolation—she couldn't drive, lived several miles out in the country, wouldn't have a phone, and went into town only once a week to the beauty parlor and the grocery—Grandma was relatively well-informed through television. The night before one of my visits, she had seen a program on East St. Louis, which had a regional reputation for being a terrible place to live, one of the poorest, most dangerous urban black ghettos.

The program had explored the effects of poverty on black children. Grandma really liked children, enjoyed their spontaneity, even their devilment. Her voice quavering with tears and anger, she said to me, "You know, it's terrible hard to get away from the way you was raised. We were raised to think—well, all I know is that anything that makes children hungry is wrong. Anything." We'd never talked about race. She knew how my parents felt. Unlike my grandfather, she never made explicitly racist comments in front of the grandchildren. Nevertheless, I knew how she felt. I'd thought that there was no use talking about it. Her "impossible" change of heart exploded one of my premises, that some things never change.

Growing up in Shumway during the 1950s and 1960s had left me with a Victorian sense of the nature of identity. Sure, everybody knew that kids were malleable, but adults' identities rigidified fairly early. A certain number of crucial decisions, and your identity was fixed. Ask George Eliot. Grandma's change was seismic in its implications for her own character and for my idea of character. Process and development apparently went on far longer than I'd dreamed. This perception intensified my attraction to African-American culture, which uses process as a fundamental premise. Ernest Gaines's *The Autobiography of Miss Jane Pittman* shows the tribe's development through the individual heroine's development over a century. Paule Marshall's third novel, *Praisesong for the Widow*, also extends the process of female identity into old age; Grandma Dehn, meet Avatara Johnson. Much as I liked the archetypal figures in *The Autobiography* or *Praisesong*, realistic characters appealed to me more. Marshall's second novel, *The Chosen Place, the Timeless People*, details the struggle of the middle-aged Merle Kinbona with feelings of unworthiness and frustration. At what point I began to link my own such feelings with social forces as well as inexplicable personal failures, I can't say.

As compared to my racial awareness, my feminist consciousness developed less through separable, dramatic incidents than through slow accretion of experience. My neurotic legacy of isolation, a treasured sense of uniqueness in every aspect, had to wear away before feminist analysis made sense. Still, a few incidents resonate. I remember my surprise at receiving a small fellowship that I nearly hadn't applied for. Then I found out that the competition had been somewhat reduced; not one of my equally qualified women friends had applied. All gave the same responses that had nearly derailed me: "I'm so bad about deadlines"; "I haven't been a research assistant"; the whole litany of personal responsibility and failure. Hearing my own self-doubts voiced by others made the abstractions of feminist analysis suddenly real and relevant. I hungered to know more about other women's experiences. Certainly most of what I could read wouldn't give me realistic details identical to my own, but differences might give me insight into others, and analogies would help me reflect on myself.

In some ways the sexist biases of the academy were on display—only three women professors in a large department, few courses on women's writing, no female research assistants. Identifying the pervasiveness of sexism in the academy, however, has taken the better part of two decades. Certainly no single graduate student could have articulated the enormity of the problem facing us as female academics. In 1978, my last year in graduate school, an experience on a committee brought home the extent of the academy's prohibition of any emotion except anger. An internationally famous scholar of premodern English literature, now dead, was inveighing against the cheapening of the Ph.D. To make his point, he challenged the male graduate student next to him to define a bibliographical term. A modernist and film specialist, the student could have replied with a whole list of terms that the eminent professor wouldn't have known. Instead, he quietly admitted ignorance. Roughly jostling his shoulder, the professor triumphed, "See there, you're getting your degree next month—and you shouldn't be!" In 1978, most graduating Ph.D.s weren't getting jobs. To the financial and psychic difficulties attendant on unemployment, the professor had just added contempt and an accusation of intellectual fraud. My colleague flinched, then assumed the mask of indifference. Through tears, I objected. The committee reaction, in itself hilarious, is part of the tragedy of American education. "Gee," said one, "it's very warm in here. We should open a window." We were in an interior room whose windows opened on a hallway. "The grad student lounge used to have coffee, didn't it? I'll go get some coffee." Afterwards the woman professor chairing the meeting explained to me that I would just have to toughen up. My reading told me something different. Increasingly, my casual reading had focused on black literature. In addition to the demand for social justice (which was what I liked about the novels in my own field, English Victorian fiction), I found there the respect for emotion and individuality that the academic context lacked.

Then, unexpectedly, I found my own face. The English building was old, continually in the throes of one or another remodeling. The latest round had consigned me to the only usable basement room, its long hallway dimly lit by a single bare bulb. Arriving before seven one morning, I left the door ajar behind me. It was too early for anyone to be in the office; as far as I knew, no one else was in the building yet. The man's voice behind me scared me badly, too badly for me to hear what he had said. Whirling in terror, I saw a black man. Reacting very quickly to what flashed across my face, he took a step backwards, away from me, and repeated quietly, "Could I use the phone, Ma'am?" He was a construction worker, a little bit early for his job this morning, just as I was. He carried the same tools that my Grandfather Brenner, the carpenter, had carried. His question shamed me profoundly. Of course, I had been afraid before I had seen that he was black. Rape is always a threat to women, always a possibility. It was rumored that a woman professor had been raped in a bathroom during a school holiday. Seeing him had increased my fear, and my face had shown him my racism. I had read Wright's "Big Boy Leaves Home" recently for the first time. I knew what my reaction had meant historically, saw in his face part of its meaning now, and felt in my shame what it meant to me. "Race" ceased to be something that had constructed other people, especially blacks. I began to comprehend myself as a racial being as well as a gendered being.

Reading African-American literature offered many joyous experiences too. The passionate claims for, and defense of, the individual in this tradition's novels moved me in the same way that Victorian novels like *Bleak House* did, but more powerfully. Dickens had wide social sympathies, but his limited view of women intruded. Eliot articulated the problems of great-souled women but offered no strategies other than submission. Certainly other traditions share with African-American literature a high valuation of the individual, but in some ways its contextual meaning there is unique. English romanticism, for example, held no attraction for me, its poets only tangentially attached to anything human. Small-town life had given me all the Byronic alienation that I cared for. African-American fiction, on the other hand, offered a vision of a valuable self inextricably connected to a cohesive community.

Reading African-American literature probably contributed substantially to the crux of my dissertation on Victorian women writers' presentations of duties to self and society; in my presentation, the romantic idea of self and society as opposing forces gave way to a Victorian view of them as mutually creative. In a minor way, the influence of African-American literature on a dissertation about canonical Victorian women writers illustrates Patricia Hill Collins's point about the overlap between Afrocentric and women's cultures. At any rate, I began to read and kept reading African-American literature because it gave me what I needed and hadn't found elsewhere. That's why I read it now too.

Reading in women's studies and in African-American criticism has over the years increased my awareness of the extent to which I am controlled and constructed by the many "isms" of class, gender, race, sexuality, and state. My privileged position in most of these allowed me to remain unaware of their shaping functions for years. Only my disadvantaged gender position spurred me to more than sporadic, abstract consideration of the others. From African-American literature, as from other literature, I often learn about experience that I can't have. In addition, I learn more about what it means to be white in the United States. Primarily, though, African-American literature speaks to me and for me of silenced experience. It articulates and confirms my sense of the persistence of injustice while also offering strategies for survival and development. From African-American literature I learned that versions of a silenced heritage can be, must be, reconstructed: if specific facts are unrecoverable, flexible interpretations will nevertheless arise. After awhile, the loss of history becomes a part of tribal history, its void acknowledged and held open by collective psychic brackets—if the story is told and retold. Talk may not be the whole of politics in the way I understood it at twelve, but if the literature is right, talk is political, and it can have political effects. The version of America that relies on the suppression of ethnic and racial difference is no one's story;

the creation of America requires many versions of real individuals' stories. To an emotional absolutist trained as a Victorianist, saying "yes" while saying "no" hasn't come easily. The stories that constitute African-American literature say that oppression kills and that people survive oppression. Wanting to know more about survival brought me here.

Acknowledgements

GIVING ALL THE THANKS owed would make a document almost as long as this study. At least these: for their encouragement and sensitive suggestions, Barbara Christian and Keith Byerman; for a crucial fellowship, thanks to Cornell University's Society for the Humanities; and to my husband Craig Kubitschek, for necessary support, including the willingness to move twice to keep me teaching and to live apart for the fellowship year. Almost all my friends contributed through refining discussion and emotional support, particularly Yvonne Brooks Grant and Molly Hite. To Judy Boss, I owe many first acquaintances with writers, including Octavia Butler. To the friends who read drafts—Debra Fried, Margaret Moore Willen, Diane Gillespie, Joan Gibson, and Alan Goodman—I am grateful for critical encouragement. Robin McCollum, the friend of my youth, wins the grace-under-pressure interlibrary loan award. For help with the ghastly grunt work as well as friendship, sincere appreciation to Dawn Downs Birge. Many students have given me continued support more important than they know. From this group, I must name a few to represent many more—Sherley Gonzales, Ed Tucker, Shari Taylor, Mari Campbell, and Connie Eberhart. And for years of discussion, as well as hours of editing, many thanks to Craig Werner.

Claiming the Heritage

I

"MY MOTHER TALKING"
Ancestral Voices and the Quest for Identity

IN THE UNPRECEDENTED CELEBRATION of black, specifically female
heritage in the late 1970s and 1980s, African-American women
writers have explored their matrilineal roots, delving deep into the
strength found there. Mary Helen Washington's article exploring
black women novelists' feelings about their real-life mothers quotes
Dorothy West's memory of her first entry into what might have
been the intimidatingly male Harlem Renaissance society: "And I
went in and began to tell them that story, making fun of those
proper people *just as my mother would. All my mother's blood came out
in me. I was my mother talking.* All of the things I thought I admired
and there I was making fun of them. *I became me*" (151, emphasis in
original). Interestingly, West feels that she is simultaneously her
mother and her self—the presence of the female ancestor allows
self-assertion, which creates and affirms the self.

Washington's article is entitled "I Sign My Mother's Name," a
literal description of Pauline Hopkins's strategem for disguising the

extent of her contributions to *Colored American Magazine*, 1900–1903 (Carby 127). In somewhat the same vein, Jamaica Kincaid links her creativity and her mother's voice: "My second book, *Annie John*, is about a girl's relationship with her mother because the fertile soil of my creative life is my mother. When I write, in some things I used my mother's voice, because I like my mother's voice" (Cudjoe 402). The difficulties of competition and separation which frequently characterize Euro-American discussion of the mother-daughter relationship are less frequent here. (West's presentation of the mother figure in *The Living is Easy* suggests, however, that she and other writers as well have complex and sometimes difficult relationships with their mothers. This exposition of mothers' central importance to the tradition does not argue that mothers are presented as unqualifiedly nurturant.) Washington has pointed out that, whereas Euro-American women authors have found their literary foremothers riddled with psychic contradictions about their right to assert themselves by writing (Gilbert and Gubar), African-American women have found their heritage, if no less problematic overall, at least more empowering to the contemporary artist.

Of the many underlying reasons for the divergence between the Euro- and African-American women's traditions, two intertwined historical causes stand out. Part of the difference in black and white women's legacies is no doubt related to the different stereotypes of their proper roles: submissiveness was demanded of all women, but black women were forced to participate in the labor from which white women of the middle class (the class that produced most white women writers) were excluded. Their capacities to create and accomplish were thus never subject to question in quite the same way as white women's, though of course the opportunity to choose work meaningful to the self remained elusive. In addition, whereas Euro-American women have until quite recently looked almost exclusively to the printed word to justify their literary endeavors, African-American women have embraced their mothers' and grandmothers' participation in oral literature.

Paule Marshall has spoken and written, for example, about the lasting influence of listening to her mothers' friends, the "kitchen table poets," informally interpret their world and their experiences in everyday conversations. Similarly, in "In Search of Our Mother's

Gardens," Alice Walker has established connections between her works and the creative accomplishments of earlier women kept by circumstance from producing art as it is traditionally understood in the academy. By abandoning the overly narrow Euro-American definitions of art, African-American women have claimed and begun to explore their historical participation in artistic creation.

This sense of empowerment applies specifically to African-American female artists and more broadly to African-American women as a whole. Erlene Stetson speaks movingly about the rediscovery through black women's studies of female forebears: "They empower me to speak. I am no longer content to feel sheer bafflement and frustration when I think that I have suffered or that I am oppressed. It is precisely that Black women's history—from servitude and slavery to freedom—tells me how to live, how to survive, and how to be" (238). The sense of concrete lessons to be learned from the past permeates the writing about matrilineal heritage.

As Washington asserts in "I Sign My Mother's Name," "The long chain of presences that inhabit the literature of black women does not convey inferiority, or submissive femininity, or intellectual powerlessness: What these mothers passed on would take you anywhere in the world you wanted to go" (161). At times the joy of recognition dominates the discussion of foremothers: "Denied the knowledge of their existence so long, I feel that my finding them is like the celebratory occasion of a company of women and their coming together, across centuries, as a family: Phillis Wheatley meet Ella Baker" (Stetson 248). The examination of one's heritage can never remain an unalloyed celebration, of course. The desire to find empowering role models coexists with the knowledge that to concentrate exclusively on them is to overlook and thus devalue the more ordinary woman's experience. One wants to see one's own experience, or perhaps an idealized version of it, while at the same time wanting historical truth. Thus, Gloria Wade-Gayles describes, in "The Truths of Our Mothers' Lives," the ambivalences of African-American women readers:

> Those of us who search in Black women's fiction for mother-daughter relationships are often disappointed by the recurring image of the cold, distant and domineering mother. We want to see mothers

embracing their daughters—loving them openly and unashamedly. We want to see mothers and daughters sharing laughter and bearing their souls to each other in moments of intimacy. And yet, we want the truths of our mothers' lives, even if those truths are sometimes "cruel enough to stop the blood." We must see them first as persons with dreams and needs no less important than ours, and then as mothers who sacrificed their dreams in order to put our hands on the pulse of freedom and self-hood. We dare today to search for sisterhood because our mothers, our "sister warrior(s)" taught us the beauty of struggle. (12)

Stetson reiterates this pain in describing her historical research: "For me, and I suspect for many other Black women researchers, the slavery period is personally the most painful and difficult to explore. The omissions, the neglect, and the deliberate distortions found in Black history in general are repeated a thousandfold in slave women's history. Moreover, this period reminds us of our traumas, insecurities, and wounds that never make sense and are difficult to convey" (244). Nevertheless, both Wade-Gayles and Stetson affirm the need to recognize the past's creation of both the personal and the social present.

This interest in real-life female forebears has an analogous fictional exploration that is clearest, perhaps, in contemporary novels set in the nineteenth century, slave narratives like Sherley Anne Williams's *Dessa Rose* or Toni Morrison's masterpiece of Reconstruction, *Beloved,* both of which chronicle intensely painful pasts. That same past, however, offers also female models of strength and commitment and sometimes of joy. Rediscovery of this past invigorates heroines of novels such as Paule Marshall's *Praisesong for the Widow*. With black women's history as with white, as with all women's history, these two parts cannot be separated; the legacy of empowerment cannot be severed from the legacy of victimization and enjoyed as the whole truth, hence the paradoxes of historical exploration and the ambivalences of women readers grieving for and praising their foremothers and themselves.

Barbara Christian's *Black Women Novelists* performed in the critical realm the same function that Alice Walker's and Paule Marshall's reminiscences did for autobiography and the spate of historically concerned novels did for fiction; it brought the connected heritage

of African-American women writers into sharp focus for the academy. Her exploration of lineage and heritage demanded the chronological approach that *Black Women Novelists* develops, and Christian's survey of the historical progression of themes in African-
American women's fiction established beyond question the existence
of a rich tradition. Interestingly, Christian has recently singled out
the theme of motherhood as one of the important focuses in the
work of Opal Adisa, an Afro-Caribbean writer. Chronology's almost
necessary focus on distinct stages and therefore definitive shifts,
however, can obscure certain kinds of continuities. Robert B. Stepto
has proposed two different kinds of journeys, for example, as
unifying motifs of Afro-American literature, and Susan Willis identifies "the single most common feature in fiction by black women
writers: that of return to community" (116). This book proposes
another continuity in the works of African-American women fictionists: coming to terms with the history of slavery and oppression as
the fundamental necessity for the construction of a tenable black
female identity.

The tradition of the African-American woman's novel consistently
asserts the necessity of recognizing—knowing both intellectually
and emotionally—the history of blacks in order to become and
remain a fully functional African-American woman. The fifty-two
years between the publication of Nella Larsen's Harlem Renaissance
novels and Toni Morrison's *Tar Baby* have seen substantial changes
in almost every area of social and personal concern, yet the barriers
to these African-American heroines' achievement of a satisfying
identity remain remarkably constant. Jadine, the deracinated heroine
of Morrison's novel, cannot pass for white as can Nella Larsen's
Clare Kendry of *Passing,* but her life is reminiscent of another of
Larsen's heroines, Helga Crane, who in *Quicksand* has the opportunity to stay in Denmark as a beautiful exotic, the ultimate objectified
Other. Larsen and Morrison depict remarkably similar temptations
and psychic pitfalls for women physically or psychically separated
from their families' and larger communities' histories. In analogous
fashion, characters better grounded in historical experience—Zora
Neale Hurston's Janie, Paule Marshall's Avatara Johnson, Gayl
Jones's Ursa—share the pains and joys of developing an increasingly

sharp definition of self, the individual's place in the community, and the community's place in history.

This sense of the past's persistence in the present is, of course, one of the strongest survivals of African cultures in African-American culture (Genovese 247–48), not only in the Western, figurative sense of past events' having set the stage for current happenings but in the much more immediate and literal sense of ancestral spirits visiting those now inhabiting the earth. This multitextured reality, then, informs the writers' and the audience's expectations. When a work fails to reproduce that texture, a novelist like Alice Walker revises; speaking of her first draft of *The Third Life of Grange Copeland*, she observes, "There was lots of love-making and courage in that version. But it was too recent, too superficial—everything seemed a product of the immediate present. And I believe nothing ever is" (Ensslen 197).

Walker's remark testifies to a sense of continuous process essential to black culture, a process that demands a very different kind of art from that of traditional Euro-America and hence a different reader and a different critic. In a pithy statement, Morrison sums up the distinctions in all three areas: "I think about what black writers do as having a quality of hunger and disturbance that never ends. Classical music satisfies and closes. Black music does not do that. Jazz always keeps you on edge. There is no final chord. There may be a long chord, but no final chord" (McKay 429). These tendencies go by various names depending upon the interests of the speakers, but "call-and-response aesthetics" seems to be gaining ascendancy. In these terms, *Claiming the Heritage* represents the Afro-American experience from 1600 forward as a great call to which nearly all African-American female novelists of the twentieth century respond.

The range of response to this ubiquitous concern is enormous. Some heroines destroy themselves in a quest for an ahistorical identity; others survive to acquire complex individual/social identities; yet others remain in process as they disappear from view. As the tradition develops, the writers deal simultaneously with their heroines' identities and their own identities as artists. Here also specific writers' strategies and figurations differ dramatically. Jessie Fauset, for example, depicts a graphic artist; Gayl Jones, a blues singer; Octavia Butler, a writer; Toni Morrison, an artist manqué, sans form. In defining their individual selves, which are also simultaneously selves-in-community, the writers use many different tropes for expressing female creativity, its forms, uses, and various fates. *Claiming the Heritage* seeks to document a recurrent theme, the interplay of history and developing female identities, enlivened by individual improvisation. The diversity of African-American women writers' responses to the call of tribal historical experience and to each other's works creates another long black song, lovelier than any that America has yet heard.

The tradition of twentieth-century African-American women's novels is obviously too big, too rich to be contained in any single study. While *Claiming the Heritage* argues that many works present female identity and historical tribal experience as inextricably linked, it does not consider that theme as defining the Afro-American women's tradition in this century, or its canon. Ann Petry's *The Street*, for instance, is not explicitly concerned with history but with the racist, patriarchal capitalism that controls Lutie Johnson's present. The wider historic dimensions of such an economic system later became the subject of a novel, Paule Marshall's *The Chosen Place, the Timeless People*, but Petry was under no obligation to highlight history. Perhaps Marshall could do so only after Petry had documented the grinding present.

Not only do some novels stand outside the thematic range, but this short study cannot include all those that do explore history and female identity. In general, I have chosen major works, centered on female characters, by major fictionists who have written more than one novel. (Thus, Toni Cade Bambara's *The Salt Eaters* does not appear, even though, as Gloria Hull's thorough explication demonstrates, its theme is pertinent.) I have also chosen to include lesser-known works such as Gayl Jones's *Corregidora* and Octavia Butler's *Kindred* rather than, for example, Toni Morrison's *The Bluest Eye* or *Sula*, in those cases in which critical commentary has already extensively examined the interplay between individual and community in a particular book. This study deals with the novels as part of a self-conscious tradition, unified in part by considerable attention to the theme of historically influenced female identities.

Claiming the Heritage explores novels that posit the fundamental necessity of knowing and coming to terms with tribal history to construct tenable black female identities. This theme appears in dual form: first, the characters' relationships to the history of blacks in the new world and, second, the authors' relationships to literary traditions. On the literal level, African-American women's works consistently assert the necessity of intellectually and emotionally understanding tribal historical experience to become and remain a fully functional black woman. On the meta-level, they document the linked strategies of persistence by which African-American women writers have communicated, written, and published.

Critical paradigms to explore the salient features of this tradition are still in the process of forming. The development of identity, particularly in relationship to community, has frequently been described through quest patterns. These critical models mirror the times that produced them, of course, and their sequence shows the academy's progression from universalist views of literature to understandings that highlight racial and gender inflections. Literary criticism has not yet produced a generalized model of the quest as constructed simultaneously by race, gender, class, and desire. A simple sketch of three paradigms—the first universalist, the second focused on race, and the third devoted to gender—and an examination of their applications to one African-American woman novelist's oeuvre will demonstrate the inherent limitations of current models to explicate this tradition.

Following Lord Raglan's *The Hero,* Joseph Campbell proposed, in *The Hero with a Thousand Faces* (1949), a monomyth to describe cross-cultural similarities in narratives of questing heroes. His schema begins with the call to adventure, the event that notifies the hero of an opportunity to defend or heal the community by journeying. A hero who accepts the challenge then crosses the threshold from the old life to the quest. In subsequent adventures, the hero frequently meets a supernatural helper with wise advice or useful tools and protection. Many of these adventures are trials or ordeals to measure the worth of the hero. If he proves himself deserving, he wins the boon for his community. With it, he returns to heal the community. This return is often problematic, for outward adventures have their inward counterpart: the hero returns, changed, to the unchanged community; some narratives show successful reintegration, others alienation. Campbell emphasizes the flexibility of this pattern, parts of which may be truncated or even absent to allow greater development of others.

Campbell's last chapter, "The Hero Today," recognizes the impossibility of a modern quest's conforming to the earlier pattern that had been set when societies were more homogenous religious units, when the hero's importance lay not in his individuality but in his role as cultural representative. The academy's recent explorations of literature centered on minorities points up the limitation. Because neither racial minorities nor women of any race have historically been allowed the role of cultural representative in European-dominated cultures, their quests must take divergent paths. For example, other than science fiction—that is, within the naturalistic mode—novels about women's quests tend to concentrate on the response to the call to adventure, that part of the quest that women's historical social conditioning has made most problematic.

Important revisions of Campbell's schema have thus come from critics considering African-American works and women's works. The issue of literacy, both in the literal sense of reading and writing, and in the symbolic sense of understanding and being able to manipulate the signs of a culture, has long been recognized as crucial to Afro-American literature. In perhaps the best-known critical exposition of literacy's interplay with identity, Robert B. Stepto's *From Behind the Veil* sets out two crucial patterns in African-American narrative: first, a journey of ascent from a symbolic South of slavery, through the means of literacy in the dominant white culture, to a symbolic North of freedom in which the sojourner lives as an articulate but isolated survivor; and, second, a journey of immersion in which the protagonist tolerates restrictive social conditions to become tribally literate and recover a sense of community, thus becoming an articulate kinsman (167). Critics considering Stepto's paradigm have questioned its breadth, asking whether its very premises of travel do not exclude many narratives by women (Awkward, " 'The inaudible voice of it all,' " 94). Without granting it universality, however, one may say that it identifies a significant pattern.

Focusing on women's works about women characters, Carol Christ proposes a four-step pattern that is less linear and more cyclical. First, the female quester experiences social and spiritual emptiness, from which the second event, the experience of connection with natural or mystical sources of energy, rescues her. That experience leads to an awakening, after which the heroine names her self anew as a part of her re-vision of the world. Her spiritual journey complete, she must then attempt the social quest to find a place for this new self.

To some extent, this sequence of critical paradigms reflects the academy's limited understandings of difference. Works have been placed in the African-American tradition (gender unconsidered, assumed male) or in the women's tradition (race unconsidered, assumed white). The male orientation of a work like Elizabeth Schultz's "The Insistence Upon Community in the Contemporary Afro-American Novel" (see O'Neale) or of Stepto's paradigm (Awkward) have been noted. Likewise, those familiar with African-American literature have noticed the Euro-American orientation of early feminist works such as Annis Pratt's *Archetypal Patterns in Women's Fiction*. Early formulations seem to overgeneralize. Sondra O'Neale's useful examination of the *Bildungsroman* by African-American women novelists develops seven descriptive criteria, only a few of which apply, for example, to any of Paule Marshall's novels (the last of which was published after O'Neale's article). Now, as race, gender, and class (and, increasingly, desire) are understood as simultaneous constituents of authors' identities and texts' meanings, reexamination of many texts reveals a complexity not yet described in critical paradigms.

Deborah McDowell is probably right to suggest that it is too soon to look for overarching unities in the contemporary parts of a tradition developing so rapidly. The first literary history of this tradition, Barbara Christian's *Black Women Novelists*, posited a clear divergence between the subject matters and approaches of early twentieth-century Afro-American women's novels and those of Alice Walker, Marshall, and Morrison. Because the earlier novelists refuted racist stereotypes of black women, contemporary novelists have been freed to explore the full emotional, sexual, and intellectual aspects of black women's experiences. This division seems valid but not wholly definitive. Without accepting even the idea of a black women's tradition of the novel, Hazel Carby interrogates the figure of the tragic mulatta (which Christian identifies as a concession to an overwhelmingly white audience) to discover African-American women novelists' subversive assertion of the miscegenation that white racism insisted on denying. Christian's distinction thus still holds, but its meaning has shifted or possibly become multiple. In somewhat the same way, this study suggests the existence of a strong continuity throughout many, not all, of the apparently diverse novels by African-American women in the twentieth century in their focus on history's importance to the formation of African-American female identity.

The whole nature of African-American female identity in these texts diverges sharply from that assumed in quest models largely dependent on European texts; this shift in the understanding of identity generates a different understanding of isolation in the quest process. Seen against the backdrop of the theme of history, the critical models of quests reveal a fundamental similarity of premise that makes them, while perhaps applicable, not sufficiently descriptive of African-American women's novels. Campbell's model sends the hero out from the community into the unknown, where he may occasionally meet supernatural guides but essentially travels alone. Christ's quester also leaves society, but, as her title *Diving Deep and Surfacing* suggests, her journey is internal and psychic rather than external and geographic. These patterns share with Stepto's journey of ascent the assumption that the quester is an autonomous self, fundamentally isolated from context. Hence the difficult necessity of reintegrating a fundamentally different self, or different concept of the self, into the surrounding society. Richard Chase, in his *The American Novel and Its Tradition,* identified the failure to reintegrate, imaged as the hero's rejection of a corrupt society, as a defining characteristic of American fiction. Isolation, set up as a crucial part of the hero's adventure and a necessity for development, functions differently in most African-American women's novels. The attempt of the tragic mulattas of Christian's schema to live without community, without historical context—sometimes a chosen, sometimes a forced decision—in large measure accounts for their tragedies; in general, female questers do not survive isolation, either of Christ's spiritual sojourners or, ironically, of Stepto's "articulate survivors."

Most of the women's novels that portray successful African-American female quests, on the other hand, accent connection and community. The quester experiences not the intermittent encounters with Campbell's supernatural guides but constant, complex interactions with a sometimes helpful, sometimes hindering context. (Stepto's journey of immersion, which begins in psychic isolation and ends in both physical and emotional community, emphasizes the constraints of community as well as its supportive aspects.) Changes wrought in the individual must take place within that individual, but the individual is always situated within a wider, constructing context.

Such a delineation reiterates elements noted in both African-American and women's cultures. Michel Sobel's *Trabelin' On: Journey to an Afro-Baptist Faith,* for example, indicates the importance of the African individual's connection to the past along with his/her simultaneous self-definition regarding contemporary community. Even with these connections, however, the individual remained responsible for establishing connections with Spirit. To experience Spirit in early Baptist churches, to find a spiritual identity, African-Americans participated in group rituals to facilitate each individual's achievement of the necessary ecstasy. The Anglican church, on the other hand, had comparatively little appeal for African-Americans because it accented isolated individual acceptance of dogma rather than active experience within a community of believers. The novelists' insistence on sustaining context sounds themes of growing prominence in revisionist, women-centered psychology.

Dealing with real women rather than literary characters, Carol Gilligan's *In a Different Voice* has claimed that women's moral decisions reflect exactly this abandonment of the abstract ethic or law in favor of negotiating concrete consequences in specific situations. Recent commentary has remarked on the similarity between Afro-centric and women's cultures. Patricia Hill Collins's "The Social Construction of Black Feminist Thought" identifies overlapping epistemologies and definitions of identity. The central task of contemporary critics may well be to honor and preserve the traditions' differences while delineating their rich potential unity.

Because they tend to underestimate the significance of difference, both traditional quest structures (Campbell) and revisionist structures (Stepto and Christ) illuminate certain aspects of this group of African-American women's novels well, but not fully. These patterns were all, of course, suggested as descriptive rather than prescriptive models; the extended following discussion of the novels of a single African-American woman writer, Paule Marshall, may demonstrate the limitations of both universalist, monomythic approaches and those that deal separately with race and gender.

Marshall's three novels—*Brown Girl, Brownstones* (1959); *The Chosen Place, the Timeless People* (1969); and *Praisesong for the Widow* (1983)—deal with the female protagonists' quests for identity in different epochs of their lives. Marshall's works both reinforce and critique Campbell's universalist schema, Stepto's racially specific theory of immersion, and the gender-specific paradigm of Christ: various parts of these complex novels conform to each of the suggested structures, but their meanings are modified by their simultaneous participation in the other paradigms; in addition, Marshall highlights age, continual process, female mentoring and its relationship to empowerment, and subsequent articulation as significant elements of her women's quests.

All three novels depict the necessity of confronting personal and social history to complete quests for personal identities. The conditions of the quest and its requirements change dramatically from novel to novel. *Brown Girl* covers six years of Selina Boyce's adolescence; *The Chosen Place*, a year of Merle Kinbona's middle age; *Praisesong*, several days in Avatara Johnson's sixty-fourth year. The forces that motivate and affect the questers naturally differ because of their ages. A typical adolescent, Selina must discover both her identity and her community. Merle has no doubts about her community, her experiences in England having confirmed her commitment to Bournehills, but she must reconcile the paradoxes of that community and heritage into a unified self. The most alienated of the three, Avey must discard both a false self and a false definition of community to rediscover her true identity.

Deborah Schneider locates the reasons for these changes in the climate of the times during which the novels were written. *Brown Girl* reflects its 1950s origin through its accent on art and individualism, Selina's distaste for community action, and her unconsciousness of the effect of sex roles on her parents' lives; *The Chosen Place* is grounded in the political activism and community focus of the 1960s (69). The changing times undoubtedly affected Marshall's artistic concerns, but another reason for the shift may be as important, particularly with *Praisesong* as an additional piece of evidence: the questers' radically different ages. Taken as a whole, Marshall's work reconstructs Campbell's linear quest into something more like Christ's cycles; no longer an isolated if lengthy or crucial incident in the quester's life, the quest is a life-long commitment. In the first two novels, the quest demands a continuous modification of individual identity.

The key experiences and significant influences differ for each quester, not simply because of their unique temperaments, but because their past experiences vary so widely. The adolescent Selina's parents figure prominently in her development, but Avey remembers hers only intermittently. In order to become an adult, Selina must battle with and become reconciled to her mother; Avey, on the other hand, contends with the apparition of her dead husband. Because at eighteen she has had time for only a few independent actions, Selina can focus on a single past deed (her intended fleecing of the Association); the novel focuses on her potential. Merle and Avatara must accept many years of painful, self-betraying or self-evading actions.

Though each quester seeks a place within a community rather than a privately defined role, each must journey outward from that community. Both *Brown Girl* and *The Chosen Place* end with the beginnings of that journey, Selina embarking for the Caribbean and Merle setting off for Kampala, but *Praisesong* details Avey's travels. Avatara's age precludes the open-endedness of the first two novels; she must immediately act on rediscovered integrity to contribute to her society. As a result, *Praisesong*'s ending shows her on the journey home. The sense of identity also changes from novel to novel: Merle and Selina have to create substantial parts of their new identities, but Avatara, in claiming her whole and original name rather than the diminutive Avey, essentially rediscovers hers. The more static nature of identity in *Praisesong* accords with the whole texture of the novel, which recalls Campbell's statement that the classical quester undertakes the journey to renew his society rather than to find himself.

In discussing the relationship between political responsibility and self-acceptance, Marshall makes a signal contribution to the modern quest. In both *Brown Girl,* and *The Chosen Place,* political commitment precedes the solidification of the quester's individual personality. When Selina casts one of her two silver bracelets into the graveyard of her neighborhood and keeps the other on her wrist, her action, like the exchange of wedding rings, testifies to her political commitment. Likewise, Merle supports "the little fella" of Bournehills in the midst of her personal fragmentation. These characters show an alternative to the tradition of *Invisible Man,* in which the invisible man remains in hibernation until he has assimilated his experience and is ready to emerge as a unified (and therefore less vulnerable) personality. To some extent, this variation may be characteristic of gender, women traditionally having had the responsibilities for nurturing, which cannot be postponed. *Brown Girl* and *The Chosen Place* recognize that, because society and the individual are mutually constructive, the unification of self cannot take precedence over political commitment to change; if personal identity is privileged, the warped culture will continually subvert the individual's gropings toward internal coherence, and the individual will never move into the second phase, commitment.

As they struggle toward the definition of community necessary to meaningful commitment, Marshall's characters become aware of overarching similarities between themselves and those from separate cultures. These unities expand in both space (outward from the individual through family and wider community to culture) and time (backwards from the individual through historical generations to the mythic past). Often these different types of unities are expressed in terms of one another, so that felt connections between family members expand to express a spiritual nexus with past generations or mythic heroes.

For Marshall, these unities constitute an inescapable context. She insists, for instance, on family resemblances in *Brown Girl* and *Praisesong.* Selina's mother, Silla, notes a similarity between her own mother and her exasperating daughter: "Yuh's just like my mother. A woman that did think the world put here for she" (*Brown Girl* 102); Selina comes to a full awareness of herself when she can admit that she resembles her mother, Silla, more than her father, Deighton: "Everybody used to call me Deighton's Selina but they were wrong. Because you see I'm truly your child. Remember how you used to talk about how you left home and came here a girl of eighteen and was your own woman? I used to love hearing that" (307). In *Praisesong*, such correspondences characterize secondary as well as primary characters, not only Avey and her great-aunt Cuney, but Lebert Joseph and his daughter Rosalie Parvay. Often the likeness is extended from the concrete present to the mythic past. A passage describing Rosalie links her to the divine: "She might have sprung whole from his head, a head-birth without benefit or need of a mother; an idea made flesh" (216). Here the description draws attention not only to the faithful reproduction of physical traits but calls up the Greek myth of Pallas Athene as well as Christ's incarnation.

Rituals reenacting past events with necessarily contemporaneous actors emphasize the characters' awarenesses of their heritages and their own importance. Myth thus becomes not the distorted history of a dead past but a living embodiment of lasting forces. Bourne-hills's yearly dramatization of Cuffee Ned's rebellion, for example, allows its impoverished and nearly hopeless people to experience a victory against oppression; the drama simultaneously recalls a past event and offers hope for the future. Avatara's decision to take on her great-aunt Cuney's role as griot retelling the story of the Ibos shows an individual consciously choosing this participation. *Praisesong* depicts the individual level and *The Chosen Place* the social level of mythic consciousness.

The richness of *The Chosen Place* lies precisely in its characters' multiple presences as individuals, cultural emblems, and persistent historical representatives.[1] Harriet Amron exemplifies the layering of character. As an individual personality, she desires total control but cannot deal with her responsibility for power; when pressed, she demands that her own emotional need for security take precedence over those of her husband Saul and over the economic needs of Bournehills. (Feeling her marriage threatened by staying in Bournehills, she arranges to cancel the grant that supports Saul's work there.) In addition to her role as insecure wife, she simultaneously represents the contemporary paternalistic American racist and a reincarnation of the Widow Shippen, her forbear who made the family fortune in the slave trade. Harriet violates the order of Gwen's household by preparing an omelet for the children with eggs that

Gwen has promised to sell. Though hungry, the children refuse to eat. Thus, Harriet is linked to the English sugar-mill owners, who refine the island's raw materials to produce a product that the diabetic islanders cannot consume. Harriet's violation is not malicious since she is unaware of Gwen's bargain, but she learns nothing from the experience and refuses Saul's analysis, which emphasizes the islanders' right to choice and self-definition. Harriet's mythic perception of her experience shows the warping of "universal" myth to the uses of political power. Of her omelet, she complacently reflects, "There was something of a miracle about it almost; the fishes and loaves" (178).

Though Marshall's characters often perceive others as facets of deities, only Harriet has the egoism to perceive herself as the savior. Her paradigm casts the islanders as sinners, inferiors, in need of saving. The great redemptive myth of Christ has become the white colonizer's flattering mirror. Campbell's chapter in *The Hero with a Thousand Faces*, "The Hero Today," indicates the modern trivialization of myth that Harriet personifies. In calling for new symbols for the new necessity, "the co-ordinated soul," he indicates the conscious mind's inability to foresee what these symbols might be. "But there is one thing we may know," he continues, "namely, that as the new symbols become visible, they will not be identical in the various parts of the globe; the circumstances of local life, race, and tradition must all be compounded in the effective forms" (389).

Marshall posits just such a racially specific myth as an antidote to the politically perverted "universal." Western myth thus constitutes only a part of the spiritual texture of her novels. Whereas *Brown Girl* generally limits the interplay of divinity and everyday reality to Selina's consciousness, *Praisesong* extends the perceptions from the point-of-view character to the controlling, creative consciousness of the narrator and the very structure of the work. Selina perceives her parents as divine, but not necessarily as Judeo-Christian incarnations. In *Brown Girl*, Selina sees her father as "a dark god . . . fallen from his heaven" (52); her mother shares this immanent presence when she is "kneading the dough for the coconut bread as though it was a world without form and she the god shaping it" (108). Later, when making love with Clive for the first time, she feels that "[i]t was as if the night had mounted her" (239). The ritual leading to Avey Johnson's rebirth in *Praisesong* is for "the Old Parents . . . The Long-time people," as Lebert Joseph calls the Vodun spirits (165). Eugenia Collier points out that Lebert Joseph himself embodies an African deity, Legba (312). The renewed belief in and experience of myth is essential to Avey's recovery of integrity.

To recover her wholeness, Avey must recognize her participation in a racially or culturally specific myth rather than a universal structure. Initially, she resists such specific identification, considering it part of the streets that threaten her family. After a dream about the death of her daughters in an incident like the Birmingham church bombing, she simply forces herself to stop dreaming for over twenty years. In a sense, Avey desires the alienation forced upon so many modernist protagonists. Even this life-long, chosen repression, however, cannot alienate the Marshall individual to that point at which the invisible man or Sula begins to function. In *Praisesong*, when the individual absolutely requires sustenance, the subconscious knowledge of kinship reemerges. During the crossing to Carriacou, the island where her true self is reborn, Avey recovers her connections to a defining element of her ancestral history, the Middle Passage: "She was alone in the deckhouse. That much she was certain of. Yet she had the impression as her mind flickered on briefly of other bodies lying crowded in with her in the hot, airless dark. . . . Their suffering—the depth of it, the weight of it in the cramped space—made hers of no consequence" (209). Avey finds her own suffering diminished, its meaning modified by the knowledge of her heritage. Marshall here re-sounds a familiar motif in African-American writing in which the somber notes of the Middle Passage occur again and again. Equiano, Douglass, Baldwin's *If Beale Street Could Talk,* Hayden's "Middle Passage," and Baraka's *Dutchman,* to name but a few, explore the Passage's literal history and figurative meanings for black identity.

The Chosen Place shares this mythic resonance, but its presentation of each person as a cultural microcosm allows it to avoid *Praisesong*'s thinness of characterization. Combining the mythos of *Praisesong* and the convincing individuality of *Brown Girl* with an added political and social consciousness, *The Chosen Place* is the most richly textured of Marshall's novels. The novel dispenses with the direct family resemblances so crucial to *Brown Girl* in favor of more inclusive connections. Merle's victimization reminds Saul of that of his first wife; Bournehills represents for him "every place that had been wantonly used, its substance stripped away, and then abandoned. . . . Bournehills could have been a troubled region within himself to which he had unwittingly returned" (100). Deep connections thus override the division of race, and the conventional Western division of external and internal realities breaks down. Likewise, the Western concepts of past and present are irrelevant in Bournehills, as indicated by the Tiv epithet at the novel's beginning: "Once a great wrong has been done, it never dies. People speak the words of peace, but their hearts do not forgive. Generations perform ceremonies of reconciliation but there is no end." The characteristic jangling of Merle's bracelets signifies both the court fool and the manacled slave. Marshall's culturally specific myth, her attention to difference, accents variety while simultaneously insisting on analogies rather than disjunctions between cultures. Campbell articulates the more conventional belief that emphasis on difference leads inevitably to isolation for each group and antagonism between groups: "[I]t is necessary for men to understand, and be able to see, that through various symbols the same redemption is revealed. . . . A single song is being inflected through all the colorations of the human choir. General propaganda for one or another of the local solutions, therefore, is superfluous—or much rather, a menace" (389–90). Marshall's vision is more pluralist: different groups may not hear a single song, but the sounds remain consonant.

Responding to the call of other Afro-American literature from Equiano, Douglass, James Weldon Johnson, and spirituals like "Go Down, Moses," Marshall explores the interactions of two minorities, blacks and Jews. The very title *The Chosen Place, the Timeless People* conflates black and Jewish self-definitions. During her speech to the Association in *Brown Girl*, Silla adumbrates the theme of similarities based on shared oppression (224). The relationship between Selina and Rachel at once develops Silla's insight and implicitly criticizes a paradigm of racial or cultural experience that does not consider gender.

Selina and Rachel share experiences, not only as women, but as minority women. As women, they are forced into constant awareness of their physical appearance; as minority women, they confront standards of beauty that deny their identities. Originally Rachel's short, badly dyed hair offends Selina's love of beauty and seems to her out of character. In fact, the hair style and color do represent a distortion of character, for they are Rachel's extreme reaction to pressures to conform to an inappropriate aesthetic. The Jewish community had perceived Rachel's long, naturally light hair as a mark of status, since she could almost pass for a gentile; the gentile community, on the other hand, scorned her as a poor imitation. Rachel's situation, of course, parallels that of the mulatta, a consistent theme in early Afro-American women's novels (Christian, Dearborn). Rebelling by cutting and dyeing her hair, Rachel refuses an aesthetic that undercuts her identity.

Selina and Merle face a different and more difficult challenge than that confronting Avatara Johnson. Selina, to some degree, and Merle, to a much greater extent, cannot use others as models because they desire selves and surrounding societies that have not yet been allowed to develop. For this reason, they must learn from others outside their immediate communities, hence Marshall's emphasis on analogues between culturally specific myths. In the first two novels, those who aid the questers must be significantly different and yet share enough sensibility or experience to make communication possible. Selina can listen to Miss Thompson precisely because Miss Thompson, as a black woman born in the American South, does not belong to the Bajan community but shares its experience of racism. Rather than guiding, the mentoring function in *Brown Girl* consists largely of sharing experience, listening to the quester's experiences and responding with one's own story.

Taken as a whole, Marshall's works vary substantially from traditional critical paradigms of the quest. Her female questers achieve energized, articulate identities, with each quester resolving the problems of her particular stage of life. An adolescent, Selina separates from her parents without rejecting them, acknowledges her community while denying its right to determine her personality. The middle-aged Merle recovers from her disappointments in her own character and her husband's personal rejection. Revitalized, she journeys to Africa to establish a relationship with their child; her renewed self-respect and consequent interest in her personal life do not signal a retreat from her political commitment, however. For Merle, Bournehills is home, and she intends to return to her political commitments there. As an older woman, Avatara must throw off the psychological bondage of many years of loyalty to a false ideal that had seemed the only means of survival. Instead of being handicaps, her age and family position grant her the authority to educate the youngest part of her immediate community, her grandsons. Marshall has thus expanded the nature and duration of the classical quest pattern. The quest is no longer an isolated, if perhaps lengthy, incident in the quester's life but a life-long commitment and, in the first two novels, a continuous modification of identity. While speaking in her own voice of her own experience, each quester addresses a wider community, until, in the final scene of *Praisesong,* the empowered woman quester becomes a griot speaking in tribal language of universal concerns.

This examination of particular works by Paule Marshall concretely demonstrates that current literary criticism has not yet developed paradigms that adequately honor difference. Black American women writers insist on both the social context that vanishes for lengthy periods in Euro-centered paradigms and a sense of history's importance that is not ever present there. As the convergence of creative writers (Marshall, Walker) and critics (Stetson, Wade-Gayles, Washington) of the 1970s suggests, specifically female historical experience affects contemporary women's identities. In literature, the emphases on history and on female ancestors converge in the figuration of the mother or surrogate mother; at the same time, both heroine and mother remain selves-in-community rather than autonomous figures. To unify these simultaneous concerns with history and the present, self and community, mother and daughter, many African-American women novelists make storytelling a central element of the female quest for identity.

In this tradition, successful female quests often rely on information from others' personal/historical narratives. Using process rather than static roles, the tale-tellers constantly shift from speakers to audience, continually participating in shaping both individual and group histories. Frequently Afro-American heroines must hear specifically female historical experience—a mother's or grandmother's story; often they must creatively reinterpret and re-present this story to escape its constraints and preserve its empowering aspects. History's legacy for black women characters, both imprisoning and freeing, is found primarily in their mothers' and grandmothers' stories.

Many of the earlier works in the tradition show young heroines without a mother, perhaps for a reason analogous to the nineteenth-century English novel's focus on the orphan or the young girl whose mother is dead: the lack of the crucial mother's concrete and symbolic importance to female growth sets the plot in motion. The list of novels whose female protagonists have lost mothers includes *Plum Bun; Quicksand* and *Passing; Their Eyes Were Watching God; The Chosen Place, The Timeless People; Tar Baby; Beloved; Kindred;* and *Linden Hills.* Recovering the historical experience figured by the mother is thus a crucial and always painful part of each character's development. Even where the mother is present, she cannot always communicate her experience sufficiently (as in Jones's *Corregidora*), and the daughter must recover the story.

Having excavated a painful, sometimes empowering black female heritage, women characters have another difficult task: deciding the use(s) of this knowledge. Any attempt to live without knowledge of the historical past is doomed, but living in the present by the rules of the past simply paralyzes, stops time. To survive whole, heroines must contextualize their knowledge of their heritage in the concrete present.

Women's quests for identity in novels by twentieth-century black women writers, then, have three essentials: the decision to explore history, the absorption of heritage, and interpretation of the past's uses in the present. The heroines' historical exploration generally centers on female ancestors, particularly mothers and grandmothers, with storytelling as the primary means of discovery. This study will set out a paradigm for this process of coming to terms with historical experience in the following chapter's consideration of *Kindred.* Like other models of quest patterns, this paradigm is intended as a flexible description. Novels may concentrate on one aspect or another, particularly as later novelists enter into dialogues with earlier writers to enlarge the tradition. Chapter 3 explores an important ancestor for *Kindred*'s depiction of a successful quest, Hurston's *Their Eyes Were Watching God,* which concentrates on the second two steps of absorbing heritage and deciding its uses.

Chapter 4 deals with the progression of successful quests in Marshall's novels from *Brown Girl, Brownstones* through *The Chosen Place, the Timeless People* and *Praisesong for the Widow.* In each of these, specifically oral narrative is crucial to the heroine's knowledge of heritage, which Marshall defines more inclusively in each successive work. In contrast to these successful quests, Chapter 5 shows the results of the female protagonist's other possible decision—the refusal to undertake a historically based quest in *Plum Bun, Quicksand, Tar Baby,* and *Linden Hills.* Questers in this tradition do not divide neatly into those who fail from lack of courage or support and those who succeed, however. The final chapter probes the experiences of an intermediate group, heroines who have undertaken historical exploration but find themselves paralyzed by their discoveries. Chapter 6 thus examines the interactions of historical understanding, motherhood, and oral narrative in *Meridian, Corregidora,* and *Beloved* as each heroine moves out of stasis and recommences her quest. Taken together, these novels from *Plum Bun* to *Beloved* constitute both a legacy of historical consciousness and meditations on that legacy, the liberating gift of free women to their daughters.

2

"WHAT WOULD A WRITER BE DOING WORKING OUT OF A SLAVE MARKET?"

Kindred *as Paradigm*, Kindred *in Its Own Write*

EXPLORATIONS OF HISTORY may seem the antithesis of science fiction, with its limitless scope for imagining futures. The past, after all, has certain fixed events and forms. Nevertheless, the paradigmatic work of the African-American woman's quest for understanding of history and self belongs to science fiction.[1] Octavia Butler's novel *Kindred* presents clearly all three parts of the female quest for a historically grounded understanding of self: the need to explore history, the process of excavation, and the subsequent interpretation of historical knowledge.

Butler presents historical exploration as literally inescapable: *Kindred*'s heroine, Dana, involuntarily time travels from present-day Los Angeles to antebellum Maryland whenever her white progenitor, Rufus Weylin, is in danger of dying. When she feels that her own life is threatened, she somehow breaks the psychic bond to Rufus and returns to her Los Angeles present. Her husband Kevin accompanies her on the third of her five journeys because they are physically touching when Rufus calls. Separated from her when she returns, he is stranded in the past for some time. From a family Bible passed down through generations, Dana remembers her genealogy and realizes that in order to preserve her own life, she must guard Rufus until he fathers her next-generation ancestor and this child, Hagar, is safely born. Time passes at different rates in the two eras; Dana spends several years in the past while only a few weeks elapse in Los Angeles. Rufus is about five years old when he first calls Dana to help him; as the story progresses, Dana ages only a few weeks while Rufus grows to manhood and becomes master of the Weylin plantation. Dana meets and has a very complex relationship with her black female ancestor, Alice, Hagar's mother. Dana resembles her great-great-grandmother in many ways, sufficiently to attract Rufus sexually and emotionally after Alice's death. Unable to persuade her to be his mistress, Rufus attempts to rape her; Dana kills him and returns to the present permanently. There she and Kevin contemplate the meaning and uses of the past in their present lives.

In *Kindred*, then, Octavia Butler uses time travel to examine the experiences of female slaves and their legacies for contemporary black women. Although the necessity of confronting historical realities is thus a premise, *Kindred* suggests the psychic realities that construct the necessity. In its depiction of the historically based female quest, the novel concentrates on the second and third steps, discovery of historical knowledge and a process of assimilation that determines its uses in the present.

THE NECESSITY OF CONFRONTING HISTORY

Kindred's central narrative details the growth of Dana's emotional understanding of slavery; its frame, "Prologue" and "Epilogue," indicates the importance of that understanding to the construction of a contemporary identity. This frame has thus far not received a great deal of critical attention, in part because the novel has not been the subject of detailed critical analysis. "Prologue" takes place after Dana's time travels. In it, Butler indicates part of the cost of her understanding. Killing Rufus disrupts the psychic link that causes the travel. When Dana rematerializes in her living room, the spatial orientation is skewed, so that her arm and the wall physically coalesce. When she pulls free (of the wall, of her past), she loses the part of her arm caught in the wall. "Prologue" ends with the hushed admission that Dana and her husband Kevin cannot account for "how such a thing could happen" (11). "Epilogue" very briefly recounts Dana and Kevin's visit, in the novel's present of 1976, to the Maryland site of the Weylin plantation. An old newspaper article informs them that Rufus's death was attributed to fire—probably the slaves' scheme to disguise the nature of his death by arson—and indicated the fate of some of those whom they had known. When Dana wonders about the numerous others, Kevin responds, "You've looked . . . [a]nd you've found no records. You'll probably never know" (264). The records of history cannot satisfy emotional cravings to trace the individual lives of those not valued, whether they be white, like Rufus's senile mother, or black, like Rufus and Alice's children. Frustrated, Dana ponders why she has voluntarily returned to the site of so many unpleasant and dangerous experiences. The finale, a dialogue between Dana and Kevin, implies the theme of the whole novel: the necessity of personal confrontation with history and the rarity of that process in contemporary America:

> "You probably needed to come for the same reason I did." He shrugged. "To try to understand. To touch solid evidence that those people existed. To reassure yourself that you're sane."
> I looked back at the brick building of the Historical Society, itself a converted early mansion. "If we told anyone else about this, anyone at all, they wouldn't think we were so sane."
> "We are," he said. "And now that the boy [Rufus] is dead, we have some chance of staying that way." (264)

Not only the literal fact of time travel but the metaphorical coming to terms with the past sets Dana and Kevin apart from all around them. The process is psychically and physically demanding and sometimes damaging; Dana loses exactly that part of her arm that Rufus is still touching as she fatally stabs him—the dead past has claimed a part of the living. On the other hand, Dana and Kevin have acquired understanding of the past, not as some procession of abstracts like "slavery" and "westward expansion," but as a collection of known individuals' experiences. They have also discovered their own capabilities and limitations under historical circumstances; their heritages become, for crucial periods, their lives.

More ambitious in scope than many other novels in this study—in part because Butler can rely upon their earlier voicings—the inner narrative of *Kindred* explores both black female and, in less detail, white male experiences. Dana's race becomes clear in chapter two, "The Fire," during her second trip; the third chapter, "The Fall," which contains the history of Dana and Kevin's relationship, reveals that Kevin is white. As these facts fall into place, the reader realizes that, although Butler concentrates on Dana's and hence African-American women's experiences, she addresses contemporary racial relationships and white men's identity as well.

The chapter titles of the central narrative—"The River," "The Fire," "The Fall," "The Fight," "The Storm," and "The Rope"—indicate events on a grand scale, archetypal or mythical. ("The River" and "The Fire" are reminiscent of Faulkner's statement about *As I Lay Dying;* he said that he had set out to show peasants progressing through the epic trials of flood and fire.) These titles echo biblical imagery, of course, as does "The Fall." The characters themselves interpret their experiences within this framework. Margaret Weylin, for example, identifies Dana's rescue of her drowning son by artificial respiration with Elisha's breath of life; Alice Greenwood names her daughter "Hagar" with conscious knowledge that the Bible shows slavery as transient. The elemental qualities of "The River," "The Fire," and "The Storm" intimate a fundamental testing, which "The Fight" carries on as the supreme assay of individual strength. Thus far the imagery conforms to archetypal patterns generally considered universal or at least broadly representative of Western culture. "The Rope" speaks to a racially specific experience, the coffle rope and the lynch noose, that indicates both the shared and the divergent natures of black and white experiences. The chapter titles thus grant Dana's and Kevin's explorations a dignity and importance beyond their individual personalities, affirming their participation in large, overlapping, not wholly congruent patterns.

At the chronological beginning of their journeys in time, Dana's and Kevin's situations indicate their need to confront the historical past. Both orphans, they are further deracinated by their ambitions to be writers, desires that their families see as incomprehensible and, worse, as threatening to economic security. Kevin's family destined him to be an engineer; Dana's, a nurse, secretary, or teacher—both gender-stereotyped roles. Dana, in fact, tries and rejects the college majors for these careers; the historical influence on her relatives' conceptions of proper training becomes clear when, in the past, Dana takes on all of these traditionally female roles that she scorns in the 1970s. When their nonconformity extends from professional to personal life, their interracial marriage alienates both Kevin's sister and Dana's elderly aunt and uncle, their closest relatives. Their alienation a product of bad luck (their parents' deaths) compounded by sexism and racism in their social context, Dana and Kevin are perforce operating as only minimally social individuals. Their alliance might seem to represent the triumphant unity of strong individuals who are wiser than their personal circles or surrounding society. *Kindred* implies, however, that no individually negotiated contract can cancel or transcend the social context. Significantly, Dana first time travels on her twenty-sixth birthday, just as she and Kevin are moving into their jointly chosen dwelling. The new house suggests the convergence of two individuals, and the birthday, of course, indicates the emergence of a new or modified self. Over the next few weeks, time traveling repeatedly interrupts the unpacking of boxes that represent Dana's and Kevin's personal pasts and integrity; each has been unwilling to sacrifice these symbolic possessions in order to move into the other's apartment. This sequence suggests that, before they can meld their possessions, much less their beings, into a coherent relationship, they must confront larger issues, the heritages of both races and both genders. The bicentennial setting (1976) broadens the theme, implying that the country itself must reexamine its history in order to have any hope of resolving contemporary racial conflicts.

At first, Dana and Kevin resist the necessity. When they marry against their families' wishes, Kevin humorously proposes that they travel to Las Vegas and "pretend we haven't got relatives" (112), but he seriously suggests the same tactic after Dana's first trip in time. Unable to explain logically Dana's brief absence (she momentarily enters the past and saves Rufus from drowning), the two attempt to evade the whole experience. Dana is aware of her desire to reject the memory because it scares her, but the strength and clarity of her feelings prevent her from denying its reality. Having seen objective proof of its reality—the river mud on Dana's clothes when she returns—but not having experienced it directly, Kevin suggests, "Let yourself pull away from it. . . . Let go of it" (17). Dana discovers, however, that she cannot escape by letting go because the past is grasping her.

Dana and Kevin thus find themselves in essentially different positions. Dana has no choice but to confront history, for she has partial control of only one part of the mechanism of her time travel, its return. Further, for her first two trips, she does not know that she can return if she feels that her life is physically threatened. Kevin, on the other hand, must consciously decide to accompany Dana and act on his decision. Butler implies that, in order to fulfill his emotional potential, the white male must explore his past, but he may sidestep the opportunity and remain functional. Finding the past so inextricably part of her present, however, the African-American woman must excavate history to acquire both insights into contemporary life and the strength to continue acting on them.

HISTORICAL CONFRONTATIONS WITH SELF

Historical knowledge changes Dana's understanding of both self and context. Her growing understanding of slavery redefines the concepts of self and community by clarifying their mutually creative processes. Partially experiencing the lives of her nineteenth-century foremothers—she is protected to some extent by her twentieth-century knowledge and by Kevin's presence—she understands how her self would have developed under those circumstances. The nature of the self that Dana discovers has occasioned some critical disapproval. In an article comparing *Kindred* with Marlys Millhiser's *The Mirror* and Phyllis Eisenstein's *Shadow of Earth*, feminist critic Beverly Friend objects strenuously to what she sees as the vulnerable if not helpless nature of this self:

> In historical truth, the life the authors describe is the unromanti-cized life that women living in those times did lead. Women did menstruate; childbirth was agonizing; biology is destiny. . . . [F]ew realize what these three novels have didactically presented: that con-temporary woman is not educated to survive, that she is as helpless, perhaps even more helpless, than her predecessors. Just as Philip Wylie pointed out in *The Disappearance*, a world of men might be strife-

ridden, but it would go on; a world of women would grind to a halt. . . . Men understand how the world is run; women do not. Victims then, victims now. And Eisenstein, Millhiser, and Butler know it. (55)

This argument harks back to the early and periodically resurgent feminist desire for positive role models, an understandable craving. With this subject matter, however, it misses the point entirely. No realistic depiction of slavery can emphasize triumphant individuality, though it may show occasional victories of the spirit and preservation of individual integrity. Understanding slavery requires both an intellectual and an emotional understanding of a social system that legally granted every physical power over blacks, including that of life-and-death, to whites. Dana's personality, formed in a considerably less oppressive society, must make adjustments to survive. The arrangements of social power construct not only expression of the self but in large measure the self itself. The self's best protection lies not in the superior individual capabilities implied by Friend but in alternate definitions of the self provided by a supportive community of the oppressed.[2]

The whole concept of "self" or "the self" remains problematic. The essentialist concept of self as a core collection of personality traits and morals, which changes slowly if at all, and which simply manifests itself in somewhat different actions over a lifetime, no longer seems tenable. On the other hand, an opposing concept of individual human beings as wholly the construct of particular, interacting social conditions has little appeal to humanists and little to do with African-American fiction. Characters with a rigid, set sense of self violate the idea of process that is central to African-American culture, and characters with no core at all are perhaps summed up in the existential nightmare of Rinehart in *Invisible Man*. Most novels by African-American women honor characters like Pilate in Morrison's *Song of Solomon*, who "threw away every assumption she had learned and began at zero" (149); they presume that stripping away social conditioning will reveal not a void but an interlocking set of needs, desires, and gifts. *Kindred* shows one fully developed character, Dana, whose irreducible self values physical life (her travel mechanism returns her to the present when she believes that her life is threatened), bodily integrity, and writing.

From these three spring a whole subset of desires and values that shape the particular contours of Dana's personality, contours that can alter in response to changed social conditions without endangering the self.

Like "self," "community" is an ambiguous, vexed term, partially because women-centered psychology's development of self-in-relation models clarifies the fact that self and community do not exist as completely separate entities. This exposition assumes that almost all of a self's manifestations in personality traits are dependent upon the nature and quality of the surrounding society, which is built of overlapping, simultaneous communities. Further, the works under consideration define "community" in varying ways. In general, "community" stands for a group to which the individual self belongs by self-selection, election, external assignment, or some combination of these. To write "a community of the oppressed" does not, of course, signify that all members have identical or even similar selves, nor that they suffer the same conditions of oppression. To take the most obvious divergence, male and female slaves experienced sexual oppression in different ways. So powerfully oppressive in numerous primary ways, slavery reinforced the group-orientation of Africans so that plantations became the sites of African-American slave communities (Genovese). *Kindred* recounts the meeting of Dana's twentieth-century self with two overlapping nineteenth-century communities: the slaves who live on Tom Weylin's plantation; and the entire Weylin plantation, black and white. Dana's story details a progressive understanding of what constitutes her core self and its possible relations to both communities.

Kindred does not romanticize the solidarity of the slave community—Dana's attempted escape is betrayed by another slave, Liza. Significantly, however, others punish the betrayer by beating her. In securing an individual prize, personal vengeance, Liza has lost much of her positive identity in the black community and some of its protection, which is the only protection available to her. Overemphasizing the individual weakens the viability of the individual. Just as she refuses to idealize the extent of community solidarity, Butler pays careful attention to the range of its accomplishments. It can sometimes ameliorate the lot of an individual—temporarily—by thievery, deception, and bargaining with the emotional attachments that perforce develop between masters and slaves; it cannot over-throw the system and thus cannot prevent the arbitrary sale of individuals, cruel punishments, or the sexual exploitation of women.

To come to terms with the system of slavery personified by her white great-great-grandfather Rufus Weylin, Dana must resolve relationships with others symbolically representing the community and the self, respectively Sarah and Alice. Developing the two relationships is neither a single process nor two separable activities; the relationships develop simultaneously and are mutually influen-tial. To see the necessity of identity within a community, Dana must experience individual helplessness; to define and maintain the self, Dana must relearn to insist on absolute individual needs even when they do not serve the community.

Before Dana can begin to understand either the slave community represented by Sarah or the historical fate of her own temperament represented by Alice, she must lose confidence in the individualist self that was cultivated in twentieth-century Los Angeles. (Thus, she does not even meet Sarah until her third visit and does not find Alice an adult until her fourth.) During Dana's first, very brief visit to the past, she acts from this isolate self (Kevin describes her as a "zombie" on the job), assertive and confident. Seeing Rufus drown-ing, she pulls him from the river, brushes aside his hysterical mother, and administers restorative artificial respiration. Had she realized fully where she was—the era, the slave state, the Weylin plantation, within range of Tom Weylin's rifle—she could not possibly have responded so efficiently. Succeeding chapters, each chronicling a single visit, introduce Dana to the diffidence that a slave must at least affect, both in defining a situation and in acting on that definition. Through experiencing these steadily lengthening epi-sodes of slavery, Dana develops a progressively more complex understanding of contextual influence on the self.

Dana's second visit, in revealing the nature of the controlling system, also exposes the limitations of her current definition of self within it. Her previous experience in the past has been entirely with whites; this trip suggests her psychic progression through her perceptions of other blacks. Her first "sight" of a black person barely qualifies as such: "There was a row of small buildings off to one side almost out of sight of the house. Slave cabins, I supposed. I thought I saw someone moving around one of them, and for a moment, I froze behind a huge spreading tree. The figure vanished silently between two cabins—some slave, probably as eager as I was to avoid being caught out at night" (33).

A "figure," "some slave"—gender as well as all other specificity remains invisible to Dana. Later the same evening, Dana is able to see more when patrollers roust a male slave, his free wife, and their child from their cabin: ". . . a moment later, three people were shoved, almost thrown out of the cabin. Two of them—a man and woman—were caught by the riders outside who had dismounted, apparently expecting them. The third, a little girl dressed in something long and light colored, was allowed to fall to the ground and scramble away, ignored by the men. She moved to within a few yards of where I lay in the bushes near the edge of the clearing" (35).

These people, no longer vaguely glimpsed figures, are the young Alice Greenwood and her parents, as Dana concludes later in the scene. Alice's proximity to Dana suggests a psychic nearing that the next actions further. As the patrollers whip Alice's father, Dana experiences the raw brutality. Her retrospective narrative contrasts her previous knowledge of such deeds, gained from television, with this experience: "But I hadn't lain nearby and smelled their sweat or heard them pleading and praying, shamed before their families and themselves" (36). Not only sight but the other senses of smell and hearing testify to the man's human reality. Dana's revulsive urge to vomit foreshadows the retching that accompanies her own later whipping in "The Fall." This brief sequence of her changing views of other blacks sketches her larger process of movement from observing those who are "other," through associating self and other, to a powerful if still incomplete identification based on shared experience.

This scene and its aftermath inform Dana of both the limits of personal action and its necessity. Here, Dana is forced to observe and know that she cannot confront the four patrollers to aid the victims. Later, when one of these men returns alone to rape Alice's mother and decides on Dana as a substitute victim, she cannot seize her chance to defend herself. Unable to muster the resolution to blind her attacker by gouging his eyes, she is saved only because her fear of death returns her to the present. Later, as they pack a traveling bag, Kevin asks Dana if she can bring herself to use a switchblade. Without hesitation, she assents. Dana has certainly confronted unpleasant racist definitions of herself and her actions before, but she has never before felt the ferocity of the attack in a context that fully empowers those definitions. To reject that definition of herself and implicitly insist on another is insurrection, and she now knows that it must be backed by willingness to use violence, "any means necessary."

The individual's powers, however, cannot compare with those of a whole community. Dana realizes in "The Fall" that she cannot rely simply on influencing Rufus (still a child, helpless because of a broken leg) to construct a decent place for herself on the Weylin plantation. To become a functional part of the plantation and the slave community, Dana works. Her aims are two-fold. First, given that the context will in short order demand it anyway, by volunteering her labor, Dana retains some control over the kind of work that she does. Second, her participation will ingratiate her with the master and allow her an entrée to the slave community. Significantly, maximizing personal autonomy and contributing to the community are not presented as necessarily opposing choices. While working, Dana supplements her meager knowledge of strategies for survival in this alien social structure by listening to "old people and children . . . or house servants or even field hands. . . . Without knowing it, they prepared me to survive" (94). Dana thus tentatively moves toward securing a place in a community by working. At the same time, she chooses work that she can tolerate, so that her choices also strengthen her as an individual. *Kindred* does not postulate an either/or choice of individual versus community interest. In return for her contribution to the community, she receives informal instructions in its norms.

Dana's participation remains relatively limited. Kevin has accompanied her this time, and although they wish to return home, their lives on the Weylin plantation flow fairly comfortably. Their nascent assimilation rests on a bogus foundation that Dana pinpoints: "We were observers watching a show. We were watching history happen around us. And we were actors. While we waited to go home, we humored the people around us by pretending to be like them. But we were poor actors. We never really got into our roles" (98). Kevin's presence protects Dana from the worst vulnerabilities of female slavery, and she only hears about the usually cruel aspects of slavery (the selling of children away from parents) rather than seeing its excesses (Kevin's later account of the openly sadistic fatal whipping of a pregnant woman and her child).

Dana's third journey to the past deepens her intellectual, distanced appreciation of slavery into an emotional, visceral understanding. Stranded in the past, Kevin has moved north, and Dana must face not only witnessing slavery but being a slave without a white male protector. The enormous destructive strength of social systems is being borne in upon her. During her interim returns to Los Angeles, she has read material on both slavery and the Holocaust. (Later, she explicitly associates Rufus and other masters with nazism.) During this visit, she witnesses horrors that she is unable to prevent or ameliorate. As the master's power begins to shift from the aging Tom Weylin to the maturing Rufus, Rufus becomes less amenable to Dana's influence. In love with Dana's black great-great grandmother Alice, he also loves the power that is his race's and gender's prerogative. He therefore refuses to accept Alice's choice of a slave husband, Isaac, in preference to being his lover. In grudging deference to Dana, Rufus agrees to conceal the source of his injuries after Isaac physically avenges Rufus's attempted or accomplished rape of Alice. Rufus can keep his promise without sacrifice because the social system works for him: the slave Isaac is caught, tortured, and sold South; Alice had been born free, but her complicity in Isaac's escape forfeits her freedom. When Rufus buys her, he gains any control over her that he had previously lacked.

Dana must confront the total inadequacy of her individual bargain with Rufus to secure a black woman's rights or even to ameliorate the consequences of unjust laws. Through caring for Rufus, Dana has experienced one part of the nineteenth-century black woman's experience, nurturance of white children who grow into oppressors. (The hope of overcoming Rufus's social conditioning by force of personality was always naive, of course, but the belief in individual power dies hard.) More painful still, because Alice cannot immediately remember the events leading to her bondage, Dana must explain them. Thus, through nursing and reeducating

Alice, Dana has experienced a relationship analogous to that of the slave mother/child and felt the terrible burden of socializing kin into slavery. Dana's conversion of intellectual knowledge to emotional understanding accelerates.

Not only the power of the self to prevail over racist and sexist oppression but the very ability of the self to persist in recognizable form becomes questionable. Dana has felt comfortably superior in mettle to the cook, Sarah, because she does not run away when her three children are sold, even though her grief nearly maddens her. Although Sarah indicates her total ignorance of how to navigate North and her doubt that free states really exist, Dana initially ascribes her inaction to cowardice: "She had done the safe thing— had accepted a life of slavery because she was afraid. She was the kind of woman who might have been called 'mammy' in some other household. She was the kind of woman who would be held in contempt during the militant nineteen sixties. The house-nigger, the handkerchief-head, the female Uncle Tom—the frightened powerless woman who had already lost all she could stand to lose, and who knew as little about the freedom of the North as she knew about the hereafter" (145).

Dana here implicitly claims two different kinds of superiority. With no sense of what their actions might have gained for her, Dana congratulates herself on her tolerance in not calling Sarah a handkerchief-head. She may be correct about the radicals' rigidity and her own greater flexibility, but her complacent analysis shares with theirs a coldly intellectual dismissal of Sarah as a type, a category, not an individual. In both ways, she identifies herself as an individual far superior to the average run of both the black political community of the sixties and the slave community.

This elitism dissipates when Dana sees the extent of Alice's injuries, the real price of an attempt at running away. Recognizing her earlier ignorant smugness, she rethinks her appraisal of Sarah. In fact, as Dana later realizes when she contrasts her own pitiful attempt at escape with Alice's, she has had certain advantages in having seen maps, and she is also able to forge a pass. Yet at this point, she has not tried to run North to find Kevin. Recognizing that, despite her advantages, her courage might fail, a chastened Dana has her first really personal contact with Sarah. Knowledge of her own vulnerability thus leads Dana to actual connections with other individuals who collectively make up the slave community.

To this point, Dana has thought of the community as a reservoir of strength which can help her save herself. In part, she adopts this view because her skills are not well adapted to nineteenth-century life. Dana must learn both tasks and social skills that even the slave children already possess. Nursing the helpless Alice gives her a sense of purpose, of contributing to someone besides Rufus in an irreplaceable way, so that she feels a more genuine sense of belonging. And with this sense of community comes an immediate ambivalence. The system of slavery, with Rufus as its major embodiment, can manipulate Dana's position in the community to its own benefit. Rufus discovers, for example, that he can ask Dana to persuade Alice to return to his bed if he points out that peaceful persuasion will avoid a beating for Alice. Soon he broadens his program, for Dana cares about others in addition to Alice. When Rufus takes over the debt-ridden plantation after his father's death, he uses Dana's skill in writing letters to ask his creditors for more time. If Dana refuses, Rufus will simply sell slaves. No longer an individual without a context, Dana ironically finds it necessary to defend the black community by preserving the Weylin plantation on which it is enslaved.

As Dana accepts her membership in the slave community, it reciprocates, despite some misgivings. Although some are jealous of Dana's assignments to work that is less taxing than the fields and some misconstrue her relationship with Rufus or her loyalty to Kevin, she wins friends. Among the house servants, Carrie explicitly affirms that Dana belongs; among the field workers, Sam James defends her integrity (237–38). Dana's ambiguous status receives some clarification when Sarah, Carrie, and a third woman avenge the betrayal that thwarts her attempt at escape. Despite its observation of her peculiarities, the community recognizes Dana as a full-fledged member deserving of its protection.

Instead of seeing herself as a separate actor, Dana finds that she shares the most fundamental feelings with other slaves now that she has had experiences somewhat like theirs. During the intense physical pain following the beating to punish her for running away,

Dana ponders her fear of more punishment and her fear that her courage will fail. Dana expresses a curious duality here:

> I moaned and tried not to think about it. The pain of my body was enough for me to contend with. . . .
> I tried to get away from my thoughts, but they still came.
> *See how easily slaves are made?* they said. (177, original emphasis)

The thoughts, the analysis, are perceived as something separate from, almost hostile to, her beaten body. Dana prefers even the physical pain to the psychic humiliation of feeling a slave's fear. Less humiliating emotions are also common property, for Dana discovers that others share her ambivalences toward Rufus: "Strangely, they seemed to like him, hold him in contempt, and fear him all at the same time. This confused me because I felt just about the same mixture of emotions for him myself. I had thought my feelings were complicated because he and I had such a strange relationship. But then, slavery of any kind fostered strange relationships" (229–30). Despite her entirely different early life and her periodic respites from slavery in the present, Dana shares with the other slaves emotional reactions to their social conditions.

Functioning as part of a community speeds Dana's redefinition of self, for she sees in Alice the danger of the isolate self in this context. Alice and Dana share a temperament; Alice's experiences without Dana's advantages inform Dana of her own probable fate under slavery. Coming to terms with Alice involves knowing and accepting herself. Butler rather heavy-handedly underlines the women's likenesses: everyone notices their physical resemblance, Sarah says that they fight like sisters, and Rufus pronounces them "the same woman." The novel's plot further emphasizes their analogous lives. Both experience rebirths into slavery. Rufus first calls Dana on her birthday, and the injuries that the previously free Alice suffers while escaping with Isaac turn her into "a very young child again, incontinent, barely aware of us unless we hurt her or fed her" (153). Both have sexual relationships with white men, although Dana chooses hers while Alice has no meaningful choice. Each cares for the other after the physical punishment subsequent to an unsuccessful attempt at escape.

These similarities coexist with substantial differences created by their divergent experiences. Alice, for instance, loses her husband to slavery. In one of the most moving scenes in *Kindred*, Alice witnesses Kevin and Dana's meeting after what has been five years in Kevin and Alice's time. Knowing that her husband has been sold to a plantation in Mississippi, Alice must witness their joy in an event that she desires but can never experience. These differences in circumstances force the personalities to diverge as Alice is consistently more damaged by slavery. To a certain extent, each woman feels the other's choices as a critique of her own; each sees, in the distorting mirror of the other, her own potential face.

Alice shows Dana a woman completely victimized by the legal system and by psychic isolation. Because Alice did not grow up on the plantation or in slavery, she lacks emotional connections to other slaves and the knowledge of social norms in the same way that Dana does initially. Her forced concubinage and its attendant respite from the hardest work, however, continue to prevent her from developing strong community ties. Like Dana, Alice probably has some say in choosing her tasks, but her choices of sewing and minding very small children reinforce her isolation.

Physically restored by Dana's nursing, Alice becomes emotionally functional again after the births of her children. Thwarted in her love for Isaac, she finds another outlet in her son and daughter. Alice fears the ambivalences developing within her, the emotional connection that she feels with Rufus just after Hagar is born. Such feelings threaten her self-defined integrity. Dana observes that the other slaves also have these mixed emotions, but Alice's isolation may keep her unaware of their true state. In anger, she projects her feelings onto Dana and reviles her as a "white nigger." Because loving the master who was instrumental in mutilating and selling her husband would destroy her identity, she tries to run away. Rufus punishes her by making her believe that he has sold her children. She must grieve alone, for Sarah cannot bear to reexperience her own grief over sold children and thus avoids Alice. Alice then avails herself of the weapon that Dana has always had and that she had thought Alice could not use—the abandonment of Rufus. Dana sees in Alice's suicide the fate that inevitably overtakes the isolated black female self of the nineteenth century.

Less isolated than Alice, Dana can call on the advantages of a twentieth-century woman's knowledge and experiences to protect herself. Alice's suicide shows Dana her own choices. Rufus simply will not allow compromise, even if his absolutism destroys those whom he claims simultaneously to love and to own. Alice's death makes him look to Dana as more than a replacement, almost a reincarnation. Having faced, at least briefly, the major tasks required of nineteenth-century black women—cooking, field work, the raising of both black and white children—Dana must now confront the most basic of racist, patriarchal oppression in Rufus's attempt to define and control her sexuality.

Kindred shows Rufus gradually exercising more power over Dana's sexuality as he grows into his adult role. When he first knew Dana, he was a child of five and she an adult of twenty-six; because of the different rates of time flow in their two eras, when the novel ends, Dana is still twenty-six and Rufus is about twenty-five. Modeling his behavior on his father's, Rufus very soon outgrows any considerate treatment of his mother. Dana's competent rescues of him preserve his respect for her longer, but his growing experience of power will not allow him to believe in the definition of a woman, especially a black woman on his plantation, which he does not author. Even before Alice's death, Rufus possessively separates Dana from any possibility of contact with the admiring Sam James by summarily selling him. This scene replays the story that Dana saw played out on her second visit, the attack on Alice's parents. Tom Weylin, who owns Alice's father, has directed him to take another wife so that his children will be slaves, not free children of a free mother. His persistence in cleaving to Alice's mother, documented by the patrollers' catching him without a pass, probably caused him to be sold. The master thus mediates sexual interactions between black women and black men, drastically circumscribing their choices. When he becomes desperate to replace Alice, Rufus defines Dana as "the same woman," and since they are black women, as his property.

Dana feels the pressure of the racist, patriarchal social context so strongly that she considers, if not internalizing its definition of her self, accepting it provisionally. Like Alice, Dana momentarily feels that she could somehow forgive Rufus almost any enormity, even rape. That thought inspires terror; she must maintain her self-definition and necessary corollary definitions. Rufus has real emotional needs for her support, but she cannot endorse or even allow his self-serving definition of rape as necessary to fulfill them. Earlier, Dana had learned to use violence against the unknown patroller's lust. Now she must learn a harder lesson, to use it against her own affection and Rufus's perverted love for Alice and genuine, if intermittent, affection for her. When the choices amount to killing her self (literally by committing suicide like Alice or figuratively by allowing the rape) or killing Rufus, Dana affirms her self. Becoming a part of the black community has been a necessity for Dana's physical and emotional survival. It cannot always protect the self, however, and no responsibility to community can obliterate the self's right to integrity.

Thus far the discussion of *Kindred* has highlighted aspects of the novel which are paradigmatic for many African-American women's novels of this century. To limit discussion to these would not only deny *Kindred* its deserved status as a unique text but would obscure important parts of its presentation of the African-American woman writer's process and progress. Whereas many novels in this tradition focus entirely on the black community, or on black women within it, *Kindred* insists on black-white relationships as a central part of its presentation.

The mechanism of Dana's time travel, her connection to Rufus, underscores the inseparability of black and white in the United States. Given their many likenesses, in addition to the facts of their blackness and femaleness, one might expect Alice to issue the summons for Dana's help. Butler's choice of Rufus, of course, avoids many plot difficulties; with Dana protecting a master instead of a slave, the power structure allows her to exist in the past, and besides, her ability to protect a slave from the likeliest life-threatening circumstances (whites' abuse) would be minimal. In addition to these plot conveniences, the choice of Rufus establishes the important theme of intertwined black and white, male and female experience. Dana must confront a submerged portion of her family history. Although she knows of Rufus's existence from the family Bible, she does not know his race and is surprised by it, just as the reader may be surprised by the rather late mention of Kevin's race. Dana's inability to develop an uncomplicated emotional attitude toward Rufus (either hatred or love alone) intimates Butler's refusal to simplify shared, mutually created historical truth.

Kindred does not explore white women's identities extensively;[3] the white male's identity receives more attention. With the focus on Dana, Kevin's progress remains less detailed. Dana narrates *Kindred*, and they are separated for all but the events recounted in "The Fall." In fact, it may seem hyperbolic to explore Kevin as representing the white male in history as the text gives no information on his ethnicity or his family's history. Nevertheless, certain descriptive details suggest his symbolic importance. Kevin's last name, Franklin, echoes that of one of the United States's most famous white founders. Further, his prematurely gray hair suggests a patriarch, especially since he is twelve years older than Dana. This difference in Kevin's and Dana's ages echoes that between Carol and her husband, insisting on Kevin's connection to the racist whom he abhors. When Kevin's face, aged by his experience of the past, matches his hair, he has assimilated his heritage.

Briefly, the reader sees in Rufus Weylin's development the nightmare of unrestricted white male power from which Kevin must divorce himself. Rufus's development shows the natural progress of a white male enjoying rarely challenged legal and social hegemony. Rufus first appears as a victim when he nearly drowns. He next emerges as a pathetic child who is physically abused by his father; Rufus, in fact, has scars on his back from repeated whipping. But as his physical maturity brings power, he becomes obsessed with control of others, through which he hopes to fulfill his emotional needs. Gradually his self-indulgence grows until his sadism, its purpose a mystery even to him, leads to Alice's suicide. A disaster for those under its control, Rufus's power never makes him happy; obedience can be enforced, but not the love that he craves.

In order to avoid damaging others and to experience any emotional fulfillment, Kevin must first eschew control. Such a program is enormously harder to follow than to articulate. Dana notes that although their "natural," physical stature is the same, Kevin as an older white male has greater social status. (He has, for example, more recognition as a writer.) He must learn to identify and refuse the privileges of his race and gender. His social conditioning works against him, of course, but his love for Dana makes him flexible.

When she refuses his casual demand that she type his papers, he cannot initially understand her anger, but he eventually accepts her decision. Even so, Dana's account contains no record of an apology or even a recognition of why his request violates a peer relationship.

Once in the past, he faces less trivial choices. While he and Dana are both playacting master and slave, he enthuses about going West to watch the building of the country. Dana's indignant comment, "That's where they're doing it to the Indians instead of the blacks!" (97) surprises him because, at this point in his development, he has not realized that merely refusing to participate directly as a slave master is insufficient. The pervasiveness and extremity of the slave system's definitions allow for no neutrality. In the past, his food is harvested by black labor and his food cooked by black women; in the present, he confidently expects Dana to serve him by typing. Kevin cannot remain transcendent, ostensibly outside of it while inevitably benefiting by this oppression, either in the past or in the present. Later, his witnessing the same kind of brutality that Dana sees in Isaac's and Alice's experiences clarifies his understanding. In connection with his change, he mentions a particular incident that focuses on a black woman and her child: a pregnant woman is strung up by her wrists and killed by whipping; her child also perishes when he or she (no sex is specified) falls from her womb. Butler's decision to have Kevin rather than Dana see this event suggests that, lacking Dana's quicker sympathetic identification—in the past, she lives with known ancestors and is subject to the punishments that she watches—he may require a greater shock to move him to action. His attitude then reveals a complete lack of self-dramatization. On their return to the present after Kevin has spent five years in the past, he accounts for his scarred forehead with, "I was accused of helping slaves to escape. I barely got out ahead of the mob. . . . I'll tell you all about it, Dana, but some other time. Now, somehow, I've got to fit myself back into nineteen seventy-six. If I can" (193). To clarify, Dana asks if he was actually helping slaves to escape. His affirmation is "angry, almost defensive" (193). Far from spinning yarns of adventure in his "look at the Wild West mode," Kevin avoids telling a story which would inevitably center on his actions and might cast him in a heroic mode. His preference for getting on with his life in the present suggests an emphasis on continuing responsibility. Clearly, the white male cannot remain morally aloof from slavery or oppression; the only morality lies in engagement.

THE USES OF A PERSISTENT HISTORY

The different natures of what Dana and Kevin have learned, consequences of their different races and genders, are symbolically present in the physical marks of their experiences in the past. (Wounds suffered in Rufus's world persist in the present.) Dana's scarred back and Kevin's scarred forehead bespeak their divergent knowledges. In confronting and rejecting the past's definition of her as sexual property, Dana has experienced victimization without becoming a victim; Kevin has both resisted his illegitimate power and accepted the mark of Cain as his heritage.

Thus, Dana and Kevin have acquired scars testifying to their accretion of experience. Dana, however, also loses parts of her physical being, two teeth in her escape attempt and most of her left arm on her permanent return to the present. The book stresses the physical, literal level; it begins, "I lost an arm on my last trip home. My left arm" (1). Given this emphasis and Dana's profession as a writer, it seems too glib merely to say that she has paid for her knowledge by losing expendable parts of herself, her initial elitism and confidence. *Kindred* does not depict compensation or a freely struck bargain, Odin's eye for a draught of wisdom. Instead, the effects of past oppression and Dana's understanding of them, and their persistence, remain a continuing limitation of her capabilities.

Kindred does not promise the smooth enjoyment of these hardwon, new self-definitions; the surrounding society remains obtuse, and no community appears to replace the slaves' mutual support, even though Dana and Kevin each have a good and reliable friend of their own gender. The inability of their contemporaries to imagine their initial shared experience as writers moonlighting at a warehouse documents the persistence of attitudes formed before the Civil War. Butler presents these characters indirectly, primarily through Dana's and Kevin's summaries of their reactions; only one speaks in his own right and then fewer than ten words. Clearly, their importance lies in the attitudes that they espouse rather than in the complexity of their natures. Dana's and Kevin's coworkers, for instance, image their relationship only in terms of their appearances, their races. A female coworker calls them the weirdest-looking couple she's ever seen, and a male constantly harasses them by mumbling about chocolate and vanilla porn, an intimation respectively of the slaves' puzzlement at Dana's love for Kevin and of Tom Weylin's salacious enjoyment of what he believes a perfectly usual master-slave liaison.

The coworkers know Kevin and Dana only on a very limited basis, but their families respond with equal rigidity to their decision to marry. The causes of the families' rejection differ, as do their expressions. Dana's foster parents represent somewhat more complex attitudes than those held by Kevin's relatives. Her aunt accepts her decision to marry Kevin, but not Kevin himself, because the children of their union will be light-skinned African-Americans. The implied self-hatred and focus on the next generation seem an ironic development of Alice's—and the other slaves'—hopes to make their children literate and then free. Dana's uncle takes another tack entirely, disinheriting Dana in favor of his church. Because he feels her love for Kevin as a personal rejection of his own black maleness, he means his action to have symbolic overtones. His actions echo those of the slaves who resent Dana's speech ("More like white folks than some white folks") and her attachment to Kevin as betrayals of their solidarity. All of these attitudes bespeak a premise that the races are and must remain essentially separate, a separation legally mandated and enforced in the past and powerfully extant in the social if not legal present. The success of Dana and Kevin's marriage is by no means assured, but *Kindred* implies that their nascent relationship has a much better chance because of their experiences in the past. Intellectually and emotionally more knowledgeable about their mutual tribal histories, they can perhaps act more wisely in their—and our—present.

To do so, they must remain aware of history without being imprisoned by historical reactions inappropriate to a different context. Their responses to each other, as well as their responses to their families and coworkers, must take into account the persistence and influence of historical events without constantly recreating them by rejecting new information. Butler presents at least one example of the necessary flexibility through Kevin's and Rufus's shared speech patterns and physical resemblances. Robert Crossley argues that these similarities indicate Kevin's and Rufus's shared character. Instead, the men's affinities show the potential for similar character development, not its actual presence. Crossley's assumption ignores the contexts in which the two men live, speak, and act, and *Kindred* explicitly points to the importance of context and speaker. When Tom Weylin threatens to "flay you alive," Dana remembers her annoyed but loving aunt's having used the same words. Clearly, the incident does not point out likenesses between the slavemaster and the aunt but rather the different contextual meanings of the same words. Kevin no doubt had the potential to become Rufus, as Dana had the potential to be Alice, given different conditions. Stronger links between Kevin and painful oppression are figured in several scenes in which, on Dana's return to the present, he unintentionally aggravates a physical injury that Dana has received in the past. As a white male, Kevin cannot dissociate himself from his heritage sufficiently to be continually supportive; at times, with no intention of doing so, he will oppress Dana or remind her of oppression.

Suggesting a positive, controlled use of historical knowledge through Dana's vocation as a writer, *Kindred* simultaneously explores the development, functions, and persistence of African-American women's writing. This meta-level of female identity modifies the meanings of each female character's experiences. Sarah's daughter Carrie provides moving testimony of the drive to communicate despite every disadvantage. Born deaf, she never learns to speak. Nevertheless, she and her immediate family develop an elaborate sign system that allows her to "talk." Significantly, Dana learns to understand her, but it never occurs to Kevin that she is capable or desirous of communication. (He is surprised to learn later that she is not retarded.) Her mute language is sign and symbol of an irrepressible black female creativity and need for connection whose first and often only audience is other African-Americans.

In many ways, *Kindred* restates the major themes of earlier slave narratives. White males control access to literacy in the antebellum Maryland setting of the novel. Slaves, of course, are forbidden literacy; white women receive little education; barely literate themselves, masters must guard their tenuous advantage. Significantly, when Dana eventually persuades Rufus to let her teach several of the slave children to read, his neighbors give him "fatherly" advice (236) to desist; patriarchal racism regards any deviation as a threat. The connections between literacy and mobility, both geographic and economic, are explicit. Dana offers, for example, to write a pass for a runaway slave (he refuses because he does not trust her, is caught, punished, and sold). Faced with Rufus's reluctance to study, Dana tries to motivate him by pointing out that if he cannot read well, others will cheat him; after his father's death, they go over Weylin's "books" (227), not his library but his business ledgers. What really persuades Rufus to learn, however, is not the economic motivation but an important underlying reason for the masters' insistence on keeping slaves illiterate, the power of the written word to open the imagination and intellect to new ideas.

Within this familiar framework, Butler uses the relationship between Dana and Rufus to examine the African-American woman writer's relationship with the white patriarchy. In the nineteenth century, the white male is shown to control access to literacy, the resources necessary to its exercise, the processes of transmission, the permissible aims for texts, and their styles and forms. At the same time, the novel images African-American women's resistance to and subversion of patriarchal racism.

The white male, who constitutes a substantial portion of the nineteenth-century audience for the black woman's texts, controls the transmission of her writing. On the literal level, Dana writes to Kevin to let him know that she is again in the Weylins' time; Rufus, having promised to mail the letters and then reporting that he has done so, hides the letters in a trunk under his bed. The location of the subverted letters suggests a link between textual and sexual oppression (a trope that Alice Walker's *The Color Purple* also uses), particularly given that Alice discovers them.[4] Further, Rufus can bend Dana's writing skills to his own uses. Using the threat of further sales of slaves if she refuses to comply, he asks her to write his creditors to request extensions for his debts. Dana's writing thus supports the current functioning of the Weylin plantation because its breakup might well be worse for the individuals involved. In order to write persuasively, Dana studies other contemporary letters and consciously adapts her style to the "stilted formal style of the day" (227), in other words, to the conventions of both nineteenth-

century white male literature and commerce. Not trusting even
these restrictions to control Dana's creativity, Rufus must approve
all of Dana's letters before sending them. Literacy itself, time and
physical resources, transmission, conventions of form, and editorial
control of content all lie with the white masters.

Faced with this monolith, the nineteenth-century black woman
salvages a tiny space—literally a page of a Bible in this work—in
which she preserves knowledge of family, and therefore of history,
for her twentieth-century descendants. Access to literacy being the
first necessity, Alice begs Rufus to allow her children to learn to
read as a Christmas present. (Though she cannot read, Alice is,
ironically, more conversant with a major Western text, the Bible,
than Rufus; she names her children after biblical characters who
outlived their slavery. Her covert resistance manipulates literacy in
Rufus's culture.) Literacy secured, Hagar records her parents' names
and her own in a family Bible, beginning the family register. This
apparently commonplace and private act has much larger ramifications. First, by allowing Dana to understand why she time travels
to this place, it keeps her from destroying her family and thus herself
by prematurely killing Rufus. Second, this very recording of the
unvalued life subverts the official order. When Dana and Kevin visit
present-day Maryland in an attempt to discover the fates of those
on the Weylin plantation, they find only newspaper reports, the
masters' understanding of social history. The newspaper gives an
account of Rufus's death which Kevin and Dana know to be false
and then lists the slaves who were sold. Of the other slaves and
Rufus and Alice's freed children, including Hagar, it makes no
mention. However cryptic, Hagar's notation testifies to her existence
and perseverance, her sustaining presence in a family that now
includes Dana.

In order to preserve, Butler implies, the African-American woman
writer generally had to encode her meanings. Once Rufus supplies
her with sufficient paper, Dana keeps a journal in which to express
thoughts too dangerous to speak; if Rufus could read the journal,
of course, it could no longer perform its function. In order to keep
her secret thoughts secret, Dana writes in secretarial shorthand.
Shorthand, developed to facilitate male-controlled commerce, is
virtually a female sign-system, male proficiency being extremely

rare. Clearly, Dana uses patriarchal tools to preserve herself, and as Butler later implies by having her considering her journal (in the present of the 1970s) as source material for stories, to further the attack on white male control of African-American women's texts.

Kindred shows contemporary African-American women with far more freedom to author their stories than their forebears, but racist and patriarchal constraints persist. Even a relatively nonconformist white male like Kevin is capable of insisting that Dana type his papers as a prerequisite to sharing his apartment. Symbolically, the African-American woman will be allowed into the white male domain only if she is willing to use her energies to replicate white male texts. Having accepted her definitive refusal, he blunders again when he suggests that they can winnow Dana's books in order to have enough space to live together in his apartment. Showing him the absurdity of the idea by applying it to his books, Dana rejects his presumption that he can decide which texts are or should be nurturant for her. Dana's education of Kevin, however important to their relationship, has personal rather than institutional ramifications. At the beginning of her time travels, Dana has had one, but only one, story accepted for publication.

The nature and forms of Dana's and Kevin's future works remain unspecified. When they return to the present after prolonged experience of the past, they find themselves unable to write, their creative powers somehow blocked. This disabling preoccupation with history, quite temporary in *Kindred,* appears in radically different perspective in several other novels, notably *The Chosen Place; The Timeless People; Corregidora;* and *Beloved.* Here, it may imply a need for new forms—as *Kindred* revises the form of the slave narrative—to voice new understandings of historical constructions of the present.

Robert B. Stepto articulated the traditional quest patterns of ascent and immersion in the same year that *Kindred* both evoked and reworked them. Clearly, in Stepto's terms, *Kindred* is an immersion narrative. Yet Butler's specification of Dana's and Kevin's West Coast residence literally redirects the paradigm of travel, suggesting more complexities, more areas to be considered as time enlarges the experiential base for the tradition's subjects. In earlier texts, the journey tends to be singular though history gives at least one example of a woman involved in multiple journeys, Harriet Tubman. Butler's use of multiple journeys adds layers to the psychological development depicted and emphasizes its nature as process. Further, *Kindred* accentuates the articulateness of Stepto's "articulate kinsman" through Dana's profession as a writer while simultaneously redefining the tribe that unites as kindred.

Kindred shifts the definition of tribe away from race and toward a cultural experience that is shared, however unwillingly or unwittingly. In the texts that Stepto describes, tribe has a clearly racial meaning. The dominant culture having defined any individual with measurable African blood as "black," the tribe consists of those blacks with a knowledge of and loyalty to African and African-American cultural traditions. The word "kindred" first appears in Butler's novel as a description of Dana's and Kevin's shared commitment to writing in the face of familial disapproval and social ridicule; despite their different races, Dana sees their common values as paramount. Here she chooses her spiritual kin. The term takes on richer meanings as Dana discovers her literal kin among the black and white Marylanders of the early 1800s. Here Butler suggests the meta-level concerned with the writer in her tradition through the development of the character. The writer must first become familiar with the bare facts, on the symbolic level, the texts of earlier generations; next, must organize those facts into categories, as Dana recognizes types of people and critics locate patterns of discourse; and third, must break down the categories into their component elements in order to rediscover complex individual people, symbolically the richness of individual texts constituting a tradition. Dana's heritage from the past encompasses Rufus and Alice—and the scribe, Hagar. Accepting this heritage without allowing it to define her (killing Rufus rather than submitting to rape), reaccepting it in the new form personified by Kevin and her cousin but still insisting on her right to self-definition, Dana figures the African-American woman writer expanding the concept of community.

This expansion, of course, is not unique in the history of African-American literature. Witness Ellison's invisible man stating/questioning, "Who knows but that, on the lower frequencies, I speak for you?" (439). Likewise the protagonist of David Bradley's *The Chaneysville Incident* finally images a past in which black and white, female and male, have a collaborative history. More like Shẽrley Anne Williams's *Dessa Rose* than these male-authored texts, however, *Kindred* differs from them in depicting the growth of a relationship concretizing the invisible man's abstract possibility. The increased tribe is not imaginatively recreated from scraps of the known past, as in *Chaneysville Incident*, but actually experienced in both past and present.[5] The acceptance of past tribes, defined and chosen by the dominant powers, merges into the denomination of the present tribe by the dominant power, the individual questing heroine/ African-American female writer.

To Dana's question, "What would a writer be doing working out of a slave market?" (53), Butler's text replies that she might be working out, first, "using the material"; second, working out as "dealing with"; third, working out as "moving away from that social definition and into others."

For the tradition of the African-American woman's novel, *Kindred* provides a literal paradigm of coming to terms with a history of slavery and oppression, a process that is in other works frequently metaphorical. *Kindred* assumes the importance of history to contemporary female identity and uses its heroine's involuntary time travel to symbolize the necessity of that confrontation. Butler does not present Dana as an arbitrarily selected time traveler; her willingness to marry Kevin implies a willingness to come to terms with complicated, historical, racially inflected and gendered identities. Dana's experience of history changes her self-definition and her understanding of context, fundamental shifts that must affect her writing. Although various novels explore different components, this tripartite pattern of deciding to excavate history, then accumulating knowledge, and finally reinterpreting it from a forward-looking perspective recurs throughout the tradition. While the divisions are by no means absolute, novels written early in the twentieth century tend to emphasize the decision itself, later novels stress the gradual acquisition of knowledge, and contemporary novels focus on the interpretation of history for present use.

3

"SAVE DE TEXT"

History, Storytelling, and the Female Quest in Their Eyes Were Watching God

Kindred both distinguishes and links oral storytelling and written works. Listening to the slaves on the Weylin plantation keeps Dana alive there; reading in her own time allows her to generalize about urges to power; writing stories will communicate her historical knowledge from a contemporary perspective. An ancestor of *Kindred*'s depiction of a woman's successful quest, Zora Neale Hurston's *Their Eyes Were Watching God*, originates several of *Kindred*'s important themes: sexism, historical education, orality, and growth into a self-in-community. As in *Kindred*, these themes are inextricably linked. The pressure from Janie's grandmother and her first two husbands to accept sexist patterns, for instance, comes from the sense that, historically, these have been the only roles available. Similarly, oral storytelling becomes the arena from which Janie's sexist husband Jody shuts her out, then the stage on which she joins in community theater, and finally the site of her self-fulfillment. Because of the different social contexts depicted in the novels—polyglot Los Angeles, 1976, versus all-black Eatonville and the Everglades, circa 1937—*Kindred* emphasizes written interpretation, and *Their Eyes Were Watching God* celebrates oral storytelling.

The sexism—and, of course, the racism—critiqued in *Their Eyes* influenced the novel's initial reviews and contributed to its marginal status for forty years. The critical reception and presentation of *Their Eyes* offers a model of the academic shift from universalism to awareness of race, class, and gender. The reviews sounded long-lingering notes of anger and dismissal. Richard Wright damned the novel as pandering images of black minstrels to white audiences; *The New Republic* complained that Hurston was incompetent to write dialect because she could not recognize rhythm as its essential component (Ferguson). So much for the first serious modern collector of oral southern black folklore. When the novel went out of print, critical works, which in large measure determine whether the academy teaches a book, echoed the initial judgments with varying riffs on the novel's and Hurston's limitations. To epitomize the attitudes of most white male critics toward African-American women's works, Craig Werner has singled out David Littlejohn's 1966 denunciation (3). Littlejohn finds Nella Larsen, Zora Neale Hurston, and Paule Marshall deficient in intellect and technical proficiency; further, he fears a kind of contagion in their works, for "the responding spirit is dulled, finally, bored by the iteration of hopelessness, the sordid limitation of the soul in the tight closet of the black imagination" (3).

The seventies began the revival of Hurston's reputation. The early years of the decade brought somewhat condescending or limited examinations rather than virulent attacks. Darwin Turner found Hurston's heroine rather simple: "All Janie wants is to love, to be loved, and to share the life of her man" (109). Turner at least saw Janie at the center of the novel; some viewed her as essentially passive and focused on other characters' struggle to control her (Giles) or on other characters entirely (Kilson). Robert Hemenway's 1977 biography, Alice Walker's foreword to the Hemenway biography and her subsequent "Looking for Zora," and Mary Helen Washington's introduction to the 1979 reprint of selections from Hurston's oeuvre—these among others reestablished Hurston as a major writer. Both Walker's testimony as an artist and other critical demonstrations highlighted Hurston as a powerful presence and influence in the African-American women's tradition.

Taking Hurston's increased stature as their premise, several critics of the early 1980s restored Janie and her voice to the center of *Their Eyes Were Watching God* (Bethel, McCredie). As part of this movement, I argued for viewing Janie as a questing heroine, an interpretation that this chapter reiterates and modifies. Recent criticism, particularly that of Michael Awkward and John Callahan, has moved ahead to larger considerations of voice in the novel, accenting its collaborative nature. This chapter seeks to integrate the critical concepts of the quest and of voice.

The rich narrative of *Their Eyes Were Watching God* welcomes many critical approaches. Including all the elements of Campbell's description of the quest, the first half of *Their Eyes* deals with Janie's initial refusal to answer the call to adventure; the second details her trials; the crucial frame concerns her return to community and resultant possibility for communal as well as personal growth. Carol Christ's three-part pattern of women's quests (experiences of emptiness, connection to natural forces, and subsequent renaming) likewise describes Janie's growth. *Their Eyes* also briefly attracted Robert B. Stepto's attention as a rare narrative of both ascent and immersion, which he dismissed on the grounds that its structure contradicted its theme. The novel's content, then, seems clearly to be about Janie's gradual growth into a different, more fulfilling identity, no matter what critical vocabulary describes it. Each of the paradigms highlights important themes, but perhaps because of their attempts to be inclusive, none of them touches on what *Their Eyes* presents as the necessary mechanism for individual growth within a community: the exchange of stories.

Hurston's training as an anthropologist with Franz Boas guaranteed her familiarity with materials similar to those from which Campbell drew his paradigm; both in childhood and as an adult who professionally collected folklore, she enjoyed and valued lying contests. Naturally enough, storytelling is crucial to both individual development and communal interaction in *Their Eyes*. Janie's call to adventure consists of her vision of the pear tree being pollinated by bees. In this vision, a real pear tree in Nanny's yard acquires transcendent significance. When Janie perceives a bee penetrating a blossom of this tree, she vicariously experiences that sexuality and thinks "so this was a marriage!" (24). This identification of marriage with total fulfillment, however, reflects her immature consciousness. The middle-aged Janie, preparing to tell her story to Pheoby, "saw her life like a great tree in leaf with the things suffered, things enjoyed, things done and undone. Dawn and doom was in the branches" (20). Clearly, the tree symbolizes the life cycle, and the seasonal change in the tree, which is now in leaf rather than in bloom, corresponds to Janie's time of life. Her initial interpretation of the tree is essentially static, focused on the social institution of marriage. Her later, more sophisticated vision centers on the balance of opposites, "things done and undone" (perhaps even the union of opposites, since the singular verb "was" indicates a singular subject in "dawn and doom"). Through her quest, Janie attempts to harmonize her daily life with her ideal image derived from the pear tree. When she returns to Eatonville and recounts her adventures to Pheoby, Janie implicitly asserts the unity of her experience and her vision. But to achieve fulfillment, she must struggle through many years during which the image remains tantalizing but seemingly unattainable.

This divorce of Janie's life from her vision of fulfillment results from her initial refusal of the call to adventure. Her temporizing stems in part from the pressures exerted by her grandmother, pressures reinforced by her geographic and psychic isolation. Indeed, the responsibility for her unfulfilling marriage, contracted when she is only sixteen, lies largely with these forces. Aware that Logan Killicks has nothing to do with the pear tree, she is led to believe, particularly by Nanny, that no matter who the marriage partner, a congruence between the image and the reality will develop gradually. Her hope of developing harmony between her marriage and the pear tree evaporates when Logan refuses to accept essential parts of her heritage, personality, and experience. As soon as she discovers that Logan "was accusing her of her mama, her grand-mama and her feelings, and she couldn't do anything about any of it" (54), she jettisons her commitment to him and seeks adventure with Jody Starks. Janie must leave Killicks to preserve her connection with her vision. As a response to its call to adventure, however, her acceptance of Jody represents only a limited understanding of its requirements.

At this point, Janie cannot conceptualize a true quest capable of uniting the quotidian and the transcendent. At the outset, she knows that Jody is not himself a part of the pear tree vision, that ". . . he did not represent sun-up and pollen and blooming trees, but he spoke for far horizon" (50). A short time later she seeks to realize her vision by disguising the concrete reality that should embody it: "From now on until death she was going to have flower dust and springtime sprinkled over everything. A bee for her bloom" (54). Janie no longer sees Jody as a vehicle but as the thing in itself. When she cannot sustain the fiction, she consciously decides to live in bad faith: " 'Maybe he ain't nothing',' she cautioned herself, 'but he is something in my mouth. He's got tuh be else Ah ain't got nothin' tuh live for. Ah'll lie and say he is. If Ah don't, life won't be nothin' but uh store and uh house' " (18–19). Janie bears complete responsibility for her own unhappiness in this marriage. Given the natures of Janie and Jody, the marriage could never have furthered a female quest, but here Janie temporizes as she did not when confronted with Logan's intransigence. Her failure of courage and imagination results in an insistence both public and private that the marriage is a success. The price of this bad faith is almost twenty years of spiritual hibernation, complete separation of concrete reality from the vision of the pear tree. She has temporarily refused the call to adventure in favor of a specious security.

As Nanny's death freed Janie from her first entrapment, so Jody's death frees her from her second retreat from the quest. Thereafter, Janie becomes an active agent in her own life; her acceptance of existential responsibility makes her truly, as opposed to nominally, free. Hurston underscores Janie's rebirth by associating her reflections on her marriages with a creation myth:

> She had found a jewel down inside herself and she had wanted to walk where people could see her and gleam it around. But she had been set in the market-place to sell. Been set for still-bait. When God had made The Man, he made him out of stuff that sung all the time and glittered all over. Then after that some angels got jealous and chopped him into millions of pieces, but still he glittered and hummed. So they beat him down to nothing but sparks but each little

spark had a shine and a song. So they covered each one over with mud. And the lonesomeness in the sparks make them hunt for one another, but the mud is deaf and dumb. Like all the other tumbling mud-balls, Janie had tried to show her shine. (138–39)

This irreverent, edited, and conflated variation of *Paradise Lost* and several Egyptian myths emphasizes both the mud and the shine. Previously Janie has been aware only of her shine. She must also accept the mud of the Everglades in order to realize fully her vision of the pear tree.

Before experiencing the community of the Everglades and Tea Cake's love, Janie must cross the threshold, separating specious safety from the risk necessary to fulfillment. She refuses offers of marriage, recognizing that their offers of "protection" amount to no more than economic exploitation. Her life alone, while it has no connection with the pear tree, has few uncertainties. Accepting Tea Cake's offer of companionship and love, on the other hand, carries tremendous risk. The community (represented by Hezekiah) warns Janie that Tea Cake will exploit her sexually and financially and then abandon her. Having internalized this concept, Janie nonetheless acts on her feeling with only Tea Cake's verbal reassurance. She cannot have an advance guarantee of his intentions; only his actions can certify his sincerity.

These actions are not initially encouraging. In Jacksonville, Tea Cake borrows Jane's money for a gambling stake without first consulting her. Alone for a day and a night with no word, Janie fears the fulfillment of the Eatonville prophecy that she will return home alone and broke. When Tea Cake returns, explains the reasons for his actions, and reaffirms his commitment to her, Janie fully accepts that relationship and its implicit call to adventure. She thus embarks on the quest to unify her life and its ideal image.

As part of this quest, Janie and Tea Cake undergo various trials and redefine their lives outside the usual social constructs. Their relationship rejects many ordinary conceptions of dominant and subordinate sex roles. Tea Cake is Janie's companion on her quest, not her master or mentor. In the Jacksonville incident, for example, she asserts her right to full participation in community activity after Tea Cake has excluded her from his party, fearing that the "refined"

Janie will be revolted. Tea Cake's action recalls Jody's prohibitions against Janie's participation in community affairs such as the wake for the mule or the storytelling sessions. Whereas Jody actively imposes a certain gentility on Janie, Tea Cake simply assumes its presence. As part of her determination to " 'utilize mahself all over' " (169), she insists that she be allowed to stand, not on a pedestal, but on the ground. This exploration of new roles continues in the Everglades, where Janie develops traditionally masculine skills such as marksmanship. Clearly, the adjustment involves more than Janie's investigation of previously male roles. Just as she works beside Tea Cake in the fields, he helps prepare supper. By abandoning traditional limitations, they approach the joyous harmony of Janie's vision.

Their lives are not, however, simply a continuous celebration. As questing hero, Janie must face trials with their origins in individuals, society, and natural forces. Janie's first trial centers on the questionable reliability of the individual closest to her, Tea Cake. She insists that Tea Cake admit that possibility when she discovers him wrestling with Nunkie, obviously responding on some level to a sexual invitation. After confronting Tea Cake, Janie accepts his reaffirmation of love, and there are no more wrestling matches. Nevertheless, she has learned that any real commitment must risk betrayal.

Janie has further preparation for her social trial through her exposure to Mrs. Turner, a light-skinned black woman who idolizes white culture. Janie very early accepts her blackness (though she at first resists it when she sees a picture of herself with white children) and later rejects Nanny and Jody's unsatisfying white system. Not personally threatened by Mrs. Turner's self-hatred and racism, Janie fails at first to understand the depth of that threat to Tea Cake and the rest of the black community. She tolerates Mrs. Turner's presence even when Mrs. Turner criticizes Tea Cake and offers her light brother as a more socially desirable spouse. Janie limits her reproofs to mild hints and a rudeness that Mrs. Turner can rationalize as the prerogative of Janie's lighter skin. Still, Janie does not fail this trial, for she accepts Tea Cake's anger and does not interfere with the community's violent annihilation of this threat to its integrity.

The hurricane, a trial generated by nature, threatens physical survival just as individual and social betrayals threaten psychic survival. Those caught in the hurricane shed their social roles: "The time was past for asking the white folks what to look for through that door. Six eyes were questioning *God*" (235). Under the circumstances, attempts to react to or protect another would endanger oneself. When Janie tries to secure a shingle to shelter Tea Cake, it acts as a sail, and the hurricane blows her into the water; when Tea Cake sees her drowning, he rescues her at the cost of the fatal dog bite. An elemental and divine force, the hurricane reduces the personality to its simplest components, forces a confrontation with physical limits. If the celebratory life in the Everglades is the "dawn" in the branches of Janie's pear-tree vision, then the hurricane is certainly part of the "doom." Up to this point, Janie has not had to contemplate the death of anyone dear to her, much less her own mortality.

The experience of the hurricane not only creates the physical circumstances leading to Tea Cake's death but also raises the metaphysical issues involved in humanity's complex relationships with nature and death. Janie has recognized fate's power during Jody's illness, but while she pities him, she has much more emotional investment in Tea Cake, whose madness and death try her strength severely. Janie ultimately accepts memory as a means of transcending death, which she perceives as a part of the natural cycle. At the same time, she expresses an immediate grief and longing that acceptance cannot obliterate: "No hour is ever eternity, but it has its right to weep" (273). Transcendent vision must expand rather than deny the concrete reality if an individual is to live the integrated life that is the reward of the successful questing heroine.

This application of Campbell's paradigm usefully explicates many elements of *Their Eyes,* but the paradigm itself cannot address other important components. Revisionist paradigms such as Christ's allow some of these submerged themes to surface. The pear tree as a naturally empowering symbol would become central in Christ's thinking, as would the hurricane's link to divine power. Further, Janie's experiences of nothingness in her first two marriages lead her to self-interrogation exactly as the model suggests, with the repetition emphasizing the cyclical nature of women's quests as Christ describes them. These experiences of nothingness correspond to the isolation of the articulate survivor in Stepto's journey of ascent.

From her childhood, Janie has been articulate in white ways; her playmates nickname her "Alphabet," and growing up in the white folks' yard assures her literacy. Still, the nickname comes into existence because " '. . . so many people had done named me different names' " (21), and Janie does not realize that she is black until she sees a photograph of herself with her friends. Janie feels the isolation of the articulate survivor when she describes Nanny's philosophy and her own compliance with it: "She was borned in slavery time when folks, dat is black folks, didn't sit down anytime dey felt lak it. So sittin' on porches lak de white madam looked lak uh mighty fine thing tuh her. Dat's whut she wanted for me—don't keer whut it cost. Git up on uh high chair and sit dere. She didn't have time tuh think whut tuh do afer you got up on de stool uh do nothin'. De object wuz tuh git dere. So Ah got up on de high stool lak she told me, but Pheoby, Ah done nearly languished tuh death up dere" (172).

Janie's experience of the pedestal previously reserved for white women, while it separates her from the community psychically, does not entail the kind of lonely trials that Campbell's quester undergoes. Janie's isolation comes from being "classed off," forbidden first by Joe and later by the townspeople themselves from participating in group rituals. Her quest also differs in important ways from the internal quest that Christ's heroines undertake.

Both traditional and revisionist paradigms share an assumption that the autonomous individual may be divorced from the social context. This premise obscures *Their Eyes Were Watching God*'s emphasis on community and individual as mutually and simultaneously constitutive. The integration of the spiritual and social quests, the most pressing issue of the Christ paradigm, never arises in *Their Eyes* because the spiritual cannot be separated from the social. Although Belle Glade differs from Eatonville and from the town in West Florida where Nanny settled, the towns are recognizably parts of the same African-American culture. To speak of Belle Glade as the landscape of idyll (Hite 267) seems to me to overlook, for instance, the victimized and victimizing Mrs. Turner, the physical violence between Tea Cake and Janie, and white control of the legal system that conducts Janie's actual trial for killing Tea Cake. These presences in Belle Glade establish continuities with the earlier scenes: Mrs. Turner may be a twisted version of Nanny and Jody; the physical violence, a milder rendition of Leafy's rape; and white control, an ostensibly protective mechanism for Janie that really alienates her from the African-American community.

In Campbell's terms, Janie's individual reward and her boon for the community consist of her full participation in a process of community expression and construction, a process from which Nanny and Jody had isolated her. As Jody's wife, Janie can participate only in extremely circumscribed ways. She first feels an unpleasant restriction when Jody refuses to let her respond to an invitation to speak on their first night in Eatonville or at its "low-life" communal celebrations. Janie disguises her only public rebellion under the cover of praise of Jody. Even then, Janie's remark, " 'You got uh town so you freed uh mule' " (92), passes without notice of its irony.

Her participation in the Everglades community contrasts dynamically with this restricted relationship to Eatonville, just as her partnership with Tea Cake contrasts with her subordination to Jody. Janie listens to lying contests and stories in Belle Glade, just as she did in Eatonville, but she begins to create and tell stories herself and, through practice, becomes good at it. These storytelling sessions are crucial to community and self-definition since they generate and develop communal tradition. Participation in this process is also crucial for the individual's self-definition since communal traditions define available roles. Janie's previous passivity, enforced by Jody and by her own avoidance of a confrontation with him, locks her into a fixed role; her active participation in the storytelling on the Glades exemplifies Hurston's vision of the relationship between communal and individual definition.

Robert Hemenway succinctly describes Hurston's attitude toward this creative process: "Hurston alone, among all the artists of the Harlem Renaissance, understood this principle of folk *process*. Folk tradition involves *behavior*—performed interpretations of the world which influence action—and it does not easily transfer to a point-oriented tradition. . . . There is no separation of subject and object, of mind and material for the creative artist" (80). Hurston shows Janie's artistic temperament, previously limited to private and escapist images of the pear tree, now expressing itself in communal creation, integrating her concrete experience and her transcendent vision.

The participation in communal story sessions constitutes a central element of what Stepto calls immersion; the tribal literacy of an articulate kinsman or kinswoman consists not only of the historical knowledge of the tribe but of competence in the tribal forms of expression. Janie creates a fulfilling self only thorugh immersion in the community of the Everglades. By emphasizing the frame story and the pattern of the quest, Hurston extends the narrative pattern to include the effects of the heroine's ascent and immersion on the community. Janie becomes an articulate kinsman; she influences an initial audience (Pheoby) and has reason to anticipate an expanded audience and extended effects for her art. *Their Eyes Were Watching God*, then, intimates a third narrative, this time a group ascent.

Group ascent would involve a community's growth to literacy and awareness of the modes of expression in surrounding white culture; its result, a literate community, would lessen or abolish the isolation of the individual articulate survivor. Although Jody's idea of establishing a post office in all-black Eatonville has the potential to aid in a group ascent, he can never successfully lead or join such a movement. Jody establishes a division between himself and the group—hence his emphasis on behavior appropriate for Mrs. Mayor Starks. Almost aspiring to the alienation that plagues Stepto's articulate survivor, the authoritarian Jody can never join, he can only command. The community accepts his material innovations, but, significantly, his assertion of superiority creates the isolation that makes his death so painful. With his position resting on the imposition of his "progressive" ideas rather than a consensus reached through many individual contributions, Jody remains a superior rather than a leader among equals.

Amiri Baraka has described the tradition of leadership in the African-American community in terms of a call-and-response pattern analogous to that of work songs composed during slavery. In this pattern, a leader's call invites a popular response, which then alters or becomes the next call. As a result, the leading voice always reflects both individual and community. Jody's big voice never issues a real call and will never evoke a response because of his implicit elitism, which the community recognizes immediately on his arrival in Eatonville:

> Jody: "Ain't got no Mayor! Well, who tells y'all what to do?"
> Hicks: "Nobody. Everybody's grown." (57)

Jody's patriarchal, child-adult or superior-inferior system finds only limited acceptance because it seeks obedience instead of collaboration. The sharing of knowledge essential to a community's preservation of its history and its continued growth relies on participatory forms. In *Their Eyes Were Watching God*, stories or beginnings of stories "call" for adventure, for response, for mutual creations. *Their Eyes* uses and examines different forms of storytelling and their divergent effects on the audience.

Their Eyes comprises a third-person narrator's presentation of Janie and her experience interspersed with Janie's direct narration to her friend Pheoby. This structure has occasioned much critical discussion, and Stepto called it a major flaw undercutting the establishment of Janie's voice. Three recent persuasive replies defend Hurston's technical choices by accenting the collaboration of voice seen as central to call-and-response; Stepto's argument, they imply, rests on an unexamined premise of articulation and hence control by a single voice. Thus, Michael Awkward in *Inspiriting Influences* maintains that Janie finds the individual voice either "tyrannical or ineffectual" and strives instead for a more effectual voice through her contribution to Pheoby's forthcoming stories. More inclusive, John Callahan's *In the African-American Grain* suggests a vision of Hurston's narrator, Janie, and Pheoby collaborating to produce the text of *Their Eyes*. John Kalb expands this idea to reconsider traditional definitions of first- and third-person narratives. He argues for the use in *Their Eyes* of a continuum of narrative technique, a breaking down of the separation usually seen between first- and third-person narrative, rather than an alternation between the opposed viewpoints. These critics thus place call-and-response at the thematic and technical center of *Their Eyes*. Building on their perceptions suggests that Hurston's originality lies in asserting the social construction, preservation, and exchange of individual and tribal histories as the key to successful female quests.

Hurston reiterates this connection with a myriad of histories, appearing in many different genres of narration. In addition to the frame and Janie's story (both third-person and first-person presentations), the novel includes inlaid texts of stories and suggestions of Pheoby's stories to follow. The inlays consist of events that Janie could not narrate: Nanny's personal narrative, lies about the mule, the buzzard's sermon on the mule's death, and an impromptu drama of courtship on the store's porch (105–9). Clearly, these function in different ways. Eatonville uses the mule as a convenient focus for its "crayon enlargements of life," material on which to exercise its collective hyperbolic narrative creativity. Making up stories on the mule unites the community in a friendly contest, allows it to criticize mean behavior of the mule's owner, and to enjoy absurdity and exaggeration. Similarly, everyone involved in the porch drama "know[s] it's not courtship. It's acting-out courtship and everybody is in the play" (105). Everybody is also in the audience, simultaneously performer and observer.

Just such a performance reconciles Tea Cake and Janie after their first serious misunderstanding. Tea Cake has taken Janie's money without asking and disappeared for twenty-four hours. Reassured that he will not abandon her, Janie still wants an explanation of his absence, an explanation that Tea Cake says she need not ask for " 'cause it's mah all day job tuh tell yuh" (181). Tea Cake appeals to "an imaginary audience"; in return, Janie plays "to the same audience" (192). These appeals, in which the lovers parody each other's positions, do not resolve the conflict. They do, however, set the stage for Tea Cake's subsequent performance, in which he "talked and acted out the story" (183). When he is finished, Janie's questions allow him to revise the story by adding that he had often wished Janie to be with him and nearly come for her three times—a crucial piece of information for his audience, both Janie and the reader. Revision thus leads to reconciliation and, more importantly, to agreed-upon premises for future behavior. His postscript empowers Janie to let him know that she wishes to participate fully in their relationship, a challenge to his old idea of her as the "classed off" Mrs. Mayor Starks. Call-and-response is restored through the communication of storytelling.

This example of negotiation and subsequent reconciliation through call-and-response contrasts sharply with Hurston's treatment of white obliteration of such African-American narrative strategies in the courtroom scenes. Although Janie's fate rests on the jury's verdict, Hurston chooses not to present directly the narrative that the jury finds so compelling. And the African-American community rejects Janie's story, striving instead to air another version in which Janie murders Tea Cake rather than defending herself. The community rejects Janie's story as a response to its exclusion from participation in the legal proceedings. Call-and-response is limited by the whites' monopoly over "calls" in the form of questions; each person testifies in turn, in a predetermined order, so that no group narrative emerges. The black community feels so strongly the need to participate that Sop-de-Bottom actually interrupts with "Mr. Prescott, Ah got somethin' tuh say" (277). By answering "shut your mouth up until somebody calls you," Prescott reiterates that the white power structure will not call to the black community. In response, the black community exercises its only power, rejection of the "official" edition of the events of their community.

The community does not rigidly continue to insist on Janie's guilt, however. Once removed from white interference, it immediately creates its own persuasive narrative of the events. When Janie calls the community to participate in Tea Cake's funeral, Sop-de-Bottom responds with a new version of events featuring Mrs. Turner's brother as the villain somehow responsible for Tea Cake's death, and the men run the hapless scapegoat out of Belle Glade for the second time. Here, as in the scene between Tea Cake and Janie, reconciliation (the agreement upon an acceptable narrative of past events) occurs in the context of impromptu performance.

More like the courtroom story than the mule stories—especially in its insistence on a single truth rather than multiple versions—Nanny's story demands its audience's attention with its claim to accuracy and historicity rather than hyperbole. It is private rather than public, for she deliberately withdraws Janie from open space by the gate to the inside of their house. The purpose of the story eschews entertainment; it aims, instead, at persuasion alone. The collective circumstances surrounding Nanny's tale—her fright at Janie's sexuality; her fear of being too old to protect her granddaughter; her previous choices to fight alone rather than marrying—

militate against collaboration. Nanny slaps her granddaughter because Janie remains silent in response to her grandmother's harangue when Janie does not want "to marry off decent like" (30). The slap both punishes and prompts Janie toward the one acceptable response, acquiescence. Janie cannot articulate her objection in terms that Nanny can respect, and her silence irritates Nanny, who rebukes her, "Don't you set dere poutin' wid me after all Ah done went through for you!" (32). Nanny frames her story, then, as a saga of self-sacrifice for her daughter and subsequently her granddaughter. Determined to persuade Janie to marry Killicks, Nanny sees her own story as providing what Janie later offers to Pheoby, "de understandin' to go 'long wid it" (19). Both Nanny and Janie offer an enlarged context through which to understand their stories and the present.[1]

Nanny's text has a powerful, continuing effect on Janie, even after Janie discards its explicit messages. Nanny offers the example of a female storyteller recounting her own experience, an example that Janie repeats. Nanny's text simultaneously supports a conservative ideology and demonstrates her own rejection of the most limiting view of women: "Honey, de white man is de ruler of everything as fur as Ah been able tuh find out. Maybe it's some place way off in de ocean where de black man is in power, but we don't know nothin' but what we see. So de white man throw down de load and tell de nigger man tuh pick it up. He pick it up because he have to, but he don't tote it. He hand it to his womenfolks. De nigger woman is de mule uh de world so far as Ah can see" (29).

Here Nanny constructs a folk tale, an imagined event that embodies the power relationships. This she follows with her vision, the sermon of "colored women sittin' on high" (32) and her own experience. Unable to realize her vision, Nanny preserves it first for her daughter and then for Janie: "So whilst Ah was tendin' you of nights Ah said Ah'd save de text for you" (32). Even while criticizing her limitations, Janie later pays tribute to her grandmother's ability to dream beyond her social realities (172).

In fact, Janie does save her grandmother's text though, of course, not in the way that Nanny meant her to, for she retells Nanny's story but disarms its potentially limiting messages by recontextualizing it in her own story. Janie tells her story under far different circumstances. Janie and Pheoby are on the back porch rather than inside the stuffy house, and Janie is demanding no particular action from Pheoby. Janie's voice and rhythm accommodate, even require, interruption and hence participation, as Nanny's did not. Much of *Their Eyes Were Watching God* recapitulates, in essence, the missing courtroom story, the explanation of how Janie came to shoot Tea Cake, this time told properly through collaboration between the narrator, Pheoby, and Janie. At the opening of the novel, Janie is already an accomplished storyteller, her experiences in Belle Glade testifying to her potential to issue calls worthy of response and to incorporate those responses in her next call. Eatonville intuited her ability when she first arrived; however, Jody quashes the communal invitation. This communal recognition is explicitly established when, in response to her comments on the mule, a bystander comments, "Yo' wife is uh born orator, Starks. Us never knowed dat befo'. She put jus' de right words tuh *our* thoughts" (92, emphasis added). Janie has talent, experience, flexibility, and communal acceptance. Her participation in storytelling belongs to the Afro-American pattern of call-and-response; her narration of her own story functions as a call to adventure for other questers. Through Janie, Hurston merges the quest pattern with the Afro-American call-and-response to form a new experience, a group quest or ascent. *Their Eyes* intimates an Eatonville with Janie and a whole group of Pheobys growing "ten feet tall" (284), traveling in company "tuh de horizon and back" (284), ever constructing and renewing both individual and community.

With this creation of a female griot, Zora Neale Hurston herself issued a powerful call to which subsequent African-American women novelists have responded in depicting the relationships of their heroines' identities and nonprint narratives. Expanding some tentative suggestions from Jessie Fauset's *Plum Bun*, *Their Eyes Were Watching God* establishes storytelling, oral narrative, as crucial to black women's quests. Hurston presents the complex relationships of three generations of women and their stories (Janie and Pheoby, Leafy, Nanny). She carefully differentiates between Nanny's purpose, the inflexible interpretation of tribal history that necessitates particular action, and Janie's aims—self-revelation, her audience's delight, collaborative construction. As a succession of critics from

June Jordan, Alice Walker, Henry Louis Gates, Jr., and Michael Awkward have noted, Hurston's fiction has served these same purposes. Wherever an African-American novel published after 1937 features a tribally literate female character helping to immerse others, Hurston's call has engendered a response, which in its turn becomes another call. Ernest Gaines's Miss Jane Pittman, Paule Marshall's Merle, Gayl Jones's Ursa, Octavia Butler's Dana—all seem to be "kissing friends" to Janie. Hurston has had such a powerful effect on subsequent African-American novels that occasionally a writer responds to a structural element as opposed to a character; thus, Toni Morrison's *Tar Baby* signifies on Janie and Tea Cake's journey to the muck. From the shout of *Their Eyes Were Watching God*—even from its echoes—come responsive, calling figurations of African-American women's historical experiences and identities.

4

PAULE MARSHALL'S WITNESS
TO HISTORY

PAULE MARSHALL'S THREE NOVELS—*Brown Girl, Brownstones; The Chosen Place, the Timeless People;* and *Praisesong for the Widow*—successively illustrate stages of the historically grounded female quest that *Kindred* portrays: the decision to investigate the historical past, difficulties in assimilating it, and a purposeful incorporation of historical past into the present self. For this reason, each heroine has feelings and experiences situations analogous to those that Dana faces. Like Dana, Selina is exasperated by her family's expectations of her, including both her probable occupation and her relationship with the tribe. Initially rejecting the heritage embodied in her mother, as Dana spurns traditionally female vocations such as nursing, Selina Boyce eventually brings both her mother's and another older woman's knowledge to the task of self-construction. Like Dana plunging into nineteenth-century Maryland, Selina, at the end of *Brown Girl, Brownstones,* embarks for the Caribbean islands of her progenitors. In *Chosen Place,* Merle Kinbona mirrors

Dana's pain and confusion at the overwhelming historical oppression that has constructed the present; lacking Dana's ability to escape to another context, she is forced to find the materials for reinterpretation of self and history in immediate surroundings. Like *Brown Girl*, this novel ends with the beginning of a journey. Merle's departure for Africa, unlike her earlier voyage to England, takes her to a site that may invigorate while it discloses its mixed histories; it incorporates the origins of free black cultures, the historical past of slavers and the personal past of an unforgiving husband, and the future in the form of Merle's daughter. As with Dana's commitment to writing, the form of Merle's life has not yet coalesced, but reinterpretation of history (retelling for Merle, rewriting for Dana) can construct a fuller version of the self. Completing the cycle, *Praisesong* links the acceptance of tribal history to the full experience of one's personal history; when Avatara almost simultaneously rediscovers both, she emerges as an avatar of her ancestral women griots. Unlike Dana, who also descends from a female griot (Hagar), Avatara knows both form and content of her historical message for the present. Unlike the earlier novels, *Praisesong* ends with the female quester's return home.

In her depictions of female quests, Marshall follows Hurston in making storytelling central. Listening to stories motivates some questers; telling stories helps to heal others; above all, the sense of community involved in the participatory interchange of teller and audience strengthens the questers' identities. In *Brown Girl*, with its adolescent quester, older characters generally tell stories to younger ones; in *Chosen Place*, the middle-aged exchange stories. Selina must absorb the narratives of her parents and their generation, and Merle must draw out and contribute to the flow of personal stories in her mostly middle-aged circle. Merle's search for her daughter, however, implies subsequent participation in the intergenerational pattern: questers do not choose one pattern or the other, but participate in each at different stages in their lives or in different roles during the same stage. *Praisesong* exalts the intergenerational narrative by making it Avatara's vocation. Both her process in claiming it and her conception of storytelling's purposes, however, diverge from those of Marshall's earlier novels and from a large portion of other African-American fiction. All three of Marshall's novels emphasize the integral relationship of storytelling and the female quest. Collaboratively constructing stories, both tribal and individual, furthers the development of both community and individual. The quester must find an empowering, participatory audience to help her articulate her own destiny within its larger destiny. Here, as in many other areas, *Their Eyes Were Watching God* initiates many "conversations" or "dialogues" with later works because it includes both patterns and implicit, or explicit, commentary on the necessary conditions for storytelling to do its work. Indeed, *Their Eyes Were Watching God* critiques some of *Praisesong*'s assumptions as Janie both "save[s] de text" (32) of her grandmother's sermon and changes its meaning by recontextualizing it.

ORAL NARRATIVE IN *Brown Girl, Brownstones*

Listening to stories broadens Selina's perspective, giving her vicarious access to experiences different from but finally consonant with her own. These narratives inform Selina not only of her parents' personal pasts but of heritage based on national culture and gender. In their examination of possible defenses against oppression, these stories distinguish effective means of self-defense from those that end in self-destruction. Initially, stories correct her typically childish rejection of a family photograph with a very young Deighton, Silla, her older sister Ina, and her short-lived brother. How could the world, much less her family, have existed before her birth? Even after this self-centeredness gives way, Selina has difficulty in believing in her parents' pictured youthful energies, particularly her mother's. Intervening harsh experience has so changed them that Selina cannot perceive her father and mother as connected to, possible developments of, the pictured youthful parents. Selina's internal image of her parents, then, has been limited by the cumulative effect of their struggles as poor Bajan immigrants. For the child, the present obliterates the past. By restoring the past, with its different potentialities, storytelling recasts the portrait and the present reality into frames of a continuous, still-developing film.

Similarly, Selina learns from stories to think beyond present-day white American definitions. For example, in one kitchen-table scene, Silla casually accepts Florrie Trotman's melodramatic tale of obeah-powered vengeance on an unfaithful husband and his mistress with,

"What you believe in you die in" (73). Florrie's story teaches the listening Selina, first, the power of a religion dismissed by white culture and, second, the agency that a wronged woman can exercise. Silla's comment asserts the effect of internalized beliefs, preparing Selina to understand the obliterative power of internalized racist images.

From Miss Thompson's narrative, Selina learns the depth and lasting impact of racist, patriarchal violence against women. Miss Thompson repelled the would-be rapist, but decades later, she still limps from the "life sore" on her leg, the unhealed wound from his attack. Selina hears this story because she specifically requests it. Having previously refused to tell it because "it ain't nothing for a child to hear" (217), Miss Thompson admits that Selina has become a woman, is nearly as old as Miss Thompson was at the time of the assault. The story might be dangerous for a child to hear, given that children simply do not have the physical strength to prevail against grown men, but it provides an adult woman with a model of partially successful resistance. Acknowledging their relationship, the older woman calls Selina "my baby, always been my baby"(218). Such gender-based unity has its limits, however. Though she may learn necessary stories from other women, Selina must follow Miss Thompson's directive to return to the Bajan community to resolve her identity within the specifically tribal context that shapes her mother's story.

Selina cannot at first conceive of her mother as an individual or of her father as part of a group, given the overwhelming reality of Silla's close connections to other Bajan immigrant women and Deighton's separation. At ten, "[s]he could never think of the mother alone. It was always the mother and the others, for they were alike—those watchful, wrathful women whose eyes seared and searched and laid bare, whose tongues lashed the world in unremitting distrust" (10–11). To see her mother as more than a minor variation of a stereotype, to realize and admit her own resemblance to her mother, Selina must hear the story of Silla's development.

Throughout *Brown Girl, Brownstones,* Selina shows an increasing interest and belief in oral narratives. When her older sister recounts that Deighton used to entertain this first-born by window-shopping with her, Selina discounts the story as a crude attempt to claim an intimacy with their father that the present set of relationships does not support. She feels it, in short, as an attempt to displace her privileged position as "Deighton's Selina." Years later, however, her father independently volunteers much the same story when he is distributing the fruits of his spending spree. Corroborated oral history acquires more authority.

This pattern of initial doubt followed by greater belief recurs especially in Selina's developing understanding of her mother's history. Set off unexpectedly by Selina's casual statement that it would be nice to live in Bimshire, Silla tells her own story of being, at ten, a field-worker driven by a woman with a whip. In even harder times, she carried heavy baskets of fruit on her head while fighting down her fear of duppies during the whole early-morning journey to market. Although the child Selina cannot articulate her response, the story becomes crucial to her: "It seemed to Selina that . . . the mother's formidable aspect was the culmination of all that she had suffered. This was no more than an impression, quickly lost in the haze of impressions that was her mind at ten. But it was there, fixed forever" (46). Critically, the story reveals her mother's capacity for fear. In her daily experience, Selina sees her mother as powerful and successful, never afraid. Although she is not a timid child, Selina must learn about Silla's original vulnerabilities. Without this understanding, Selina would be unable to use Silla's example to resist internalizing racist definitions. Selina witnesses, for instance, her mother's skilled handling of a dangerous machine in the war-time factory. This incident gains greater resonance when Deighton loses his arm to just such a machine. Silla herself emphasizes her self-preparation, the careful watching to learn how to operate the machine long before she is given access to it. The industrial world that frightens the child Selina and mutilates Deighton was not always congenial to Silla, however. Selina knows from Deighton's story of their courtship that Silla was once a shy country bumpkin completely lost in the confusing underground maze of the subway (117). Such stories help Selina finally to recognize in her mother's present countenance the expression of the young mother in the family portrait, to see the past's continuing presence and the present's existence as part of a sequential process rather than a static state.

Selina's reaction to her first prolonged experience of racial insult (inflicted by a white woman) shows her identifying both the primary danger and the primary means of resistance. Running from the assault until she is exhausted, she finds that she can see her reflection by street light in a vacant store's window. She sees, however, not with her own eyes, but with those of the oppressor. Not surprisingly, the false image magnifies flaws: "Above all, the horror was that she saw in that image—which had the shape and form of her face but was not really her face—her own dark depth. Her sins rose like a miasma from its fetid bottom." (291). Feebly she attempts to use individual assertion to deny the image, striking the window without sufficient force to break it. The persistence of the window's image reveals to her the power of the oppressor: "their idea of her was only an illusion . . . it would stalk her down the years, confront her in each mirror and from the safe circle of their eyes, surprise her even in the gleaming surface of a table. It would intrude in every corner of her life" (291). Almost simultaneously, she grieves and subconsciously identifies her only real defense, tribal identification and unity: "She cried because, like all her kinsmen, she must somehow prevent it from destroying her inside and find a way for her real face to emerge" (291). Her initial response is to seek an individual's comfort and support, the old dream of personal transcendence of social circumstance, here personified in Clive.

Selina's disappointment in Clive does not doom her, however, because of her new self-definition and access to other models. Feeling united to other blacks by an experience that she knows to be tribal rather than individual, Selina "was one with Miss Thompson. . . . One with the whores, the flashy men, and the blues rising sacredly. . . . And she was one with them: the mother and the Bajan women, who had lived each day what she had come to know. How had the mother endured, she who had not chosen death by water?" (292–93). Selina here affirms her unity with an African-American woman of a somewhat different tribe (Miss Thompson) and with black men. In the end, she claims membership in the group that she has always striven to transcend, Bajan women, and identity with an individual she has sought to deny, her mother, Silla. Selina now has an explanation for Silla's sudden rages which does not rely on Silla's innate pathology or on Deighton's and Selina's failures. She has been prepared to accept Silla's complexities and her heroism by the gradual accretion of years of storytelling.

Beside this account of integration into the tribe and defense of the individual by storytelling, *Brown Girl, Brownstones* examines what happens when the griot abandons his stories or when the individual does not respond to them. In the parental generation, a fundamentally European religious narrative displaces the potentially supportive tribal stories; in Selina's generation, the individual is left without structure, in an existentialist nausea. The senile Miss Mary and her broken-spirited daughter exemplify both of these themes. An Irish immigrant who worked as a servant, Mary prattles continually of the day-to-day doings and sayings of her employer's family; she never speaks of her own activities with her daughter or of her own experience, except as tangential to the white middle-class family's life. Mary's substitution of her employer's family's experience for her own leaves her unmarried daughter Maritze easy prey to a Christian structure that demands complete self-sacrifice for women. Venting justifiable anger on her mother rebounds on Maritze, undercutting her sense of worth with the guilt inherent in the system that demands her passivity. Because it allows her to venerate a part of herself through worship of the Blessed Virgin, however, even Maritze's fanatic Catholicism is preferable to Deighton's conversion to Father Divine's cult.

For whatever reason—an education that detached him from his mother, early separation from his father, preferential treatment that encouraged elitism—Deighton cannot conform to the norms of immigrant Bajan society sufficiently to remain a member of the community. He appears as part of a group only in his description of his childhood games, never as an adult. He reacts with both rage and glee to his invisibility in the United States; he is angry that he cannot get a job commensurate with his talents and training but jubilant that his illegal entry prevents him from being drafted. His growing alienation from Bajan structures, coterminous with his increasing internalization of racist images, culminates in his move to Father Divine's settlement.

Father Divine gives him a vocabulary through which to vent his resentment of Silla and other women along with a religious justification for doing so: "God is your father, your mother, your sister, your brother, your wife, your child, and you will never have another! The mother of creation is the mother of defilement. The word *mother* is a filthy word" (168). Ostensibly, this patriarchal structure would allow Deighton to asssume an authority that is denied him socially. Selina recognizes in the Divine cult the patriarchal structure of the Challenor household. There, Beryl's father simultaneously exalts himself and obliterates his daughter's personality. Just as the Challenor home can accommodate only one dominant male, Father Divine's system allows only one leader, and Deighton's position must perforce be that of a follower. Selina sees that, whereas Beryl's father has set himself up as a god in his own home, Deighton has accepted a definition of himself as a child in another's dwelling. When Deighton rebukes Selina for calling him "Daddy" and instructs her to say "Brother Boyce" (171), he accepts his own infantilization and rejects forever his adult male role. Forcibly deprived of even this self-definition when he is deported, Deighton kills himself by plunging into the sea before his ship reaches Barbados. Deighton's suicide makes clear the consequences of a refusal to articulate and communicate one's experiences. Accepting the narrative of an exterior, oppressive power structure leaves oneself and one's heirs spiritually bankrupt.

In reiterating these themes through Clive's character, Marshall widens the depiction from first-generation immigrants to subsequent generations. With no religious narrative to substitute for his tribal tales, Clive may well kill himself sooner than Deighton. Clive recapitulates Deighton's frustration with racism, his misogyny, and his resultant immaturity. On a seaside cliff, he makes a gesture toward suicide that anticipates Deighton's fatal leap: "[H]e pitched forward as though shoved from behind by some powerful invisible assailant. His body began a swift drop . . . his hands frantically grasping hold . . . saved him from striking his head and somersaulting into the water" (266). Clive's "powerful, invisible assailant" assaults every black character in *Brown Girl, Brownstones*. Clive survives, for the moment, "crouched on the last narrow ledge at the water's edge, his hands desperately gripping into the rock, his big loose body bent almost double and his head bowed between his knees as though he were retching" (266)—a semifetal position. To save him, Selina forms her plan of betraying the community by defrauding the Association of scholarship money, a kind of replay of her father's and mother's machinations with the money from the sale of Deighton's inheritance.

Strengthened by the stories that she has heard and unconsciously absorbed, Selina eventually realizes that her real defense against racism resides not in Clive but in the whole of the community and specifically in her female mentors. No longer afraid of similarities to Silla, she plans a trip to the Caribbean and justifies it from her mother's example: "Remember how you used to talk about how you left home and came here alone as a girl of eighteen and was your own woman? I used to love hearing that. And that's what I want. I want it!" (307). Listening to stories has enabled Selina to understand her parents, to know her female vulnerabilities and strengths, and to respect her tribe as she embarks on the journey to be her own woman.

NONPRINT NARRATIVE in *The Chosen Place, the Timeless People*

In *The Chosen Place, the Timeless People,* personal narrative constructs or reconstructs both self and its social context. Every character in the novel is shown to be a profoundly social construction; in the beginning, the more sympathetic characters feel helpless to combat or deal with the larger context's effects on them and others. Because telling a story involves not only recalling a particular action but supplying enough context so that the listener and the teller can interpret it, storytelling offers an individual some power, however limited, to characterize the context as it has "characterized" (made the character of) the storyteller.

In keeping with his culture and his gender, Saul Amron's initial approach to storytelling is abstract. He reacts to the climactic demonstration of the impoverished Bournehillians—the carnival reenactment of Cuffee Ned's rebellion—with an explicit, abstract disquisition on the uses of history for oppressed people. Seemingly without recognition of the role of shame in victims, Saul recommends recovery of historical events, "[They] must at some point, if they mean to come into their own, start using their history to their advantage. . . . You begin, I believe, by first acknowledging it, all of it" (315). His rationale relies on direct application of past strategies to present realities: "Because many times, what one needs to know for the present—the action that must be taken if a people are to win their right to live, the methods to be used . . . has [sic] been spelled out in past events" (315). The emotional aridity of Saul's accurate insight constrasts sharply with the power of the lived understanding of Bournehills in general and that of his auditor, Merle, in particular. Though it does not add to Merle's more sophisticated understanding, Saul's version of the insight is important because conversation, the sharing of stories, re-creates the teller as well as the listener in *The Chosen Place, the Timeless People*. Marshall replaces the generational storytelling of *Brown Girl, Brownstones* with the narratives of intragenerational friendship. Potentially, these narratives contribute to a mostly oral alternative history, one that opposes the printed texts of racism, colonialism, fascism, and other oppressive ideologies.

The tension between printed and oral histories comes to the fore early. Merle's last collapse was occasioned by losing her job as a history teacher at the high school because she told the story of the Pyre Hill rebellion instead of concentrating on the textbook's English version of English history. The problem with the dominant culture's text is not so much factual inaccuracies as its false claim to comprehensiveness. Merle's room, with its greater inclusiveness, gives the lie to official history. A microcosm of the island, Merle's bedroom contains many old paintings and engravings—the printed history in effect selects those works depicting the planter class's plantations while veiling or removing the dominant drawing, a cross-section of the slave ship that enabled the planter class to come into being. Oral narrative, at once defensive and subversive, finds many forms: Merle's telling Anancy folklore stories to orphaned children, the theatrical reenactment of Cuffee Ned's rebellion during carnival, folk rituals and songs surrounding ostensibly Christian feasts like All Souls' Eve.

Marshall does not, however, posit oral history as a simple or sufficient alternative to oppression. No one form can critically undermine a dominant ideology created by economic forces and embedded in some measure in individuals' psyches. Marshall purposefully underlines the limitations of oral opposition by juxtaposing two events, Ferguson's attempt to confront the English owners of the factory and Merle's folk stories. Merle has been telling orphaned children tales of Anancy, "who, though small and weak, always managed to outwit the larger and stronger creatures in his world, including man, by his wit and cunning" (224). Saul listens to the end of one of these stories after witnessing Ferguson's abortive attempt to make the owner, Sir John, take responsibility for keeping the factory operable. As the owner of the only outlet for Bournehills sugar cane, Sir John is not himself a great power, but he represents colonial power and more or less consciously uses it: "One of those small men who succeed in giving the impression of height and size because of the stiff-shouldered, military bearing they affect and a certain impatient, imperious air. Sir John was dressed as if for a safari." (220). In Sir John's presence, Ferguson's usual eloquence is literally muted; he leaves without being able to say a word. Although Ferguson is one of the most senior, experienced workers, Sir John cannot remember his name. Clearly, neither the story of Cuffee Ned (which he loves) nor the Anancy tales enable Ferguson to confront Sir John; on the larger scale, individuals from Bournehills cannot hope to prevail, as individuals, against imperial power and its texts.

Marshall prophesies neither victory for defeat for Bournehills, but her depiction of group participation in narration holds some hope. Every year Bournehills holds an overnight vigil and songfest on All Souls' Eve. Practical work is accomplished—the villagers tend to the graves—but while they work as individuals, they sing as a community. Although the texts of their songs are European, Marshall highlights the singers' revoicing, which "transformed the bleak joyless Protestant hymns of mourning into songs of celebration and remembrance, joyous songs" (268). *The Chosen Place, the Timeless People* takes the cliché of singing loudly enough to waken the dead and affirms its essence. The living community always achieves at least the appearance of victory over the grave: "Because toward dawn . . . the gray shreds of morning mist that could be seen rising from the graves could have well been the ghostly forms of the ancestral dead who, in answer to their summons, had emerged from their resting place to stand at their sides" (268). This presentation of ancestral persistence and support immediately precedes the account of the carnival, another Bournehills ritual.

Carnival embarrasses the island bourgeoisie intent on drawing tourists because, every year, the Bournehills community insists on dramatizing Cuffee Ned's rebellion. Its actors offer not only the plot but communal song explaining and constructing the meanings of the action. So moving is this performance that it momentarily transforms the audience into a single people despite its class divisions. The carnival song narrates Cuffee Ned's triumph and his crushing defeat, definitive as far as the governance of ths island is concerned, but it ends with him confident that "in dying he would be restored to the homeland and there be a young warrior and hunter again" (288). Cuffee Ned's faith in his reincarnation—and Bournehills's yearly communal re-creation of it—speak to Saul's sense that only a complete revolution could restore Bournehills to its former vitality. The individual's reincarnation may or may not occur; the ancestors may or may not emerge as wisps of mist to stand beside their progeny; but the community can re-create Cuffee Ned at will, when it realizes the will.

Cuffee Ned, of course, failed in his larger aims. The history of an oppressed people cannot honestly be presented as a panorama of great and unqualified victories, nor can the personal history of individuals situated in unjust social structures resound with their moral victories. For the oppressed, subjugation tends to destroy the individuals' beliefs in themselves as decent human beings and thus dissolves the basis for moral action; for the oppressors, unearned power engenders a false sense of superiority that requires continuing self-deception. Honest personal narratives, therefore, are inevitably shot through with shame, either the shame of the victim, the shame of the criminal, or the two combined since internalized stereotypes produce the behavior from which they are supposedly distilled. Social and personal awareness lead to a guilt and shame so overwhelming that every major character in *Chosen Place* is paralyzed, his/her vital processes stopped, a microcosm of the wider social world frozen in its life-denying patterns of oppression.

While admitting the limited power of any oral oppositional means—folklore, theatrical performance, group song—to change political structures, *Chosen Place* strongly affirms the necessity of individual and personal storytelling. Merle's Anancy tales may not directly prepare the children for Ferguson's ordeal, but another oral history suggests the genre's wider powers. Saul's mother, a Sephardic Jew and therefore something of an alien even within a predominantly Jewish area, frequently recalled her tribe's sojourn over several continents. Her account is mostly fictional, but its value lies beyond its factual accuracy, for in Saul's mind, it takes on "the proportions of an archetype, a paradigm, in his youthful imagination" (164). Moving beyond tribal history, his mother's narrative "also came to embody, without his realizing it (the story working its powerful alchemy on him when he had been most vulnerable), all that any other people had had to endure. It became the means by which he understood the suffering of others" (164). Merle makes clear that, although Jews and Bournehillians may have had analogous histories as oppressed peoples, not all Jews have Saul's empathy. Telling stories to people who are "most vulnerable," the children, is an irreplaceable part of constructing a more just social order with more empathetic individuals. Again, narrative empowers not only the audience but the teller, for storytelling becomes the primary means of moving beyond personal paralysis.

Telling one's own story does not solve its ambiguities or absolve one of guilt. To be unable to tell one's story in *The Chosen Place, the Timeless People,* however, is to be paralyzed; to tell it dishonestly is to be doomed. The novel maintains sympathy for the mute. In fact, silence may be a stage, albeit a lengthy one, in an individual's evolution. When the novel opens, Merle, Saul, and Harriet are all unable to speak about important parts of their experiences, and Allen's self-recognition silences him. Allen never reveals his homosexuality, even to Vere, whom he loves, or to Merle, who offers him sympathy and emotional support. He feels such shame at the discovery of his true sexuality and his subsequent masturbation while Vere makes love to a woman in the next room that he cannot voice his true nature. Aware of his real self but unable to communicate it, Allen continues half-alive. Knowledge alone does not empower.

In contrast to its relatively sympathetic presentation of the voiceless, *The Chosen Place, the Timeless People* damns those who consciously falsify their stories. Marshall identifies a crucial connection between social power and dishonesty, a theme developed through the characterization of Harriet Amron. Harriet fears the historical excavation involved in honest storytelling. She evades responsibility for the use of her power in, for instance, her contribution to her first husband's creation of nuclear weapons. When her dreams inform her that she shares "credit" for his invention, she leaves him immediately and suppresses the memory. This evasion does not come solely from her individual quirks, however; it comes with the territory of power. As part of a privileged class, Harriet has no examples of successful self-examination. Her father's attempt to interrogate history begins in retreat and ends in disaster. Unlike Ellison's invisible man, Harriet's father never emerges from the basement where he has retired prematurely from the practice of law to research Lorenzo de Medici. Preoccupied with a prime mover in the emergence of political strategy and the modern state, he abandons his family. He shows precisely the ideal of the quest that Marshall refuses, the insistence that construction of the self precede other commitments. To construct the self first is to renege on commitments that are always already there.

With no models for taking responsibility for her unconscious impulses, Harriet repeatedly lies in telling the story of her carnival experience. Like the official histories, its factual details are all correct, but her narrative is incomplete and false because it omits her own feelings. Saul invites her again and again to tell him what happened; he knows that, in some sense, the experience was a watershed for Harriet and hence for their relationship. To his call, she responds only that she was frightened by being caught in the midst of drunken teenagers playing soldier. Her narrative conceals her racist rage that the carnival participants ignored her directives and her racist certainty that they would, like lemmings, force one another into the sea. Juxtaposed with Harriet's power to affect the economic development of Bourne Island, the incident shows her fear of the islanders' collective power, her characterization of them as animal and instinctual rather than rational, her resultant contempt, and her continued insistence that she should guide them. Although she acts on this racism consistently, she cannot admit to it.

A frank discussion of a more inclusive version of the story might have headed off the later crisis that occasions her suicide. The climactic scene in which Saul five times demands to know if she has caused the end of the Bournehills project telescopes their discussions of the earlier carnival experience. Harriet denies her responsibility (and culpability) for many individual actions that, together, constitute her past. As much as either Merle or Saul, Harriet is caught in a repeating pattern fueled by her drive for control over others and her fundamental dishonesty. Her suicide stems directly from her recognition that she has repeated with Saul the essentials of her first marriage. Ironically, in fleeing from her mother's example—Harriet sees her as a weak southern belle, a suicide without the courage to act directly—Harriet embraces it. Her personally dishonest narrative becomes a part of an imprisoning false social, political, and economic history.

If false narrative betokens death, and muteness gives evidence of death-in-life, true storytelling offers some small hope. In a climactic scene, Saul and Merle trade their stories of failure. Saul recounts the circumstances of his first wife's death in the Honduras bush, partially the result of his professional preoccupation. Merle reveals that even after she marries and knows her husband's abhorrence of lesbianism, she persisted in taking money from an English woman with whom she had had an affair. Discovered, she felt judged and immoral, and she neglected both her infant daughter and husband, who returned to Africa with their child. Saul and Merle see these failures as emblematic of permanent character flaws that make them unfit for marriage or parenthood or any other responsible role. His story told, Saul really mourns Sosha for the first time, able now to admit her dying accusations about his grandiose notions of changing the world for the poor. Clearly in return, Merle reveals her shame and anger. The changes are not immediate, but in a matter of months, Merle defies Harriet as she did not defy her English lover, and Saul understands that he can return to the United States instead of hiding from further experience in the bush.

Exchanging stories can enable such emotional progress for two reasons, one grounded in the audience and one in the self of the storyteller. The acceptance by another of one's story—and the trust that it will meet with this acceptance so that one can articulate it in the first place—is transformative. The presence of a trustworthy audience makes possible, even necessary, an articulation. The transformative power of stories does not depend on the revelation of secrets, however. The reader first learns of Merle's losing her job teaching history, for example, when Leesy mentions it to Vere.

Later, Merle retells the story to Saul. Everyone on Bourne Island knows the outlines of Merle's English experiences, and she knows that Saul knows them before she speaks. In the presentation of *The Chosen Place, the Timeless People,* the importance of personal stories lies not so much in the specific information as in the narrator's construction of self and surrounding context.

Even when a story's general outlines are common knowledge, both storyteller and audience can benefit from a retelling. Thus, although the islanders know Merle's actions in England, they do not know Merle's complex motivations; they cannot, for she herself does not know them until she retells her story to Saul. Earlier she says, "I don't understand me, you know. . . . I haven't a clue, for instance, why I lived as I did in England, all the damn foolish things I did there which caused me to lose the two most important people in my life" (228–29). When talking with Saul, she complicates her earlier picture of herself as a bad mother and of her husband as a hard but fair man; she now understands her actions as those of a woman affected by colonialism, by the difficulties of communication between an African male who has escaped many of colonialism's ravages and a Caribbean woman who has suffered them. In telling her story, she constructs herself as less vile and her husband as less saintly than in the earlier, silent version that caused her breakdown and recurrently paralyzes her. Because personal narrative necessitates a construction or reconstruction of the self-as-character, it offers power to the storyteller.

Sometimes the events recalled in personal narratives have more immediate implications for the audience than for the teller. Stinger tells Saul, for instance, the story of abandoning his first, good wife and children for love of Gwen, his current wife. Stinger is mystified by the necessity to give his first wife pain, but he knows himself to have been helpless in his passion for Gwen. Saul offers no comment on the story because Stinger talks while they are driving, and their arrival precludes discussion. Stinger's story might have many resonances—it could be a warning to Saul about his feelings for Merle; it could be a request for forgiveness; it could indicate that causing pain, even great pain, is inevitable if one lives fully. Its meaning may well shift each time that Saul remembers it, but in great pain and stress, after Harriet's suicide, he remembers. Like his mother's tale of her tribe's wandering, like Merle's story of her disastrous marriage, Stinger's voice will return when his story is relevant to Saul's emotional life.

Telling one's own stories and listening to others' narratives release one from the illusion of extreme grotesqueness, from the illusion of uniqueness. Harriet's unwillingness to give up this fancied uniqueness, paradoxically defined also as normality, prevents her both from connecting with those who might aid her, like Merle, and from being able to tell her story truthfully. The guilt and shame that prevent communication of one's story are in some ways egotistical. In Marshall's works, the audience cannot, after all, transcend the social conditions that contribute to personal failure and must itself therefore fail. Those failures must be told individually—must be sung collectively—before victory songs can be composed.

AVATARS AND ARCHETYPES: *Praisesong for the Widow*

In response to the call of Hurston's *Their Eyes Were Watching God,* *Praisesong for the Widow* further develops its story of African-American male tragedy and, while retaining the centrality of the female griot, changes the nature of her experience and subsequently of her story. In *Their Eyes,* the men's experiences are tangential to the development of Janie's character. Infrequently, the narrator reveals a man's motivation even though Janie is not aware of it. Janie hears, for example, only Logan Killicks's contempt for her, but the reader is privy to his fear that she will leave him. Likewise, the impact of Janie's public verbal rebuke of Joe Starks is clear, even though neither Joe nor Janie could articulate it. What Joe Starks's way of living has cost him, the reader hears only through Janie's plain speaking as Joe lies dying. Joe rejects Janie's version; his last words order her from his room. Hurston's emphases here help construct her focus, the telling of Janie's story, including her suffering from the demands of Joe's world view.

With Janie's story a part of the tradition, Marshall can reinvent Joe's story and have her female point-of-view character realize its pain. When Janie runs away with him, Joe Starks is Jody; their bed, a daisy field for playing. *Praisesong*'s Jerome Johnson was originally Jay; his nickname later vanishes, along with all other playfulness, including the Johnsons' enjoyment of sex. The circumstances of these grim metamorphoses differ greatly. Always desirous of being a "big voice," Joe Starks commands from the top of Eatonville's social hierarchy. His cruelty to Janie comes from his need to preserve his social advantages. In contrast, Jay's truncated personality as Jerome comes into being precisely because of his responsibility to others, not because of his selfishness. Working two jobs to support his two children and the accidentally pregnant Avey, he nearly opts for the streets instead of the family as he sees all of their personalities being deformed by economic pressure. Once having chosen his family, he cannot limit the changes; constant work leaves him emotionally ever more distant, politically ever more conservative, particularly toward those unwilling to sacrifice what he has. Part of Avey's internal journey consists of recognizing and mourning, not only her loss of Jay, but Jay's loss of Jay. If *Their Eyes* is a circle with a center, *Praisesong,* with its two focal points, is an ellipse.

In several ways, *Praisesong* diverges from *Their Eyes* and its descendant, *Kindred.* The griot's motivation for undertaking her journey, her reasons for telling her story, the story's content, and the context in which she tells it all differ from Hurston's presentation and also from Marshall's own earlier novels. In *Their Eyes, Brown Girl,* and *Chosen Place,* each heroine undertakes a quest because she is conscious of a lack that may be supplied within the framework of experiences that a new place or new companions can supply. *Kindred* shows no such conscious decision, but if Dana's marriage to Kevin is to have a chance of being fulfilling, she must have a self fully grounded in history; deciding to marry Kevin is in effect a decision to embrace historical experience. Significantly, her white ancestor calls her just after her marriage to a white husband. *Praisesong's* heroine responds to a psychic or spiritual bond to an ancestor, just as Dana does, but the timing of the ancestor's call has no thematic justification in the character's actions. Avey has not recently made and is not contemplating any important changes in her mode of life. The spiritual call of Great-Aunt Cuney during the cruise thus seems arbitrary. In *Praisesong,* the mechanism for plot movement appears completely outside the character, in the spiritual realm, rather than simultaneously within and without as in *Kindred.*

As part of this shift, *Praisesong* offers very little dialogue or direct narration by a character compared with Marshall's earlier novels.

Instead, *Praisesong* focuses on memory, on internal process rather than dialogue. Processes that in the first two novels develop in community, here develop within one individual. This increased emphasis on internal process is facilitated by a shift in characterization. Earlier situated so satisfactorily within day-to-day activity and specific people, archetypal significances now obliterate individuality. For these reasons, using Campbell's archetypal heroic quest to explore *Praisesong* illuminates more and suppresses less of this novel than it does of *Brown Girl* or *Chosen Place*.

In *Chosen Place*, both action and conversation always reflect particular circumstances and experience. Saul's borderline neglect might not have had a horrible effect on another woman, but his wife's health has been ruined by a concentration camp; similarly, Harriet's offer of money might have annoyed another Bournehills woman, but it infuriates Merle because it re-creates scenes from her earlier affair. Characters experience current events, in short, from perspectives constructed by their entire previous lives. Interactions thus involve considerable complexities in which class, culture, gender, and desire are always actively present.

Instead of the earlier novels' presentations of communicative process and the development of understanding, *Praisesong* postulates instantaneous understanding between individuals from different cultures, classes, and genders. Avatara need not narrate any of her experiences or disclose any of her internal processes in order to enjoy telepathic communication with Lebert Joseph. For him, there is "no thought or image, no hidden turn of her mind he did not have access to. The events . . . which she withheld or overlooked, the feelings she sought to mask, the meanings that were beyond her—he saw and understood them all from the look he bent on her" (171). When Avey's stamina falters—her ability or willingness to express her own story, so crucial to Merle's survival and to Harriet's demise—*Praisesong* excuses her because transcendent spiritual communication obviates the necessity: "The man already knew of the Gethsemane she had undergone last night, knew about it in the same detailed and anguished way as Avey Johnson, although she had not spoken a word. His penetrating look said as much" (172). Lebert Joseph, of course, represents a divinity, Legba, "who possessed ways of seeing that went beyond mere sight and ways of knowing that outstripped ordinary intelligencce (*li gain connaiss-ance*) and thus had no need for words" (172). Avey, however, displays the same clairvoyance, for she senses his complete knowledge of her. Clearly, Avey becomes Avatara, a horse for the Vodun spirits.

Avey and Lebert Joseph are intended to be embodiments, however. Certainly Avey's body must be purified by purge before she can be transformed into a griot. Spirit cannot speak to spirit in the earlier novels except through embodiments in particular individuals. Throughout *Praisesong*, particularity is simply unimportant; this is why Avey can shuck off the years of experience that destroyed her husband, internally transformed him from Jay to Jerome, with no effect. This abandonment of individuality in favor of the simply archetypal makes the novel's progress too predictable and weakens the ending.

As particularity diminishes, so does the need for call-and-response. In *Their Eyes,* Janie's motivation for storytelling includes self-revelation and friendship for Pheoby; in *Praisesong,* Avatara reacts to her sense of tribal responsibility, joyful kinship with both the ancestors and future generations, represented by her grandsons. Janie's narrative tells her own personal experience, in the context of her mother's and grandmother's histories; Avatara plans to communicate tribal myth rather than her own life. As griot, Avatara plans to retell the story of the Ibos' return to Africa word-for-word as she received it from her Great-Aunt Cuney. This great-aunt tolerated no questions, and the story is evidently complete in itself, with no commentary or additions needed. But Avatara should be aware that listening to the story did not prevent her later alienation, that it gave her no clue as to how she should deal with her pregnancy, her marriage, or her husband's slow suicide. Disturbingly, she plans the same exact experience for her grandsons that she has had with her great-aunt. This re-creation suggests that the story's message is finished, complete; the griot's tale need not incorporate Avey's experience. True, the Bournehills carnival reenactment also repeats itself, but as a communal rather than an individual performance; it takes place in a context of storytelling that also includes folktale and personal revelation. *Praisesong* makes invariant both the role of griot and the griot's message.

In *Their Eyes Were Watching God,* Hurston had laid out the problems inherent in fixed rather than dynamic conceptions of storyteller, tribal and individual experience, and listener. Other novels in the tradition also affirm the need for ongoing process.

5

BIRTHRIGHTS
Passing, History, and Ancient Properties

SINCE THE 1937 PUBLICATION of Zora Neale Hurston's *Their Eyes Were Watching God,* the successful female journey of immersion has been a recurrent theme in African-American women writers' novels. This immersion has necessarily involved acknowledgement and new understandings of historical events. Before Hurston in the twentieth century, however, the theme of attempted disengagement from history was prominent. Earlier heroines with mixed racial heritages, like *Kindred*'s Dana, face a hostile social context much closer in time and social assumptions to the Weylin plantation than to the 1970s in Los Angeles. The synthesis of heritages that Dana seeks both internally and in her marriage to Kevin, while not readily achievable, is not an absolute social impossibility. Having lived their heritages, Kevin and Dana demonstrate a knowledgeable, flexible support for one another; further, each has at least one supportive friend. The rigid society depicted in novels of the Harlem Renaissance allows no such synthesis. Nella Larsen's *Quicksand* details the choices open to a woman of mixed heritage who is too dark to pass, all of which entail denial of one part of her racial identity. *Quicksand,* in other words, details the milieu surrounding heroines who can't pass: a society both legally and psychically Jim-Crowed.

With synthesis impossible, with social circumstances requiring that one deny part of her identity, choosing that part became a subject for literature. Three major Harlem Renaissance novels, two of them by women, center on passing, so that in literary history the theme and the Renaissance novel seem permanently linked (see, for example, Amritjit Singh). Considered passé already by the 1930s, the theme's exploration of ambivalences toward and sometimes rejection of black heritage certainly found few sympathetic readers between the Renaissance vogue and the 1986 reissue of *Quicksand* and *Passing* in the American Women Writers Series. Critic and writer Sherley Anne Williams succinctly sums up the progression by noting that, at the end of the Harlem Renaissance, the black bourgeoisie as subject "passed out of fashion"; its replacement became either the naturalism of Richard Wright or Zora Neale Hurston's celebration of "the rich verbal and musical culture of the black masses—music and lore that the black middle class deplored as examples of the backwardness of the lower classes and as reminders of the slave past" (69). Williams here accents the early twentieth-century black middle class's abandonment of historical experience and record, the perceived impossibility of enjoying both middle-class status and historical continuity.

In the novels of the early twentieth century, passing is intimately related to an African-American protagonist's ability to become or remain middle class. This movement into the middle class entails a fundamental difficulty: the traditional African and African-American sense of self rests on a self-in-community; in contrast—in opposition—the traditional white, European, middle-class sense of self, generally described as "bourgeois," insists on privatization and compartmentalization. Williams's characterization of Richard Wright in "Roots of Privilege"—ironically a major force in the erasure of the middle class as literary subject—highlights the incompatibility of African-American vernacular and the autonomous self: "In *Black Boy*, Wright literally and figuratively renounces oral culture and black tradition for personal autonomy" (71). Given this fundamental incompatibility, the passing heroine who "ascends" into the middle class automatically suffers the isolation of Stepto's "articulate survivor," literate in the dominant culture but without the connections and support of immersion in African-American culture, including a working knowledge of the African-American past. "Black middle class" has often been represented, in short, as an oxymoron.

For fifty years, the perceived narrowness of focus in novels about passing—one individual at a time, and that one sufficiently literate in white ways (including formal education) to attain middle class status—appeared self-indulgent. Other artists were attempting apparently larger themes. To some, rescuing blacks from the vise of economics and the law seemed paramount. Following Jean Toomer, others tried to preserve a threatened folk culture. After the advent of the Black Aesthetic, others voiced the experiences of disparate classes of African-Americans nevertheless united by a culture preserving African heritages. To perceive passing as a smaller issue—a purely personal decision, an elitist theme because it concerns a choice open to only a few—ignores the social context that defines the issue.

The trope of passing depicts more than a privileged individual's purely personal decisions; it investigates an individual's relationships with history. Constructing "passing" as a set of attitudes toward the middle class and concomitantly toward the past reveals a continuity between the woman-authored novels of the Harlem Renaissance and a number of major works by women fictionists of the 1980s. In her 1985 review of Gloria Naylor's *Linden Hills,* Andrea Lee's *Sarah Phillips,* and Notzake Shange's *Betsey Brown,* Williams notes the resurgence of literary interest in the black middle class. To this short list could be added Toni Morrison's *Song of Solomon* and *Tar Baby.*[1]

African-American women novelists have not so much resolved the perceived clash of racial and class identities as explored their ramifications for black women. Early novels tend to explore the fate of individuals striving to become, in Stepto's terms, articulate survivors; novels of the 1970s and 1980s, on the other hand, limn second- and later-generation middle-class African Americans who have been raised without immersion in the historical black experience. Unlike the predominantly male examples whom Stepto examines to create his critical paradigm, however, two of the three female "articulate survivors" of the Harlem Renaissance—Helga Crane of *Quicksand* and Clare Kendry of *Passing*—do not survive. (Further, the narrator of *Passing*, Irene Redfield, clearly does not survive whole.) Angela Murray of Fauset's *Plum Bun* lives, but she rejects the notion of passing in favor of reimmersion. Gloria Naylor's broader focus in *Linden Hills*, a subdivision rather than a single character, allows her to explore, for both genders and a variety of temperaments and sexualities, the costs of conformity to ideals of the isolated self. The black middle class becomes, in her work, a parody of a community that is profoundly nonnurturant, its inhabitants sterile or suicidal. One of the great journeys of immersion, Morrison's *Song of Solomon*, shows the development of a middle-class male's emotional understanding of his family's historical past and his corollary development of personal responsibility. These developments, however, peak quite near the end of the novel so that Milkman never demonstrates the integration of his experience of immersion and his middle-class standing. The immersion journeys of middle-class women, a muted theme in *Song of Solomon*, come to the fore in *Tar Baby*. Paying homage to both Nella Larsen and Zora Neale Hurston, *Tar Baby* reexamines the presentation of immersion in *Their Eyes Were Watching God* by redrawing the map of the South via Larsen's *Quicksand*. Morrison reiterates the disconnections imaged in the earlier works; simultaneously, she demonstrates surprising shared local loyalties that cut across these splits by showing identities to consist of complex imbrications of class, gender, and nationalities.

Quicksand AND ILLEGITIMATE IDENTITY

The novels of the Harlem Renaissance generate the premises that the later novels develop and explore. Nella Larsen's *Passing* shows the decision to live ahistorically, to truncate all relationships with one's heritages, and the inevitable doom which that refusal of history entails; Jessie Fauset's *Plum Bun* explores a tacit commitment to that detachment, one that the heroine rescinds as its disadvantages become clear. Larsen's earlier novel, *Quicksand*, indicates the conditions that make passing an either/or choice of heritage. American culture of this period insists on a false segregation of historical events, allows for no synthesis of black and white experiences, even when their interactions are evident in the very body of the mulatta heroine.[2] Passing does not entail the construction of a false history but, as *Passing* indicates, the obliteration of the past with no replacement:

> "What about background? Family, I mean. Surely you can't just drop down on people from nowhere and expect them to receive you with open arms, can you?"
>
> "Almost," Clare asserted. "You'd be surprised, 'Rene, how much easier that is with white people than with us. . . ."
>
> "You mean that you didn't have to explain where you came from? It seems impossible." . . .
>
> "As a matter of fact, I didn't." (158)

The black woman who passes into the white world moves into an ahistorical void where she has no antecedents, only the illusorily secure identity of connectedness to the white world through liaisons with white men.[3] The women in this position thus suffer from all the vulnerabilities of the traditional white woman's identity without any of the supporting network of kin or preserved historical wisdom.

Barbara Christian's *Black Women Novelists* has traced, in Nella Larsen's *Quicksand* and *Passing* and Jessie Fauset's *Plum Bun*, the connections between passing and the tragic mulatta theme. White, southern literary representations of the mulatta in the nineteenth century frequently presented her as "caught between two worlds, and since she is obviously the result of an illicit relationship, she suffers from a melancholy of the blood that inevitably leads to tragedy" (16). In Christian's analysis, *Quicksand*'s Helga Crane continues this general tradition, albeit with some important changes. Helga finds herself an image rather than an individual in both black and white worlds; this objectification, in conjunction with the repression of her sexuality demanded by the black middle class, means that "[the mulatta] is doomed in Larsen's novels to become a self-centered, oppressed neurotic or a downtrodden, half-alive peasant" (53). Thus, Christian details the fate of the individual in a particular set of social circumstances, the segregated black and white worlds portrayed in this novel from the 1920s.

Some more recent interpretations exclude the context in order to condemn the personal shortcomings that they present as responsible for Helga's unhappiness and, eventually, her death. Mary Lay makes the case most succinctly: "Helga fails as a woman, as an individual, as a black, not because of her environment but because of choice and personality" (486).[4] Similarly, Lillie Howard disputes Hortense Thornton's sympathetic reading by insisting that Helga has acceptable alternatives personified by Robert Anderson, Anne Grey, and Audrey Denney. In her view, the Danes show Helga that "there is something precious, to be valued about her Blackness; Anderson again showing that undisciplined sexuality may cost too much, Miss Denney's independence" (232). Howard considers Anderson a viable alternative, but Larsen presents him as a fundamentally limited person who is threatened by his own sexuality, unable either to act on it or to repress it sufficiently for consistent action. The Danes only superficially value Helga's blackness; as several critics commenting on Olsen have noted, what they really value is its utility to them as a figure of the exotic Other (Christian, *Black Women Novelists*, 52; Wall 102).

Both Howard and Lay argue that Helga should accept Anderson's pragmatic observation that "[m]ost people achieve a sort of protective immunity, a kind of callousness" toward the "lies, injustice and hypocrisy . . . part of every ordinary community" (Larsen, *Quicksand*, 20). First, the text seems not to present Anderson as a model, for he does not take his own advice in regard to staying at Naxos; Helga later meets him in Harlem. Second, their position is tenable, but it values social adjustment at a cost that seems too high, a cost that a good deal of the African-American tradition also refuses. When the title character of Alice Walker's *The Third Life of Grange Copeland* considers his lost childhood sensitivity, he considers important parts of his human capacity lost with it:

> "When I was a child," he said, "I used to cry if somebody killed a ant. As I look back on it now, I *liked* feeling that way. I don't *want* to set here now *numb* to half the peoples in the world. I feel like something soft and warm an' delicate an' sort of *shy* has just been burned right out of me. . . .
>
> "The trouble with numbness . . . is that it spreads to all your organs, mainly the heart. Pretty soon after I don't hear the white folks crying for help I don't hear the black." (210–11, original emphasis)

In Grange's view, the trouble with numbness, with developing callousness or protective immunity, is that insensitivity cannot be selective, either for one's own experience or for that of others. An entire African-American genre—the blues, as described in Ellison's famous statement in "Richard Wright's Blues"—advocate neither denying nor blocking pain, but keeping pain alive in order to transcend it "not by the consolation of philosophy but by squeezing from it a near-tragic, near-comic lyricism" (90).

Even if one grants these critics their donnée in the acceptance of individual personality as the primary focus, their analyses ignore some crucial factors in the formation of Helga's character. The isolation that both characterizes and destroys Helga has several sources. First, though she does not abandon Helga physically, Helga's mother Karen withdraws emotionally. Her death, when Helga is only fifteen, deprives the girl of competent female guidance into adult sexuality. Further, Karen's experience could not be a direct guide for Helga because the immigrant white woman's experience was not coincident with a black American woman's. Helga's ambivalences toward her own sexuality are not just those of any other middle-class black woman struggling against racist stereotypes of the wanton; her own illegitimacy emphasizes the risks of sexual involvement (McDowell, Introduction, xxi). Because the whole question of legitimacy involves social affirmation that must greatly influence character development, this last issue suggests the inseparable nature of personal development and social conditions, in short, the need for a contextual critical approach.

Several configurations within *Quicksand* support Hazel Carby's identification of the mulatta as African-American literature's insistence, in the face of racist denial, on the reality of miscegenation. (Not surprisingly, Carby offers one of the best contextual explanations of Helga's alienation.) The participants in miscegenation, Helga's parents, are absent or dead in the novel's present. Their absence allows others to deny their own connections to miscegenation. Confronted with Helga's claim to kinship to her uncle Peter, for instance, Peter's new wife stammers a confused repudiation: "*Well*, he isn't exactly your uncle, is he? Your mother wasn't married, was she? I mean, to your father? . . . And please remember that my husband is not your uncle. No indeed! Why, that, that would make me your aunt! He's not—" (*Quicksand*, 28–29). The world of the black middle class, as imaged through Anne Grey, is no less exclusive. Theoretically an exponent of black culture, Anne in fact rejects it while imitating the white middle class. She nevertheless hates whites and considers it "an affront to the race . . . for any Negro to receive on terms of equality any white person" (48), especially for any black women like Audrey Denney to consider white lovers. Helga chafes under this hypocrisy: "Sometimes it took all her self-control to keep from tossing sarcastically at Anne Ibsen's remark about there being assuredly something very wrong with the drains, but after all there were other parts of the edifice" (49). Helga's memory of the Scandinavian Ibsen at this point surely reasserts her Danish mother's experience as counterpoint to Anne's denial of miscegenation.

Larsen further adumbrates these initial disavowals of miscegenation—refusals to synthesize black and white historical experience—in each segregated world through parallel black and white characters acting as aunts to Helga. The symmetrical figures of Mrs. Hayes-Rore and Katrina Dahl develop additional aspects of the positions outlined by Anne Grey and Mrs. Peter Nilssen. Mrs. Hayes-Rore and Anne are kin, aunt and niece, and Mrs. Hayes-Rore introduces Helga to Anne's household by saying that Helga has lost her mother, thus making it clear that she is acting in place of the absent female relative. The Danish Katrina Dahl, the sister of Helga's mother, is willing to recognize her niece publicly. Although they are more sympathetic to Helga than their counterparts, each of these women insists on the suppression of a crucial part of Helga's history and thus her identity.

Mrs. Hayes-Rore inquires about Helga's "people" and then rejects Helga's evasion with, "If you didn't have people, you wouldn't be living. Everybody has people, Miss Crane. Everybody" (39). After hearing Helga's story, however, Mrs. Hayes-Rore counsels her to conceal half her heritage: "And, by the way, I wouldn't mention that my people are white, if I were you. Colored people won't understand it, and after all it's your own business. When you've lived as long as I have, you'll know that what others don't know can't hurt you. I'll just tell Anne that you're a friend of mine whose mother's dead. That'll place you well enough and it's all true. I never tell lies. She can fill in the gaps to suit herself and anyone curious enough to ask" (41).

Ironically, this is Clare's strategy in *Passing,* to allow others to construct a fictional history for her, but here Helga is passing for someone whose family history of miscegenation occurred in the unknown past. Larsen indicates the representative nature of Mrs. Hayes-Rore's motivation: "The woman felt that the story, dealing as it did with race intermingling and possible adultery, was beyond definite discussion. For among black people, as among white people, it is tacitly understood that these things are not mentioned— and therefore they do not exist" (39).

Not surprisingly, acting on this advice initially makes Helga "feel like a criminal" (42). Before long, however, she makes what turns out to be a very temporary truce with her psyche and, during this time, considers this suppression to be an act of vengeance on the white world: "For her, this Harlem was enough. Of that white world, so distant, so near, she asked only indifference. No, not at all did she crave, from those pale and powerful people, awareness. Sinister folks, she considered them, who had stolen her birthright. *Their past contribution to her life,* which had been but shame and grief, she had hidden away from brown folk in a locked closet, 'never,' she told herself, 'to be reopened' " (45, my emphasis). The ambiguity of the locked closet—whether it encloses shame or brown folk—bespeaks the impossibility of resting in this solution. Larsen situates Mrs. Hayes-Rore's advice in another way. This lecturer on racial issues constructs her speeches as "patchworks of others' speeches and opinions" (38). Clearly, her derivative ideas cannot contribute to any kind of progress.

Katrina Dahl's relationship with Helga reiterates her brother Peter's treatment of their niece. Peter has given Helga money, not really in the expectation of helping her permanently, for he believes that her black blood makes her incapable of industry and foresight. His generosity, then, is meant to undercut her self-image while reaffirming his superiority.[5] Katrina and her husband Poul acknowledge Helga in far more public ways than Peter, taking her into their home and buying her clothing. Their apparent welcome, however, barely conceals their commodification of her. As Carby notes, they hope that her marriage will give them access to the artistic circles that will cloak their class with culture's mantle. Further, this com-modification rests on a definition of Helga as the exotic Other (Wall 102). The costumes in which the Dahls dress Helga emphasize her difference, occlude her sameness. On her arrival, Helga sees a neighbor as "doll-like" and the streets as "toy-like" (*Quicksand,* 66). The nature of her experience in Denmark may be summed up, particularly in light of Larsen's earlier evocation of Ibsen, by noting that she is, indeed, in a Dahl house.

Helga has attempted to comply with the demands of the social context that she obliterate part of her heritage. As stubbornly persistent as her skin's testimony to miscegenation, however, it will not be gainsaid. When Peter writes his abominable note to accom-pany his conscience money, which will allow Helga to go to Denmark, her surprising reaction indicates the historical past's presence in the individual's consciousness: "Here the inscrutability of the dozen or more brown faces, all cast from the same indefinite mold, and so like her own, seemed pressing forward against her. . . . Then she was overcome by another [irritation] so actual, so sharp, so horribly painful, that forever afterwards she preferred to forget it. It was as if she were shut up, boxed up, with hundreds of her race, closed up with that something in the racial character which had always been to her, inexplicable, alien" (54–55).

Rational thought will never explain the Middle Passage, for that is the experience conjured here. Helga may forget this particular incident, but her emotions forever express themselves in a vocabu-lary inflected by racially specific experience. In the Gammelstrand, Copenhagen's marketplace, "Helga's appearance always roused lively and audible, but friendly, interest, long after she became in other parts of the city an accepted curiosity" (76). Ironically, an old Danish countrywoman there, having asked what nature of human being Helga is, refuses to believe in her black heritage because her appearance is not stereotypical.

Her experience on the marriage market is a cross between that of the American black women on the auction block and that of women sold as mistresses at the Creole balls. When her aunt first cross-examines her about her progress in leading Herr Olsen to a pro-posal, Helga "had a feeling of nakedness. Outrage" (79). Unlike her forebears, Helga is able simply to ignore Herr Olsen's proposal that she be his mistress, to pretend misunderstanding. When he proposes marriage, however, her earlier feeling of physical discomfort and shame returns in "a stripped, naked feeling under his direct gaze" (86). Olsen accuses her of selling herself to the highest bidder as she chooses between her suitors, and she extends the explicit metaphor: "I'm not for sale. Not to you. Not to any white man. I don't at all care to be owned" (87). Helga's limitation of her statement "to white men" clearly demonstrates her feeling that the discussed bondage goes beyond that of any married woman of the time to her husband and would be specifically that of a black woman married to a white.

This interpretation has so far foregrounded race rather than gender, yet Helga's own explanation highlights their melded significances. As Christian remarks, "her tragedy is specifically a female one. She is destroyed by her womb" (*Black Women Novelists* 53). Throughout, *Quicksand* demands our attention to gender. The stereotype of miscegenation in much African-American literature represented a black woman and a white man, in part because, under slavery, this configuration was much likelier and in part because the reversed configuration would result in free children rather than slaves, as children followed the legal status of their mothers. *Quicksand*'s inversion of this standard trope of miscegenation can be explained as a biographical matter, that Larsen's father was West Indian and her mother Danish, but such an observation does not explore the functions of the inversion in the text. Like any other artist, Larsen transforms autobiographical material as she uses it— her father died when she was a small child; Helga's father deserts Karen and Helga.

Quicksand highlights not only Helga's father's absence, but the absence of his story. First, he is never named, and this in a novel that names even the most minor of actors. Both Anne Grey's maid Lillie and Katrina Nilsson's maid Maria, for example, are named although Lillie never even appears and Maria speaks only once. Second, the alert reader perceives that Helga gives varying versions of his never-elaborated story. Her initial account, rendered to Robert Anderson when she is leaving Naxos, characterizes him as "a gambler who deserted my mother" (21).[6] A day later he appears in her thoughts as "that gay suave scoundrel" (23). After hearing motifs from "Swing Low, Sweet Chariot" in a performance of Dvorak's *New World Symphony*, has caused Helga to decide to return to American, she revises her portrait:

> For the first time Helga Crane felt sympathy rather than contempt and hatred for that father, who so often and so angrily she had blamed for his desertion of her mother. She understood, now, his rejection, his repudiation, of the formal calm her mother had represented. She understood his yearning, his intolerable need for the inexhaustible humor and the incessant hope of his own kind, his need for those things, not material, indigenous to all Negro environments. She understood and could sympathize with his facile surrender to the irresistible ties of race, now that they dragged at her own heart. (92)

But, of course, it is her own heart that Helga knows, not her father's. Later fiction, such as Claude McKay's "Truant" and Ann Petry's *The Street*, examines various intertwined psychic and economic motivations for their African-American male characters' desertions of their families. *Quicksand*, on the other hand, implies that desertion results from America's ideological insistence that black and white realities remain mutually exclusive. On the social level, this untenable separation falsifies American history; on the individual level, it obscures forever the character of the deserter, who remains a cipher.

One effect on the female story of inverting the trope of miscegenation is to emphasize the isolation of the resulting daughter and the helplessness of the mother to protect her. As a young woman, Helga understands clearly why her protest, as a six-year-old, against her mother's marriage or remarriage to a white man could not be honored. Disastrous for Helga's psychic health, the marriage nevertheless represents an economic necessity if this immigrant white woman is not to abandon her mulatta child: "Even foolish, despised women must have food and clothing; even unloved little Negro girls must be somehow provided for" (23). The marriage reestablishes or recognizes the hegemony of white male patriarchy within the family, which is Helga's immediate context, as it reigns in the larger social context.

In acute critical analyses of patriarchy's effect on Helga's sexuality, Christian locates Helga's difficulty in expressing her sexuality in the internalized restraints of the middle class; McDowell finds not only Helga but Larsen ambivalent about sexuality, unable in this novel to go beyond middle-class conventions. Certainly the narrative voice at times condemns sexual feelings per se, yet the novel presents a complex analysis of European patriarchy's deformation of women's sexuality. Three elements of the opening chapter suggest a specifically Euro-American patriarchal enclosure of women's desire, Helga's attempt at sexual freedom, and the ultimate ability of the system to reinscribe all such individual forays.

The first chapter is set in Naxos, a black school dependent upon white financing. This dependency makes "respectability" essential, not only conformity to white middle-class values but a conservatism that goes so far beyond them that it becomes irreproachable. This regime constructs only unsatisfying outlets for Helga's sexual desires. Under its influence, Helga's fiancé, James Vayle, loses his vitality and thus his original appeal. Vayle's name has rich implications. In *The Souls of Black Folks*, Du Bois uses the figure of the veil several times. His "Forethought" refers to "the two worlds within and without the Veil." Describing his initiatory experience of difference, Du Bois writes, "Then it dawned upon me with a certain suddenness that I was different from the others; or like, mayhap, in heart and life and longing, but shut out from their world by a vast veil" (2). "Vayle," then, suggests the insistent separation of black and white worlds, the very separation that rives Helga's psyche.

As McDowell notes, "Naxos" is a play on the word "Saxon," and it also designates the island that in Greek mythology is dedicated to Dionysus (*Quicksand* 243). Exploring this latter signification, one recalls that Dionysus was worshipped primarily by Greek women. Middle-class Athenian women (all of them married, of course) were not normally allowed to leave their homes. During the spring celebration of Dionysus, however, they gathered outside the city for their orgiastic rites. These rites provided a space, however circumscribed, for female expressions of desire. The origins of Dionysus suggest difficulties; he was transferred from his mother Semele's body to Zeus's thigh, and Zeus bore him, as he also bore Athena. Whereas Athena sprang from Zeus's head, Dionysus emerged from the thigh, a sexualized part of the male body. Dionysus is thus a figure of female desire removed from the female and mediated through the sexuality of the male. Female sexuality at Naxos will be defined by men and thus closely constrained.

In Larsen's presentation, twentieth-century black women have lost even the access to less-mediated expression of female desire that Athenian women were allowed. The mythic significance of Naxos and the historical experience of Athenian women help to construct the meaning of Helga's conversion experience, the imagery of which McDowell rightly interprets as sexually orgasmic (Introduction xx). The text accentuates the connections between the church service and the Greek ritual: "Little by little the performance took on an almost Bacchic vehemence" (113). As the focus shifts from the performance to the participant, the correspondence is reiterated: "She felt herself in the presence of a nameless people, observing rites of a remote obscure origin" (113) and "[S]he felt an echo of the weird orgy resound in her own heart; she felt herself possessed by the same madness; she too felt a brutal desire to shout and to sling herself about" (113). What distinguishes the Harlem church from the Bacchic orgies as a site of female desire, however, is the presence of the male director, the Reverend Pleasant Green. Religious structure has become an elaboration of patriarchal structure so that "a kind of transcendent women's room" (Wall 104) cannot, in actuality, transcend. Like the symmetrical aunts, the novel's two preachers complement each other. The first, an eminent white minister, crystallizes Helga's dissatisfactions with Naxos by giving a racist sermon congratulating the Naxos audience on knowing its (subordinate) place. This preacher speaks for white supremacy, and the second represents and promotes patriarchy.

The crucial first chapter symbolically foreshadows the refusal of European patriarchal definitions of her sexuality that accompanies Helga's conversion experience. As Helga considers her dissatisfactions with Naxos, Larsen's description of an otherwise gratuitous incident clearly has sexual overtones: "A sweet smell of early Southern flowers rushed in on a newly-risen breeze which suddenly parted the thin silk curtains at the opened windows. A slender, frail glass vase fell from the sill with a tingling crash" (3–4). The flaring of the curtains and the subsequent destruction of the vase represent sexual excitement's effect on the labia and the breaking of the hymen in sexual intercourse. Larsen here uses a familiar literary constellation. At least from eighteenth century forward, glass—particularly the vase—in the English literary tradition symbolized female chastity. Pope's "The Rape of the Lock" employs the figure, as does the famous china scene of Wycherly's *The Country Wife*. In the nineteenth century, George Meredith reiterated it in *The Egoist*. These are, of course, all from a European tradition; the culture constructing—indeed, dictating—the definitions of race and gender, as well as their expressions, throughout *Quicksand* is shown to be European.

Although the form of Helga's revolt is foreshadowed, its immediate motivation only gradually becomes clear as she experiences the psychic effects of both black and white societies's refusals to allow her to synthesize her heritages. Throughout *Quicksand*, Helga has sudden glimpses of barely remembered parts of her experience. She remembers a childhood trip to Denmark, for example, only after her decision to go there again. As each world defines its interest in only part of her heritage, she internalizes its standards and represses some part of her own experience. Helga plunges into sexual experience as an anodyne to the pain of continued consciousness. Her consciousness—racially doubled in the Du Boisian sense, doubled again by her femaleness—cannot be healed, only obliterated. Ironically, Helga's single apprehension of her own past as a unified experience occurs as a direct result of her disastrous flight into sexual experience, the delirium following a difficult birth. Acute illness frees her consciousness to include simultaneously her mother, Robert Anderson, Anne Grey, Audrey Denney, the Dahls, and many others of her acquaintance, a state that she finds "refreshingly delicious, this immersion in the past" (129). Such refreshment exists only in the psyche cut free of the dictates of this social context, the psyche on the verge of extinction.

"WRITING HISTORY WITH A BRUSH": JESSIE FAUSET'S *Plum Bun*

That very freedom to transcend what is felt to be a limiting context allures Angela Murray, the heroine of Jessie Redmon Fauset's *Plum Bun*. Compared to *Quicksand*, *Plum Bun* is in most ways a lesser novel because it displays a fundamental confusion of genre, being neither romance nor realism. *Plum Bun*'s heroine, Angela Murray, decides after her parents' death to move from Philadelphia in order to pass in New York City, necessarily leaving her younger, darker-skinned sister Virginia (Jinny). In New York, she studies art and experiences the difficulties of passing while simultaneously acting morally. Angela denies her sister after not having seen her for two years, because of the unexpected appearance of the rich white bigot (Roger Fielding) whom she hopes to marry. Not successful in bringing him to a proposal, however, Angela becomes his mistress. When he breaks off the relationship, Angela turns to the artistically talented and morally earnest Anthony Cross. Anthony reveals his mixed racial heritage as a reason for separating from Angela, and by the time that Angela reveals her own racial inheritances, Anthony has become engaged to Virginia. An African-American student in Angela's art school loses a scholarship when the awarding committee becomes aware of her race, and Angela, who has also won a scholarship, surrenders hers by revealing her own heritage. The long-suffering Jinny makes up the scholarship money to send Angela to France for further study. On Christmas, having overcome the various barriers to marriage with the man whom she has always loved, Jinny sends Anthony to Angela.

Carolyn Sylvander's perceptive study argues persuasively that the early critical condemnations of *Plum Bun* dismiss it too readily as adolescent romance. She cites in particular Arthur Davis's conflation of the perspectives of the narrator/author and the main character, Angela Murray. In her view, Angela's construction of her own life in terms of a romance or fairy tale becomes merely a stage of her development; Fauset is writing not a romance but a *Bildungsroman*. This view of Fauset's text, as a critique of sentimental romance, is further supported by Joseph Feeney's and Sylvander's explorations of the title's nursery rhyme as the novel's major ironic structuring device—an analogue, incidentally, to Toni Morrison's use of a reading primer to structure *The Bluest Eye*.

While a necessary corrective, Sylvander's perspective overlooks major strains in the novel. First, if the heroine's development does not correspond entirely to that in a sentimental romance, the presentation of her parents—Junius's rescue of Mattie from the leering white ogre, their happy-ever-after ménage, and Mattie's death from grief immediately after Junius's demise—conforms exactly to white nineteenth-century norms of romance. The daughters' names, Angela and Virginia, highlight the traits associated with the Cult of Womanhood. Then again, the method of foreshadowing seems peculiarly old-fashioned: every Sunday, while playing "The Dying Christian" for her father's pleasure, Angela's sister Virginia anticipates losing her sibling, and she later does when Angela decides to pass. Notwithstanding its brief, more candid presentation of other female characters' sexuality, Fauset's portrait of lassitude and passivity as the defining characteristics of Angela's sexuality shares more with famous nineteenth-century texts like *The Mill on the Floss* than with the much franker *Quicksand*. The tidy Christmas-present ending confirms the reader's sense of sentimental closure. It is not only Angela who remains ambivalent about sentimental romance.

The question of Fauset's own ambivalence aside, Angela's initial attraction to the "romance reading" of her own experience is intimately connected to her decision to pass. The sentimental romance plot relies on the meeting of selves whose wisdom and sensibilities, far from being a product of the social context, transcend its limitations. Because of the pure woman's moral influence, these merged selves create an escape from hostile or immoral society, the home-as-sanctuary so privileged in white nineteenth-century literary discourse. As both means and preservation of escape from a social context, the romantic love of the sentimental novel denies core premises of most African-American experience and discourse.[7]

Angela Murray's desire to marry in accord with the plot of sentimental novels is but one facet of her overall desire for the isolate self, which she images as independent. As this desire sharpens, she paradoxically becomes committed to the Angel-of-the-Household conception of woman's moral influence, which requires the submersion of female self and contentment with diffusive influence rather than direct action. Both of these force her to ignore the historical experience of African-Americans and, in so doing, to abandon her knowledge of her parents' lives.

In Angela's mind, a person perceived to be black is immediately contextualized; not only are opportunities limited, but questions of wider responsibility to the race quickly emerge. Angela pursues the phantasm of total individuality, which she locates as the privilege of whites: "I'm sick of this business of always being below or above a certain norm. Doesn't anyone think that we have a right to be happy simply, naturally?" (54). Whites can enjoy happily and simply, apparently without social construction. Angela thinks that in passing, "she would be seen, would be met against her new background or rather, against no background" (93). But as the painting metaphor indicates in this novel about an artist, such a situation is impossible; background always exists. As she puzzles over the right she has seized to be "free, white, and twenty-one" (88), her thoughts run directly into another inescapable social category that limits her—gender. Less rebellious here, she considers running a salon and then moves directly to the idea of marrying a rich white man and exercising power by proxy.

Angela's attachment to romance, with its focus on the isolated couple, causes her to misapprehend a crucial bit of her familial history. With Angela in tow, Mattie occasionally passed in order to enjoy freedom of movement, never, however, denying fundamental parts of her integrity. On one of these expeditions, Angela and Mattie see Junius and Virginia but do not speak. Angela later ponders the power of social conventions that could make her mother pass by her beloved husband. Mattie does not worry about Junius, knowing that he understands both the temporary nature and the frivolity of her passing. She does worry, however, about the damage that might have occurred if Jinny had observed their failure to acknowledge her, and she immediately resolves not to risk her younger daughter again. The complex of family relationships and responsibilities does not strike Angela, for whom the romantic dyad is all.

Angela cultivates the isolation that she thinks will free her to join the mainstream of American life. In doing so, she willfully re-creates the circumstances that harried her mother. As a poor orphan with no family, Mattie experienced in turn the female alternatives of her generation: live-in servant, seamstress, ladies' maid. This latter position had two advantages, sufficient wages and occasional periods of free time; its disadvantages include a vulnerability to predatory white males. Marriage to the protecting Junius removes her from the danger of sexual exploitation. Junius and Mattie together manage to give their daughters enough education to escape these roles, but the orphaned Angela separates herself from the protective community and particularly from her surviving sister. Ironically, the resultant loneliness makes Angela vulnerable to the blandishments of Roger Fielding. The text does not definitely state that Angela knows of her mother's history, but Jinny loves to hear the stories repeated, so the opportunity would seem to have been present. At any rate, either from lack of interest or lack of understanding, Angela opts for the isolation shown in her mother's experience to be inimical to the African-American female self.

Angela's attitude toward her heritage as a whole suggests that it exists or vanishes at her pleasure. She literally sells her inheritance (the parental home) to finance her adventure in passing. When she returns for a brief visit to Philadelphia, she is very hurt that the current owner spurns her request to reenter the house and perceives her as "white trash" (363). It never occurs to her that passing means precisely the forfeiture of both that kinship and the public avowal of the memories concerning that house.

Angela entertains, in general, remarkably cheap ideas of history's effects on the individual's present. Not surprisingly, these ideas are linked to the sentimental romance's presentation of the woman's role. When Anthony Cross[8] first reveals his belief in the importance of his own history for their relationship, Angela tries to silence him: " 'Anthony, those men, those enemies that killed your father,—did you kill one of them?' She had her arms about him. 'You know it's nothing to me. Don't even tell me about it. Your past belongs to you; it's your future I'm interested in, that I want.' " (184)

On hearing about his father's lynching and mutilation and his mother's subsequent fear and hatred of black heritage, Angela settles on a "fantastic notion" (286): she will restore his belief in humanity by revealing that she is passing, but only after he feels secure in her love. In this state of mind, she dreams of the power of love to obliterate past as well as present social context and thus history itself: "She would cajole him into forgetting that terrible past. Some day he should say to her: 'You have brought me not merely new life, but life itself.' Those former years should mean no more to him than its pre-natal existence means to a baby" (293). The implied infantalization of Anthony and the puerile "cajole" combine oddly with the divine power of creation; Angela persistently valorizes the womanly role in the sentimental romance tradition. Fauset underlines the connection between Angela's specific reaction here and the habits of thought necessary to passing: "An old story it was, but in its new setting, coupled with the fact that Angela for years had closed her mind to the penalty which men sometimes pay for being 'different,' it sounded like some unbelievable tale from the Inquisition" (286). Soon after Angela's arrival in New York, she evaluated as superficial the conversation in a fashionably intellectual drawing room; it contrasts forcibly with "the picture which she saw in her mind of men and women at her father's home in Opal Street,—the men talking painfully of rents, of lynchings" (116). Once an automatic standard of comparison for her, this heritage has, by the time she responds to Anthony, receded to the remoteness of seventeenth-century Europe.

Whereas Angela attempts to sever her relationship to history, Jinny sees in it the resources to articulate her experience. In discussing with Angela the latter's refusal to acknowledge her, Jinny "remembered that it had been possible in slavery times for white men and women to mistreat their mulatto relations, their own flesh and blood, selling them into deeper slavery in the far South or standing by watching them beaten. . . . Perhaps there was something fundamentally different between white and coloured blood after all. . . . '[P]erhaps there is an extra infusion of white blood in your veins which lets you see life at another angle. If that's the case I have no right to judge you. You must forgive my ignorant comments' " (168).

Jinny remembers historically what the decision to be white entailed and permitted; her harsh statement here justifiably calls her sister to account for the contemporary manifestations of that choice. In the finale, Jinny's carefully preserved heritage, her share of the money from the sale of the house, salves the sting of the withdrawn scholarship by making possible further study in Paris.

Angela's attempt to live ahistorically does not satisfy her, but neither does it mire her in quicksand. *Plum Bun* depicts less absolute conditions than are found in *Quicksand*. First, Angela's isolation is never as severe as Helga's; she has a sister and long-time acquaintances. Second, however uneasily, the context admits the existence of people of mixed race, and only the irrevocable bigots like Fielding attribute their talents to white blood. Nearly all of the press treats the revelation of Angela's passing in accordance with the usual social stereotypes, but the novel shows a single exception even in this public sphere. Several of Angela's white friends reaffirm their friendship, so that individual personality and action are seen to have some effect on one's social reception. Third, perhaps because slightly changed social conditions permit it, Angela never completely rejects her past. When she selects a name to pass with, out of a lingering sense of loyalty to her parents, she chooses the only slightly altered "Angèle Mory."

In addition, Angela has an important defense that Helga lacks. Whereas Helga clearly possesses a highly developed aesthetic sense, Angela trains that sense into a career. Throughout *Plum Bun,* Angela thinks of her painting as distinct from art, as a means of earning a living rather than entering the realm of the great. To some extent, this conception is necessitated by her ideals of femininity, but it also realistically assesses her aptitude. At all points, Angela is aware of the weakness of her commitment to her talent. Contrasting it early on with Anthony's steadfastness, "She was ashamed, for she knew that for the vanities and gewgaws of a leisurely and irresponsible existence she would sacrifice her own talent, the integrity of her ability to interpret life, to write down a history with her brush" (112). In Angela's thought, Fauset testifies to art's power in demonstrating the past's persistence in the present.

Angela's equivocations about her art have roots not only in the feminine role but in her attempts to deny history. As Sylvander points out, Angela's best work sketches a representative of the folk (170). Similarly, Miss Powell's award-winning entry is entitled "Street in Harlem." Angela's trained talent takes her beyond Helga Crane's limitations, for Helga can only buy the beauty that she longs for; her creativity has no outlet beyond arranging her beautiful objects or costuming herself in what others have made. Angela, on the other hand, can create. Both what she chooses to create and her changed methods suggest an increased understanding of art's meanings. At the beginning of her New York sojourn, Angela unselfconsciously and openly sketches derelicts in a park. Later, feeling connections between their loneliness and her own, she realizes the arrogance of appropriating others' experience and assuming her own superiority: "How fiercely she would have rebelled had anyone from a superior social plane taken her for copy!" (240). She continues to use these people as subjects but respects their dignity. Her portrait of her mother—drawn from "vivid memory," as well as a photograph—suggests a source of art in what her decision to pass had previously repressed. In short, whereas Helga can unify her experience only in delirium, Angela can express her past in painting; she can "write history with a brush."

WOMEN WITHOUT FACES: GLORIA NAYLOR'S *Linden Hills*

As its title suggests, *Linden Hills* broadens the focus of the Harlem Renaissance novels from a single main character to the spirit of a place encompassing several important characters. *Quicksand* and *Plum Bun* invest Helga Crane and Angela Murray with a weight of representation; not merely individuals, they participate in the literary tradition of mulattas and are means of investigating intersections (of race, class, and gender) not unique to themselves. The broader focus of *Linden Hills* means that the women characters can demonstrate commonalities yet respond differently to their experiences. (The single character to bear the weight of representativeness is Willie Mason, the only working-class male in this upper-class African-American enclave.) Differing from the earlier works in genre, *Linden Hills* is strongly allegorical. Partially because of its close relationship to Dante's *Inferno,* three male characters play crucial structural roles: Luther Nedeed/Satan, Lester/Virgil, and Willie/Dante.[9] As owner of the real-estate corporation and funeral-parlor director, Luther Nedeed controls the lives and deaths of the men as well as the women in the hell that is the exclusive housing development of Linden Hills. A poet, Lester has grown up in Linden Hills but maintains his friendship with another poet, Willie, who grew up and lives in neighboring Putney Wayne. Together they traverse Luther's domain during the week before Christmas, observing and participating in several crucial events. The novel's end includes both the fiery deaths of Luther Nedeed and his wife Willa Prescott Nedeed and the survival of Lester and Willie—and their friendship.

Linden Hills does not directly present racial oppression though its roles in the historical development of the locale is clear. Instead, the novel concentrates on the internalized oppression of its relentlessly upwardly mobile African-American characters, the required denial of particular histories necessary to rise in class. Luther Nedeed provides impetus for this process of completing the stages of self-erasure. Two male characters striving to rise in corporations, Maxwell Smyth and Winston Alcott, suppress parts of their beings so completely that they consider them obliterated. Smyth, for instance, begins by trying to obliterate racial markers: "He would have found the comments that he was trying to be white totally bizarre. Being white was the furthest thing from his mind, since he spent every waking moment trying to be no color at all" (106). Progressively, he works to obliterate all physical reality—regulates temperature so completely that he never gets hot enough to sweat in his attempt to make weather vanish, starves himself so that his shit literally does not stink. Naylor emphasizes the unity of all these manifestations: "To even the most careful observer, this man seemed to have made the very elements disappear, while it was no more than the psychological sleight-of-hand that he used to make his blackness disappear" (102). Alcott denies another essential element of physicality, his homosexual desire. The text emphasizes the futility of these endeavors: if they succeed, the character's physicality vanishes—the state usually designated as "dead"—if they fail, the return of the repressed will completely disrupt the lifestyle necessary to residence in Linden Hills.

Within this framework, the contemporary women characters battle emotional and spiritual starvation. Of the four women portrayed in some detail, only Ruth/Beatrice escapes Linden Hills, content to live in comparative poverty and to give up the security gained from both familiar materialities and children. She sacrifices these in order to maintain emotional connections with her husband, who has recurrent breakdowns. Two of the other female characters, Roxanne and Laurel, represent different stages of their common developmental process, which is opposed to Ruth's. Aware of her status as a commodity, Roxanne controls her entire self-construction and self-presentation rigorously, confident that she can manipulate herself and others to maintain her career and also marry black and well. (Given the context and the available men, "black" describes nothing important; the man whom she desires, and who is beginning to love her, has selected Maxwell Smyth as his mentor.) Laurel has married black and well, only to discover that her presentation of image to others has deprived her of self-image. Desperate to find this self, she stares at the photographs recording her life. Laurel has sold what Willie's grandmother called the silver mirror set in her soul and therefore sees no face when she searches for her essence.

These women do not experience isolation in the same ways that Helga Crane and Angela Murray do. These families are both more complete and longer-lived than in the earlier novels. Roxanne lives with her mother and brother Lester, her father having died after she attains adulthood. Although Laurel's mother dies during her childhood, her resentment of her stepmother is not grounded in physical or psychological abuse or neglect. Not only immediate family but historical knowledge embodied in older relatives remains accessible. Laurel's grandmother, Roberta, endeavors to offer the necessary love and support. Early on Roberta recognizes Laurel's emotional vulnerabilities and attempts to work within rather than against the child's temperament. Unable to keep Laurel from dangerous drainage ditches, Roberta makes sure that she is taught to swim; knowing that life brings many unpleasant experiences that must be dealt with rather than evaded, Roberta tells Laurel folk tales that metaphorically suggest strategies for managing the hated stepmother. Unlike Pilate, another bearer of folk wisdom, Roberta is no alien in the modern world. Roberta offers practical material aid as well as spiritual counsel, supplying the money to send Laurel to her chosen university, Berkeley. Although Laurel's process of self-estrangement is not presented in the same detail as Maxwell's or Winston's, Roberta is critical of Berkeley; she knows that there Laurel became a stranger to her. Formal education confirms and further exploits Laurel's initial vulnerabilities, which in Linden Hills become self-hatred focused on the body.

During the breakdown leading to Laurel's suicide, Roberta finds Laurel obsessively listening to Gustav Mahler's compositions and wishes aloud that Laurel would listen instead to Bessie Smith and Billie Holiday. Laurel focuses on the concrete details of their lyrics— "Jim Crow, unpaid bills, and being hungry" (236)—and rejects them. Roberta's rejoinder shows her desire to create female ancestors, and a model of survival, for her granddaughter: "You ain't going through nothing much more different than what they went through. . . . What they *say* is one thing, but what you supposed to hear is 'I can' " (236). Recognizing that her granddaughter is too emotionally remote from the blues sensibility to find it healing, as she had been too separated from the folklore earlier, Roberta does her best to adjust to her granddaughter's emotional vocabulary: "Baby, get up and put something else on by that Mahler man. Maybe this time it'll get a bit more clear, and I can find something else to say to you" (237). The more Roberta tries to involve Laurel in Christmas preparations and in the community, however, the more Laurel feels her emptiness. The soul's mirror cannot be replaced from outside. Laurel's destruction of her face by diving into an empty swimming pool merely makes visible her spiritual devastation.

Ironically, the fourth contemporary woman, Willa Prescott Nedeed, overcomes much more severe physical isolation to reclaim her own face. Willa shares Laurel's inability to learn from the experiences of older women in her family; she remembers having dismissed her Great-Aunt Miranda, the powerful and empowering title character of *Mama Day*. For all but the last portion of *Linden Hills*, she is locked in the cellar of Luther's house as punishment for his deluded notion that she has cuckolded him and borne him a bastard son. Like the Invisible Man in his Harlem basement, Willa conducts an investigation of personal experience to determine its meaning. Unlike the Invisible Man, however, Willa must first excavate the history of her predecessors, not the female ancestors of her bloodline, but the women who occupied her social position as the wife of the Luther Nedeed of their respective generations. In this way, Naylor significantly widens the scope of historical excavation from the earlier tradition. Social class in this version assumes a much more powerful determining effect on experience, for a woman's literal female ancestors are shown to be less important to her contemporary identity than other women who occupy her social position.

Willa discovers and examines these three women's historically and personally specific experiences of oppression and, simultaneously, their efforts to survive. Luwanna Packerville's exact situation is not replicated in the following generations of Evelyn Creton Nedeed and Priscilla McGuire Nedeed because she is literally Luther Nedeed's slave; Luther frees their son and makes him her legal master.

Symbolically, however, the same relationships echo through the generations. Luther keeps Willa in the cellar to reimpress upon her through her very food and water that "[w]hatever she had been allowed—upstairs or down—was hers not by right, but as a gift" (68–9). The women are wives or, more exactly, mothers. Having fulfilled Luther's single requirement of incubating a son, they struggle in a familial context that has no ability to recognize their personalities or talents. This limited context cannot be expanded, for race and class rigidly circumscribe them. (Even the earliest, Luwanna, explicitly comments on this conjunction.) In addition, the various Luthers (all reincarnations of the same spirit) isolate their wives, quarreling with the ministers, for example, and then forbidding the women to attend church. This combination of isolation, lack of function, and complete lack of recognition kills the women slowly. Their spiritual and physical deaths resonate in the contemporary female characters' experiences. Laurel is frightened when she returns to her Linden Hills house and finds it complete without any contribution from her. As the wife of the master controller of Linden Hills, the mistress of the house at the bottom of the hill from which increasing prestige paradoxically descends, Willa has the role to which all of the women of Linden Hills aspire.

Each of the three women who perish leaves the text of her struggles, literally written records. The first, Luwanna, initially models her text on a patriarchal authority. At first, Willa cannot make out the events of her predecessor's life, for she expects chronological succession in the handwritten entries made as marginalia in Luwanna's Bible. After some time, she realizes that Luwanna entered her experiences on the pages that covered analogous experience—the shift of her master from her father to her son, for example, between 1 Kings and 2 Kings, which deal with changes in the rulers of Israel. Willa also finds first what she later takes as Luwanna's conclusive word, "There can be no God" (125). Without the biblical God, Luwanna no longer structures her experience with the Bible as subtext.

In her depiction of all three women as fully responsible participants in their own destruction, the *Inferno*'s archtraitors because they betray themselves, critic Catherine Ward locates Luwanna's flaw in allowing her husband to destroy her faith in God. *Linden*

Hills does not seem to have the same conception of God as the *Inferno,* however. The preacher who may himself be a lost soul because of his uncontrollable lust, Michael Hollis, retains a more pertinent idea of God. (His presumably damned state would, of course, be no bar to his knowledge of God; part of the torment of the damned, according to Catholic theology, lies in their knowledge that contact with God is possible and that for them it will forever be unattainable.) Hollis never experiences religious zeal in established churches. When visitors from store-front temples visit his prestigious church, however, he remembers what made him a minister: "What had drawn him was the power that was possible between people; together they created 'God'—so real and electrifying you could believe that once it was a voice that shook mountains" (177). Of course he cannot experience such ecstasy with his Linden Hills congregation, for it relies on faith, emotional connections, and intimacy—exactly the elements lacking in Linden Hills. Luwanna's declaration, "There can be no God," then, may well testify to her loss of all human connection, for only through the human can the divine be known.

The remainder of Luwanna's experience forces Willa to recognize her own anomie and its sources in the hollowness of her marriage. After she stops making biblical entries, Luwanna writes letters to herself, and replies, in a written version of Pecola Breedlove's schizophrenia. These letters show her creating the only possible human connection for herself. Luther has insisted on hiring someone to cook and clean, important parts of Luwanna's sphere of activity; when he tries to deprive her of gardening too, she has a public tantrum to preserve her sole remaining creative outlet. (She illustrates the lost artist of Alice Walker's "In Search of Our Mother's Gardens.") Luwanna's final self-addressed letter reveals that she expects to make the same reply to the meaningless greeting of her husband and son for the 665th time the next day; she has kept track by making indelible marks on her body, one for each greeting. Having marked herself with the number of the beast of Revelations, Luwanna vanishes from Willa's and the reader's recall, her fate unknown.

Her successor, Evelyn Creton, maintains closer ties with traditionally female texts, cookbooks and recipes, which finally offer no more solutions than the Bible. At first, Evelyn tries ancient female wisdom, the sprinklings of herbs that she hopes will conjure her husband and marriage into something recognizable. Failing there, she sublimates her desires for intimacy, sexual and emotional, and for creative expression into cooking. She becomes bulimic before the disease was recognized, consuming huge quantities of food followed by huge quantities of laxatives (the same push-pull that Roxanne experiences). As the narrator points out, the body does not allow such simple trade-offs. Little by little, Evelyn loses necessary trace minerals and nutrients—just as her spirit is gradually fading, her physical self is gradually losing its necessary sustaining elements. Her despair requires a quicker resolution, however, so on December 24, she records a purchase of prussic acid, obviously for suicide.

Willa recognizes a version of her own experience in Evelyn's careful records. Against the obsessive recording of ingredients bought—the first indication of how central consumerism must become to the women of Linden Hills—Willa sets her endless purchases of cosmetics to lure Luther. In desperation, Evelyn tries a sepia dye on her skin, the inverse of the bleaching creams that both Roxanne and Willa use. The problem does not rest in the colors of their skins, however; their husbands do not desire and will not supply the intimacy that they require. With the isolation of class imposed by these same husbands and their sons, carefully made suspicious and then indifferent to them, each of these women must try to endure that contradiction in African-American culture, the isolate self.

Priscilla McGuire's legacy is at once more appealing initially and more ominous. Whereas Luwanna and Evelyn articulate their own stories in some fashion, Priscilla leaves Willa only a book of photographs, not the product of her creativity. The first several years of these pictures show a woman of obvious vitality, her sense of fun revealed in various subtle subversions of the serious poses. The pictures predating the birth of her child are accompanied, however, by only a newspaper clipping that announces her betrothal—a formal, public text identifying her as someone's daughter, someone's intended wife. Some of these photos have outdoor settings and record a freeze-frame of activity; the later pictures, in contrast, have the repetitive static pose situated indoors: a seated Priscilla, Luther standing, her son either seated on her lap or standing at her other side. In addition, Willa perceives that the men cast progressively larger shadows on Priscilla's face. These photos are labeled in her handwriting, but her text describes only the age of her child ("Luther, 1 year") even though she is present in each one. This self-denial reflects increasing denial by the context and finally results in a self-obliteration like Laurel's—in picture after picture from the final years, Priscilla removes the representation of her face, filling in this blank in the last picture that Willa examines with her single self-authored, self-referential word, "Me."

This blank horror inspires the imprisoned Willa to live up to her name by insisting on her own face. When she cannot remember it, she deliberately makes a mirror by positioning herself under the light with a pan of water to make a reflection.[10] Drinking the water then symbolically shows her imbibing her own spirit. Reassured that her disintegration has not reached the irreversible stage of her predecessors', she reconstructs herself by thinking through the processes that account for her current state of emotion and position in the cellar. This section of the novel is the most problematic for the feminist reader or, indeed, for any reader interested in contextual issues. First, Willa decides that she is responsible for her own plight, an insight that she expresses concretely, "It happened because she walked down into this basement" (279). Most readers would have no difficulty in accepting Willa's interpretation if it merely asserted her participation in the events leading to her imprisonment, but it insists on her sole responsibility:

> And since the Prescotts conceived a baby girl with healthy leg muscles and tendons, she had started walking down them [stairs to the cellar] from the second she was born.
> If she took it a millimeter beyond that, her thoughts would smash the fragility of that singular germ of truth. Its amber surface quivered in her mind, a microscopic dot of pure gelatin, free from the contamination of doubt or blame. That action was hers and hers alone. The responsibility did not lie with her mother or father—or Luther. (280)

Second, when Willa decides that the means to reverse her predicament consist simply of walking back up the stairs, she must also decide what nature of creature will do the walking; and her decisions are profoundly disquieting. The process of self-determination is explicitly imaged as both biological and beyond biology:

> . . . she breathed in. In, past the brain cells, where memory mingles with desire and night images are formed. In, past the heart tissues that beat out the rhythms of human limitation. . . . She breathed in to touch the very element that at the beginning of time sparked to produce the miracle some called divine creation and others the force of life . . . her body a mere shelter for the mating of unfathomable will to unfathomable possibility. And in that union, the amber germ of truth she went to sleep with conceived and reconceived itself, splitting and multiplying to take over every atom attached to her being. That nucleus of self-determination held the tyrannical blueprint for all divisions of labor assigned to its multiplying cells. Like other emerging life, her brain, heart, hands, and feet were being programmed to a purpose. (288–89)

That purpose is to keep house: clean, mend, dust. The connection of primal, biological reconstruction with women's traditional domestic duties is in itself disturbing. In addition, housework makes not only an anticlimax but a descent into bathos after the heightened poetic language of this passage. The novel repeatedly images the re-created Willa as a wingless Queen ant, driven by instinct. It is difficult to believe, at first, that Naylor is not being intentionally parodic. However, in a conversation with Toni Morrison, Naylor—who believes in the literary artist almost as a medium for the transfer of extant characters to the page—professes puzzlement over Willa's self-definition but clearly accepts it as worthy of respect. The way out of this impasse cannot be simply the somewhat grudging feminist reappraisal of the 1970s, that the traditional role for women deserves respect but that individual women must be able to choose it freely from a range of socially acceptable options. Among other objections, this choice would probably be defined and defended as "homemaking" rather than "housekeeping." Also, housekeeping would not be constructed as a biological instinct but as a profoundly social choice. A more fruitful approach, given the novel's emphasis on process, would be to interpret Willa's dedication to housekeeping as a first step in personal reclamation. To acquire the power to walk back up the stairs, she has to create a self-image that grants her agency. To claim her existence and dignity, she must create her own order in what she finds around her. In short, she is simply following the Carlylean dictate to do the duty that lies closest at hand because others will be present when it is finished. Wingless queen ant now, she will be another creature at another time.

The novel supports this interpretation in two ways. First, it undercuts Willa's presentation of the responsibility for her imprisonment as solely her own; second, it shows that Willa's identity is already more complex than that of a queen ant, for she is an artist emergent. To adopt Willa's literal terms, she may walk down into the basement under her own power, but she has "started walking down them since the second she was born" because social constructions direct her and lock the door behind her. Although she has not grown up in Linden Hills, Willa acquires the same hatred of her physicality that characterizes its inhabitants: "Her feet were the only part of her body that she didn't grow up despising" (277). She recognizes her own attention to the approved body image for women—slim thighs, taut waist—and her dismay over her weight gain in Evelyn's superabundant baking and subsequent dosing. Like all the other Nedeed wives, she has been chosen for her vulnerability. Luther remains single for ten years in order to be able to choose from never-married career women. The arrogant strut of their college days gone, their self-image rapidly blurring, ". . . at thirty, the only thing they envisioned for their future was dying alone. Marriage was a sigh of relief at that age. She had been a teacher, an accountant, a chemist—but now she could be a woman. And she'd quickly forget the foolish dreams that she'd had for a mate ten years ago. She was more than willing to join the life and rhythms of almost any man—and for a man like himself, she'd bend over backwards" (68). Women can still be women only within marriage.

That Willa recognizes parts of her own experiences in those of Luwanna, Evelyn, and Priscilla argues for social pattern rather than exclusively personal failure. This part of her exploration of women's history—seeing self in what had been safely (and failed) Other—is so painful and threatening that Willa, at first, violently rejects it: "She wasn't like these other women; she had coped and they were crazy. . . . But there was nothing wrong with her. . . . And there just couldn't have been anything wrong with what she had wanted.

A home. A husbband. Children. . . . No, it wasn't wrong. It wasn't sick. If there was any sickness, it was in this house, in the air. It was left over from the breaths of those women who had come before her" (205).

Despite her intimate knowledge of their torture, she blames the victims. Identification with them requires a rejection of so much of her social context that she prefers isolation and a belief in personal failure. In the rage through which she denies her historical counterparts, she destroys parts of their legacies, stopping only when a photo album opens to show a young and vital Priscilla. The photograph testifies undeniably to Priscilla's actuality, her positive presence in the world. Anger and denial forgotten, Willa is powerfully drawn to female joy and its fate.

In responding to this common fate of the Nedeed wives, Willa becomes a creative artist. At first, she remains an audience, though an active one. In this stage, she concentrates on exploring Luwanna's strange story and its correspondences to her own. With the second story, however, Willa becomes not only audience for Evelyn but creator. From Evelyn's details, Willa constructs an entire character. She begins to imagine the storyteller as "such a proper woman. The careful and meticulous handwriting formed the vision of quiet dignity and immaculate grooming. This woman never had a curl out of place, a ribbon knotted loosely, a stick of furniture not glowing with lemon oil" (187). Similarly, with Priscilla's pictures, she constructs a subject consonant with the materials but not really necessitated by them. Only after exercising her creativity in this way—constructing the historical experience of a particular class of African-American women—can Willa re-create her face. Willa's explanation of her predicament in the locked basement, whatever its limitations, conforms to Naylor's public definition of the writer/ artist. In "Famous First Words," Naylor describes the nature of fiction: "Fiction should be about storytelling, the 'why' of things is best left to sociologists, the 'how' is more than enough for writers to tackle, especially beginning writers." *Linden Hills*'s description of Willa's thought processes as she prepares to leave the cellar echo this diction: "She pushed away what had happened or why it happened. If there was any hope for her at all, it rested solely on the how: How did she get down in that basement?" (278). Willa's nascent artistry dies with her in the inferno caused by Luther, but its emergence makes sense of the close psychic connections between her and one of the structural, point-of-view male characters, the poet Willie Mason.

Willie's connections to the female characters are frequently underscored. As a working-class, extremely dark-skinned male, he shares with them the marginalization in the Linden Hills perspective. Willie is tied to Willa not only by their similar names (Naylor is at pains to specify that his birth certificate reads "Willie," not "William") but through subconscious communications. Willie's dreams of a surreal clock clearly play on the basement clock so maddening to Willa. His connections to the other women include the dream voice telling him that he has no face and his discovery of Laurel's body. As Luwanna has responded to greetings 665 times, so Willie has memorized 665 poems. He creates the first line of the 666th on the same day that Luwanna orders prussic acid, and as her order presaged a great change, his creation precedes a fiery catastrophe. Finally, and perhaps most crucially, Willie accidentally slides the basement bolt so that Willa can simply walk out the now unlocked cellar door.

Willie experiences Linden Hills in many of the same ways that these women experience it. Initially, he is dazzled by its display of wealth, but soon he feels its lack of spontaneity, just as each of the Nedeed wives has felt its absence in Luther, particularly in regard to sexuality. As he becomes aware of his connections to these women, he experiences strong ambivalences. Like Willa rejecting her similarities to Luwanna and Evelyn, Willie temporarily falls back on denying his bonds to women, relying on stereotypes of old wives' tales and superstition to discredit them and assert his own superiority (273). Aware that the connections lie too deep for conscious control, that they will continue to haunt him in his dreams if he does not articulate them, he resolves to experience the pain of creation for its relief. To do so, he must overcome the stifling effects of Linden Hills. His creativity seems located in both his face and his genitals: "His poems only made sense in his ears and mouth. His fingers, eyes, and nose. Something about Linden Hills was blocking that. And to unstop it, he would have to put Linden Hills into a poem" (275), and "If [his dream images] were anything, they were that: the first line unborn. It came with an expulsion, a relief that always felt like ejaculation" (276). Like Willa, Willie eschews the "why" when he puts Linden Hills into a poem: "It would take an epic to deal with something like What has this whole week meant? He'd leave that to guys like Milton" (275). When Willie leaves other questions to Milton, he articulates Willa's fate; the first line of his new poem is "There is a man in a house at the bottom of a hill. And his wife has no name" (277). She has a name, of course, for in the next line Naylor, for the first time, reveals Willa's name to the reader, but she has no identity. Just as Willie's name is unacceptable to Lester's upper-class mother, so is Willa's name irrelevant, unknowable within this social context.

The African-American working-class male poet has the potential to articulate not only his own experience but the lives of other marginalized groups, particularly women. To realize this potential, he must consciously consider his historical role. Thus, before Willie can complete his poem, he must develop his position not only toward Linden Hills in the present but toward its history; his confrontation with a traditional historian implies the development of a politically committed, engaged artistic aesthetic. Willie and Lester meet Daniel Braithwaite, a professional historian, at the site of Laurel's suicide. The author of a three-volume history of Linden Hills, Braithwaite has rather expected Laurel's death or, at least, is not surprised by it. Committed to objectivity, he describes his eyes as the camera's lens and history as "a written photograph" (261), a telling metaphor in view of Priscilla's photographs. His function is to record, not to act. Braithwaite's is culturally a male perspective on history, as Willa's is a female perspective. He is connected to death, first in the trees that he kills to gain an unobstructed view, in his presence at Laurel's death (she is, of course, named for a tree), and most importantly in his attachment to stasis. Braithwaite has no personal experience of the observer's effect on the observed, for no one in Linden Hills has read his books. This situation confirms his view that history is the sum effect of the actions of impersonal social forces; an individual neither can nor should attempt to affect the course of events. As Willa's theory of history is reductionist in its valorization of discrete individuals' responsibility, so is Braithwaite's theory reductionist in its erasure of the individual and concomitant elevation of abstract social forces.

Willie rejects Braithwaite's views, insisting instead on the duty of the individual to resist even apparently invincible social constructions. Familiar with the recurrent bar fights occasioned by the frustrations of poverty, Willie details the aware individual's responsibility to try to defuse the unmistakable signs of tension that presage an always potentially fatal fight. His position implicitly identifies Braithwaite—and all dedicated to his view of history—as Laurel's murderers: "So you make a joke, you buy one of them a drink—you do *something* to keep the steam down. Even though you know that next week the same thing will probably happen again—different faces maybe, but the same damned thing. And it's gonna keep going on, 'cause Putney Wayne won't change and those paychecks won't change. But you still say to yourself, 'It would be a crime to let this happen.' And I don't care how you want to break it down, there was a crime committed out there today" (257).

Willie's position here directly contradicts his earlier attempt to affirm his masculinity by denying his intuitive connections with women (intuitive, but with origins in identifiable social similarities). One must oppose the workings of social violence in every individual instance—bar or basement—no matter how frequent the repetition because discrete individuals are valuable. Willie's poetry is oral, hence his emphasis on memorization of poems. His dedication to orality continues a major strain in African-American art, and his poem about Willa's name shows his participation in call-and-response; he responds half-consciously to a sound he cannot identify, her grieving cry mourning the death of her child. A manchild so thoroughly integrated that his artistic creation is not only sexual but more thoroughly physical, Willie will fulfill his personal, interventionist responsibilities in part by producing activist, African-American art.

The evolution of Willie's aesthetic does not, however, close *Linden Hills*. The novel's last line describes Willie and Lester walking together away from the inferno. Their final conversation suggests a crucial element in Naylor's depiction of African-American art and the African-American community. Willie and Lester, lower-class and upper-class, dark-skinned and light-skinned, oral and print artists—the doubling contrasts could be continued indefinitely. They supply each other with the human contact that Luwanna finds only through schizophrenia. Critic Michael Awkward has developed a reading of African-American women's narratives in which female self-division sometimes defends the self, as in *Their Eyes Were Watching God*, and sometimes confirms its destruction, as in *The Bluest Eye*. In his view, these splits manifest "double voicings," a literary adumbration of W. E. B. Du Bois's famous double consciousness. At times, the double voicings are those of the narrative voice(s) versus those of a point-of-view character. Specifically, his reading of *The Women of Brewster Place* concludes that it differs most radically from its major distaff source, *The Bluest Eye*, in denying Morrison's resolution of the double voicing. Especially through Luwanna's letters to herself, *Linden Hills* evokes *The Bluest Eye* much more directly than *The Women of Brewster Place*. Because its major themes concern the social masking required to take part in upper middle-class life, *Linden Hills* necessarily shows doubling. One resolution of this doubling lies in Laurel's fate: the face behind the mask disintegrates, and the singleness left is only the social role. Another resolution appears in Willa's emergence from the cellar only to be destroyed by Luther. Persistence of doubling rather than its resolution characterizes survival in *Linden Hills*.

The narrative of *Linden Hills* employs a series of technical double voicings like those that Awkward points to in other novels. For instance, the major focus shifts between Willie and Lester's experiences and Willa's; Willa's sections are further divided between her viewpoint and, one at a time, those of her three predecessors. Awkward maintains that *The Women of Brewster Place* affirms the multiplicity of the black community by preserving the double voice, to which it should be added that, in the case of *Linden Hills*, the doubles remain strongly linked. Willa's essence lives on through her connection to Willie. Willie and Willa are not the same any more than he and Lester are the same: class and gender separate Willie and Willa; class and temperament keep Willie and Lester distinct. Their different, even opposing perspectives persist in their last recorded conversation, when they telegraph their attitudes toward the decision of Linden Hills residents not to call the fire department when Luther's house becomes an inferno. When Willie says, "They let it burn," Lester replies, "But they let it burn" (304). They walk to a fence, "each with his own thoughts" (304). Given each one's character development, the reader can imagine those thoughts. For Willie, with his characteristic concern for individuals and his grief at Willa's death, her fate, if not Luther's, is the primary fact; he cannot believe that neighbors would watch, like Braithwaite, and not intervene. Lester, to whom the struggle against the materialist values of Linden Hills is primary, rejoices that the community has let the epitome of social achievement go up in smoke. This difference, like many of their differences, might lead to bitter division; instead, when they reach the fence (the barrier), in an image repeated several times throughout the novel, "Hand anchored to hand, one helped the other to scale the open links" (304). In this last described event—not the final event—Naylor carefully avoids identifying the helper and the helped. Double voices persist, their linkage constructing the multiplicity of historical continuities that make up the present.

HURSTON'S MUCK, LARSEN'S *Quicksand*, AND MORRISON'S *Tar Baby*

Gloria Naylor may have decided to concentrate on the story of Willie's rather than Lester's development—that is, of a working class rather than an upper middle-class African-American male—because an extraordinarily powerful version of the latter had been written earlier by one of her acknowledged mentors, Toni Morrison. A classic journey of immersion, Morrison's *Song of Solomon* foregrounds a male quest for an identity understood to be historical and in need of historical information. Female experience remains mostly a backdrop, and, curiously, when Milkman's sister must change her way of life, her liberation has little to do with historical knowledge. In contrast, Morrison's next book has two main characters, male and female, rather than the single male of *Song of Solomon*. In a complex reworking of *Their Eyes Were Watching God, Tar Baby* revoices many of the earlier novel's concerns and complicates them enormously. Individual identities become interlocking and interactive; every response is the result of particular combinations of historically constructed race, gender, and class. With unitary conceptions of "the folk" thus no longer tenable, the female journey of immersion changes greatly.

In part because *Song of Solomon* uses Milkman as its most frequent point-of-view character, it cannot present as much complexly rendered female experience as *Linden Hills* depicts. Milkman requires emotional education before he perceives women as human beings. Naylor chooses to incorporate women's processes into a male-framed and even male-centered novel by showing the working-class poet as intuitively sensitive to middle-class women. Morrison, on the other hand, presents no such natural sympathy or empathy that is engendered by analogous experiences. Guitar Bains's purposeful separation from attachments to women is part of his political agenda; nor does the only other working-class male with a major part, Henry Porter, demonstrate concern with women's roles or experiences. Women presented in detail are likely to be those women who capture Milkman's attention precisely because they remain outside his world—those in Pilate's household. Pilate figures largely in Milkman's world because, although her life cannot offer an alternative for him, she opposes Macon's values. To Milkman, Hagar is interesting mostly as a sexual object, and his thoughts do not often focus on her. The narrator must perforce tell the story of her despair at his abandonment. Hagar's doomed quest, like Pecola's desire for blue eyes, comes from a conviction of personal ugliness; it focuses not on race but on class.

Class expectations become the Procrustean shaper for women in *Song of Solomon*, for their experiences critique the journey of ascent. Robert Stepto's schema of ascent begins in an enslaved community and ends with the protagonist's literacy in the dominant culture, in freedom for the articulate survivor. The journey of immersion may circumscribe one's freedom but has the rewards of becoming "tribally" literate, grounded in the culture of one's ancestors. Macon Dead has made the journey of ascent, as had, presumably, his wife Ruth's father, Dr. Foster. (Pilate simply eschewed the journey of ascent.) Ruth and her children—Milkman, First Corinthians, and Lena—are born with the fruits of ascent, the girls' names being the only vestiges of traditional African-American culture.

In her examination of women and ascent, Morrison focuses the critique of ascent by serial images of transportation. First, she associates First Corinthians with that exemplar of conspicuous consumption, the large and expensive automobile. Early on, Morrison shows Corinthians and Lena fantasizing that they are princesses riding in a carriage during the joyless Sunday rides in Macon's Packard. (Their fantasy does not clash, incidentally, with Macon's reasons for selecting the car, but Macon's cautious, property-conscious driving does not garner the envy that he assumes.) Later, prospective suitors choose women other than Corinthians because she lacks "drive"; having been a passenger all of her life, she gives no impression of energy to contribute to a relationship, or toward a journey of ascent. To get to the maid's job that she cannot admit to having, Corinthians must ride more plebeian transportation, the bus. Finally, when her only chance for sexual and emotional fulfillment appears ready to leave if she cannot overcome her class prejudices, she surrenders by lying on the hood of his dilapidated car.

Enjoying her first self-esteem, generated by their affair, Corinthians considers this man, Henry Porter, "A perfect example of the men her parents had kept her from (and whom she had also kept herself from) all her life because such a man was known to beat his woman, betray her, shame her, and leave her" (202). Now, with the exception of leaving, Corinthians knows all these activities to typify her eminent father's behavior. The journey of ascent makes no meaningful difference for women in how men treat them, and their ascent cannot give them lives that are satisfying in themselves. Corinthians's literacy, her Bryn Mawr education, has simply prepared her to be a suburban lady of leisure, a position that does not exist for African-American women of her generation. Ascent thus permits her only a life of decorously making rose petals from scraps of red velvet, hardly enough to stand against Porter.

This complete reconstruction of values, the rejection of ascent, however, occurs in an entirely different way in Milkman's more prominent development. Whereas Milkman requires an immersion in the historical past of his family, Corinthians both recognizes the emptiness of her life and fills it without recourse to history. To some extent, her perception of the hollowness of ascent may be tied to the female role. As a proper woman not in her first youth, she lacks Milkman's easy access to sex; in addition, making rose petals offers fewer distractions than Milkman's exercise of genuine if limited power in his father's business. For her, the first step is to get a job, an activity. That the activity is demeaning and requires her to deny her education does not matter; with the job, Corinthians breaks free of the enforced infantilization demanded by her role. Instead of collecting an allowance, she learns responsibility and earns her own money (191). Corinthians is aware that, when Porter challenges her to be a "grown-up woman," she has no models (197), yet she manages to break from her middle-class values. Corinthians acts completely independently, her sources of strength unspecified. Unlike Milkman, she neither extrapolates from historical example nor learns new values from an immersion in the culture that preserves that history.

In the far more complex milieu of *Tar Baby*, historical confrontation is a necessity for women as well as men. In many ways, *Tar Baby* shows the persistence of the premises that *Quicksand* lays out as America's conflicting imperatives. The child of African-American middle-class servants, Jadine is educated by Valerian Street, their wealthy white employer. She then faces the same either/or choice faced by Helga, in terms just as stark. In speaking to Valerian's wife, Jadine "was uncomfortable with the way Margaret stirred her into blackening up or universaling out, always alluding to or ferreting out what she believed were racial characteristics. She ended by resisting both" (64).

As in *Quicksand*, the pressure comes from African-Americans as well as whites. As Son says, "There are no 'mixed' marriages. It just looks that way. People don't mix races; they abandon them or pick them" (270). In return, Jadine adamantly articulates the creed of ascent: "You stay in that medieval slave basket if you want to. You will stay there by yourself. . . . There is nothing any of us can do about the past but make our own lives better . . . you don't know how to forget the past and do better" (271). The individualist credo of "any of us" (as opposed to "we") and the admonition to forget bespeak an incompatibility between upper middle-class life and historical memory which can only be conceived of as embarrassing, limiting. *Tar Baby* limns a world predicated on this kind of individualism with the predictable result of profound loneliness.

Jadine owes her education, her literacy in European ways, to a man comfortably well up in the hierarchy of racist capitalism. It is important that he inherits his wealth rather than making it himself; even if he were a "self-made man," his progress would rest on historical privilege, but Morrison emphasizes that historical events rather than his own talents have given him his position. Jadine's own position shifts schizophrenically between being the foster daughter sitting at Valerian's dinner table and being the servants' niece, served by her uncle. Like *Linden Hills*, *Tar Baby* is set around Christmas, probably to accent the hollowness of the holiday in both its spiritual and familial aspects. Hesitating on the brink of maturity, Jadine has come to the island to consider which career to pursue—actress, model, wife of a rich European. Her indecision or, to phrase it positively, her openness are reminiscent of Janie Starks's psychic state after Jody's death.

Son's arrival exposes the island society's inherent contradictions that earlier have been finessed. An "undocumented man," he literally has no visa, but figuratively he exists beyond the usual descriptions of class, both being and intending to remain a variation of the invisible man. Son feels a kinship with the laborers who perform Valerian's most menial work. When Valerian casually announces their dismissal at Christmas dinner, the subsequent confrontation shatters the superficial peace of the household. Ondine and Margaret's battle, if not later resolved, at least has some beneficial results. The chasm between Valerian and Son, however, cannot be bridged: "The man who respected industry looked over a gulf at the man who prized fraternity" (205).

Son's arrival crystallizes racial issues that had earlier been obscured. When Margaret finds Son, her terror goes beyond finding a man to the specific fear of having found the black rapist of racist ideology literally in her closet. Valerian immediately changes Son's proffered name from William Green to "Willie," the diminutive establishing his own authority. On this Caribbean island, Valerian has re-created a plantation, complete with the infantilization of the house servants who are Jadine's Uncle Sydney and Aunt Ondine; significantly, Sydney, Ondine, and Jadine share the surname "Childs." For Jadine, Son brings an alternative at once attractive and annihilating.

In both general situation and specific character, *Tar Baby* reiterates elements of *Their Eyes Were Watching God*. Analogues to Nanny, Sydney and Ondine sacrifice to support an orphan child linked to them by blood. Like Janie, Jadine is an orphan raised in the white folks' yard; she must choose between Valerian's individualistic capitalism (Jody) and Son's fraternal, agrarian alternative (Tea Cake). Like Tea Cake, Son is uninterested in material goods and indifferent to literacy in the European mode (a point underscored when Jadine translates the French text accompanying the photographs of her modeling high-fashion clothing). Again like Tea Cake, he offers Jadine a sexual fulfillment unparalleled and unavailable in her previous experience. Class divisions within the black community echo those in *Their Eyes* though their basis differs somewhat, color of skin having given way to degrees of literacy. Jadine's experiences separate her considerably from Sydney and Ondine. They, in turn, do not bother to learn Gideon's name, referring to him only in terms of his function of Valerian's estate ("Yardman"). Island women remain so undifferentiated to them that they not only call them all "Mary" but actually fire and rehire Thérèse several times without realizing that they have seen her before.

The crucial similarity, however, rests in the restatement of the immersion narrative of *Their Eyes*. As newlyweds, Janie and Jody enter the all-black town of Eatonville; as new lovers, Janie and Tea Cake head for the muck of Florida. Morrison conflates these two events so that, within days of their sexual and emotional coming together, Jadine and Son visit first New York and then Son's all-black hometown in Florida, Eloe. When they are still on Isle de Chevaliers, their first conversation about Eloe echoes the famous conversation between Jody and the townspeople of Eatonville. The original includes Jody's comment, "Ain't got no Mayor! Well, who tells y'all what to do?" and the laconic reply, "Nobody. Everybody's grown" (57). Subsequently, Jody makes the physical improvements, such as the addition of a streetlight, that mark the transition from rural, agrarian society to the urban and, coincidentally, middle-class creature comforts. Morrison constructs a similar dialogue:

> "No shacks in Eloe."
> "Tents, then. Trailer camps."
> "Houses. There are ninety houses in Eloe. All black."

"Black houses?"
"Black people. No whites. No white people live in Eloe."
"You're kidding me."
"I'm not."
"Black mayor?"
"No mayor at all, black or white."
"Who runs it?"
"Runs itself."
"Come on. Who pumps the water, hooks up the telephones?" (172)

The conversation continues in this vein, Son's voice describing, Jadine's mocking. In relation to the source, Jadine has taken Jody's part, insisting that the running of a town requires a hierarchy and assuming the importance of urban comforts. The gender role of the source has been not reversed but altered. In *Their Eyes*, both question and reply belong to male speakers; female rather than male in *Tar Baby* speaks for ascent, assumes the power of the articulate survivor re the African-American community.

This alteration is one of several that profoundly refigure the ascent and immersion narratives of *Their Eyes Were Watching God*. Characters change their values, develop into narrower or broader versions of their original capabilities in *Their Eyes*, but the depiction of constant self would be compatible with nineteenth-century realism. *Tar Baby*, on the other hand, has a modernist or post-modernist sensibility that includes the multiplicity of identities within an individual. As Barbara Christian has noted, *Tar Baby* includes direct and detailed considerations of class and gender as well as race. Each identity here consists of complicated, cross-cutting, and always shifting sets of relationships. Thus, any simple description, even though perfectly accurate within itself, will be inadequate. Many of the characters' descriptions of each other are offered in powerfully emotional contexts, which readily lead to oversimplification. At one point, for example, the narrator sums up what Jadine and Son object to in one another, what each of them sees as the trait that spoils their attempted rescue of the other: "Mama-spoiled black man, will you mature with me? Culture-bearing black woman, whose culture are you bearing?" (269). Neither of these describes accurately on the literal level. Son's mother died when he was a child; as a model, Jadine does not so much bear as wear culture. On the more figurative level, Son is never shown as enjoying any particular female spoiling, and Jadine has no demonstrated interest in children, the gender-specific meaning of "bearing" which Son soon makes explicit. The clichés truncate the described personalities, but they nevertheless name real traits—particular assumptions about how women will act (tending pie tables, in Son's dream), particular assumptions about what culture is better (Picasso rather than nameless black artists, in Jadine's opinion)—from a foreign perspective. Because every identity is made of multiple parts—including nationality, race, class, and gender—every allegiance or alliance almost necessarily simplifies and so is temporary.

As opposed to *Their Eyes,* which takes as its setting a rural locale and the contrasting Glades, both in the southern United States, *Tar Baby* emphasizes its international scope. National identity thus becomes an issue. As native islanders, Gideon and Thérèse see all of the other major characters as primarily American, with the possible exception of Son; Thérèse does not acknowledge the existence of whites and does not speak to African-Americans. Despite the mythic overtones of his status as undocumented man (the Huck Finns, Nigger Jims, Calibans, Staggerlees, John Henrys), Morrison shows national identity as inescapable. Son remembers that once, fishing with a Swede and a Mexican—the text identifies them this way, solely by nationality and later gender, without names—he lost his temper and, suddenly violent, smashed an offending fish to death with his fist. He had just previously been musing on the repellent violence of the United States as presented to him in exile, via shortwave radio and the foreign press. The Mexican presents him with a map of the United States, Uncle Sam's mouth full of the corpses of children, and pronounces him *"Americano. Cierto Americano. Es verdad"* (167). Because context cannot be translated, Son remains, even in exile, a native son.

Isle de Chevaliers presents, in particularly stark form, the power structures of national domination, race, capitalism, and patriarchy that also operate in the surrounding world. These systems generate conflicting hierarchies, and thus the relationships between individuals shift radically, depending on which system takes priority. At times, for instance, class takes priority over race. Thus, Jadine willingly volunteers "nigger" when Margaret hesitates over an appellation to describe the black man in her closet (129). Race then reasserts itself as a primary category when Margaret advances to "gorilla," a term too repellent for Jadine to endorse. Gender also has powerful claims. Concerned primarily to humiliate Margaret, Valerian invites the unknown black man who has frightened her to sit down to the family dinner. The next day Son repays the compliment, establishing a connection across race and class by demeaning women. As with plants, with women, he says; "You have to jack them up every once in a while. Make em act nice, like they're supposed to" (148). Lest the reader take this as ironic, he then immediately offers Valerian a joke about "three colored whores who went to heaven" (148), a particularly telling detail because he first calls Jadine a whore and then a white when her beauty threatens him. Obviously, Son and Valerian share too little to form an enduring friendship, but a temporary truce can be constructed over woman as the common Other.

Many interactions between the governing systems do not simply pit one against another but show overdetermined relationships; Sydney and Ondine's dismissal of Gideon and Thérèse demonstrates both national domination and class snobbery. In another case, class overrides both race and gender. In their first discussion of Son's disruptive presence in the house, before he has become attractive to her, Jadine offers the following comment to Margaret's implicit suggestion that the women must "do something" to overpower Valerian's will: "What? We're the only women. And Ondine" (128). The afterthought is chilling, particularly since Ondine is Jadine's aunt and protector, the family relationship resounding in their shared surname and their similar given names. Further, Margaret shares this occlusion of Ondine's womanhood. Worried that Son intended to rape her, Margaret cannot conceive that Ondine might also be victimized (130). A brief comparison of Son's and Ondine's explanations of Ondine's silence about Margaret's physical abuse of her son clarifies both the frequently oversimplified nature of the characters' understandings of each other and Morrison's insistence on their multiplicities. Son's explanation to Jadine, "She's a good servant, I guess, or maybe she didn't want to lose her job," centers on class. Perhaps because class divides him and Jadine, Son makes this type of statement. "Good servant" implies loyalty to a class system, and "lose her job" refers to the lower-class person's vulnerability, but either possibility makes class the operative system. Speaking with Margaret, Ondine, on the other hand, mentions gender first: "It was woman stuff. I couldn't tell your husband and I couldn't tell mine" (240). Soon she qualifies with class: "If I told Sydney he might tell Mr. Street and then we'd be out of a job—a good job" (240–41). With a final, "I don't know now what I thought, to tell the truth," Ondine finally recognizes the unrecoverable nature of such overdetermined decisions.

If individual identities exist in such multiplicity, then a unitary concept of "the folk," such as Hurston implicitly proposed, can no longer be tenable. Accordingly, the abstract here has concrete representatives disparate in locale and makeup. *Tar Baby* reexamines the folk as a collection of individuals, each of whom has plural identities. Just as the individuals have discontinuous identities, so too does the tribal heritage have multiple facets and effects. Unlike the unconditionally nurturant muck of the Everglades, *Tar Baby* shows traditional black culture to have unexpected quicksands identical to the swamp sinkhole that almost claims Jadine.

First, different characters locate the folk in different places; second, the same folk setting affects participants in profoundly different ways, especially when their gender differs. Every night, for example, without later remembering it, Sydney dreams about Baltimore's Morgan Street and awakens refreshed. Jadine remembers Morgan Street too, but for her it has a dual function. On first seeing Son, she identifies him with the denizens of Morgan Street, African-American men who do not try to "make it," who do not undertake a journey of ascent but consciously decide to remain as much as possible outside the system of the dominant culture. On Morgan Street, however, after witnessing a man beating a female dog in heat, Jadine decides that female sexuality inevitably leads to vulnerability and punishment (123–24).

This duality of male independence and female subjugation characterizes each location of the folk. (It is worth remembering that, in Stepto's formulation, ascent and immersion begin and end in an enslaved community, not in one that is free and fully functional.) The culture of Gideon and Thérèse might be viewed as a less Americanized and therefore less corrupted alternative than could be found in either Baltimore or Eloe. Gideon has conversations with Thérèse only when they are working at Valerian's estate; at home, such give-and-take does not exist (149). Even on the mythic level, *Tar Baby* shows such sex segregation—on Isle de Chevaliers, the blind male riders course through the terrain; the women of the swamp remain motionless in the trees. Jadine notices these same realistic manifestations of segregation as the first salient aspect of Eloe society.

Further, her insight regarding female sexuality and punishment is confirmed in a particularly disturbing way. Son has shown an extremely violent reaction to his wife Cheyenne's unfaithfulness. Although he does not intend her death, his decision to drive a car through their ramshackle house makes severe injury at least probable. Michael Awkward has recently drawn attention to the critical occlusion of Tea Cake's violence toward Janie; in amplifying the level of violence and clarifying female sexuality as its target, Morrison refuses to collude with critics and writers who desire to see folk values as simply redemptive. In this highly problematized context, it may be a mistake to take at face value Thérèse's damning comment to Son that Jadine has "nothing in her parts for you. She has forgotten her ancient properties" (305). In support of accepting Thérèse's characterization, critics Dorothy Lee and Eleanor Traylor both use Morrison's dedication of the novel to the women in her family who "knew their true and ancient properties." Perhaps. But Thérèse's statement recalls the thoughts of the swamp women watching Jadine's struggles in quicksand: "The women hanging from the trees were quiet now, but arrogant—mindful as they were of their value, their exceptional femaleness, knowing as they did that the first world of the world had been built with their sacred properties; that they alone could hold together the stones of pyramids and the rushes of Moses's crib; knowing their steady consistency, their pace of glaciers, their permanent embrace, they wondered at the girl's desperate struggle down below to be free, to be something other than they were" (183). For Jadine to stop struggling, for her to join these women, she must die in the swamp. The swamp women do not offer the "grounding" folk presence of the Glades workers in *Their Eyes,* and Thérèse's echo of them is also suspect.

Thérèse represents a shrewd voice from a particular perspective. Although the details of her understanding are incorrect, her perceptions of American women's attitudes toward maternity are to some extent borne out by Valerian's first wife's abortions and Margaret's abuse. Her perception of American class relationships, that the rich eat the poor, also has some metaphoric truth—witness Jadine's shampoo made from placenta products. No inerrant oracle of a natural, unconstructed folk, however, Thérèse views reality from as partial a perspective as the other characters. When she is entertaining Gideon with her version of what is going on in Valerian's household, "The more she invented the more she rocked and the more she rocked the more her English crumbled till finally it became dust in her mouth stopping the flow of her imagination and she spat it out altogether and let the story shimmer through the clear cascade of the French of Dominque" (108).

Her "invented story," the product of "imagination," filters through a very particular dialect, the French of Dominique. In addition, her version does not satisfy Gideon, who sees that she has omitted a salient feature of a credible explanation: "While you making up your story about what this one thinks and this one feels, you have left out the white bosses. What do they feel about this? It's not important who this one loves and who this one hates and what bow-tie [Sydney] or what machete-hair [Ondine] don't do if you don't figure on the white ones and what they thinking about it all" (111).

Thérèse's partiality—her dislike and disregard of whites—has shaped or deformed her story, depending on the framework of the listener. Thérèse's home lies outside the direct control of Valerian and the forces symbolically associated with him; she does not literally live in his house but in a community into which he will never set foot.

Women living outside this type of enclave perforce exist without community buffers in a racist, classist patriarchy. *Tar Baby* has no Pheobes, no intimate relationships between women. Jadine ostensibly has friends in New York, and their names are listed once or twice, but Morrison does not dramatize a single scene including them, nor does she include any direct quotations of dialogue. Instead, the women's relationships, like all the rest in the novel, emerge as impermanent if not transient alliances made from partially overlapping experiences. Almost no exchanges between the three major female characters are triangulated, because Jadine, Ondine, and Margaret share very little; instead, the meaningful exchanges come from pairings: Jadine and Margaret, Ondine and Margaret, and finally Jadine and Ondine.

Jadine and Margaret have the dubious opportunities of extremely beautiful women. Jadine's professions, modelling and acting, formalize and make more permanent Margaret's position as beauty queen. Neither woman's mother can help her negotiate this treacherous territory, for Jadine's is dead and Margaret's is too removed, too much in awe of her daughter's appearance, to offer guidance. Margaret married Valerian at seventeen; at twenty-five, Jadine has a chance to marry Ryk, a wealthy European. Jadine's Christmas present for Margaret aptly symbolizes Margaret's position and Jadine's prospects: a chain of gold coins. This richly ironic symbol simultaneously reaffirms and undercuts historical racial roles. Valerian has earlier referred to Margaret's "buying" a poet to bribe their son into making a Christmas visit; her position as white slaver is thus asserted. At the same time, Margaret herself willl wear this chain, for she is enslaved to Valerian's wealth. The wealth represented by the gift would in the nineteenth century have bound Jadine to a white master or mistress; in the mid-twentieth, it may bind her to articulate survivorhood.

The differences in their possible futures probably stem in part from their belonging to separate generations and in part from their original class positions. Upper middle-class expectations of married women having changed in the meanwhile, Jadine would probably not have to endure the imprisonment in leisure that was Margaret's fate. (Ondine recognizes this influence on Margaret's behavior toward her son when she explicitly identifies Valerian's responsibility: "He kept her stupid; kept her idle. That always spells danger" [279].) Her education will spare her Margaret's humiliation brought on by the socialite who, on hearing that Margaret's school was South Suzanne High School, patted her stomach and told her, "Get to work, fast, sweetheart" (58). While Jadine's education allows her a wider range of socially acceptable roles, however, they may offer no more fulfillment. In addition, Margaret has no wisdom to offer the younger Jadine, for Margaret's buried past has incapacitated her for years, and at novel's end, she has just embarked on an exploration of her own.

The two women who do belong to the same generation, Margaret and Ondine, have in crucial ways been pitted against one another by racism and class; nevertheless, their long history in the same houses brings them closer even if it does not unite them. Margaret originally thinks of Sydney and Ondine as "the coloreds," but any impulse toward separatism weakens as her loneliness in Valerian's mansion grows. Valerian divides Margaret from Ondine, instructing his young wife that her duties lie in guiding the servants, not in socializing with them. Originally, their shared secret (Margaret's abuse of her son) further separates them, but when Ondine reveals the truth, Margaret is freed to develop herself—and, tentatively, to have a more genuine relationship with Ondine. Margaret initiates the first conversation that explores the past. She reproaches Ondine for having used the knowledge to build an evil-white-woman/good-black-woman dichotomy but subsequently apologizes for her insults during the Christmas quarrel. Although relieved to have the truth now "speakable," Margaret would like to share responsibility for her actions, not with the patriarch Valerian, but with Ondine, who refuses:

"You should have stopped me."
"You should have stopped yourself." (241)

Part of Margaret's assignment of responsibility to Ondine comes from a false premise—Margaret had assumed that at the time in question, when she was a nineteen-year-old mother, Ondine had been thirty-five or so. In fact, Ondine was "twenty-three. A girl. Just like you" (241). Margaret instantly understands the importance of the correction and asks Ondine's forgiveness; her error exemplifies the tendency dissected in Sherley Anne Williams's *Dessa Rose* of white women to look to black women for mothering.[11] Ondine's revelation has freed Margaret, who, in its wake, drops the perfect grooming that characterizes the false femininity of the beauty queen. The direction and degree of her development remain uncertain, but in contrast to Valerian, she is newly energized. What she can offer Ondine is also unclear. With Valerian's illness, the white patriarchal structure has loosened its grip, and between the slackening fingers, where race and class do not interfere, there may be space for honest communication, a rarity in this novel's milieu.

Ondine's second bit of truth-telling, with Jadine, has less certain results. Ondine communicates how hurt she and Sydney are at Jadine's desertion of them after the Christmas contretemps. Earlier, Ondine has exulted in the lack of tension between herself and Jadine: "a 'child' whom she could enjoy, indulge, protect and, since this 'child' was a niece it was without the stress of a mother-daughter relationship" (96). At this crisis, she feels that she has made a mistake in not emphasizing daughterhood: "Now you didn't have a mother long enough to learn much about it and I thought I was doing right by sending you to all them schools and so I never told you it and I should have. You don't need your own natural mother to be a daughter. All you need is to feel a certain way, a certain careful way about people older than you are" (281).

Ondine recognizes that she has implicitly relied on the strength of family bonds while underestimating the effects of class (schooling). In her vision of the night women baring their breasts, Jadine has seen both her mother and her aunt among her accusers. Already defensive, she understands her aunt's statement to be a demand that she "parent" Ondine; significantly, her diction shies away from "mother." She has felt the responsibility before, musing about her future: "More and more Sydney and Ondine looked to her for solutions to their problems. They had been her parents since she was twelve and now she was required to parent them—guide them, do the small chores that put them in touch with the outside world, soothe them, allay their fears" (91). The words "required" and "chores" bespeak obligation, but Ondine speaks the language of feeling.

To Jadine, the bitch in heat seen as the defining image of her sexuality, the frightening vision of the night women, the loss of her mother, and the scorn of the African women in yellow all segue into one another: "No matter what you did, the diaspora mothers with pumping breasts would impugn your character" (288), as indeed, Thérèse does. To some extent, Jadine Childs shares Meridian Hill's inability to be a mother. Whereas Meridian expresses with the wider community the nurturance that she is unable to expend on her own child, Jadine is unable to identify a larger community for herself. Jadine mulls over Ondine's words and decides, "A grown woman did not need safety or its dreams. She *was* the safety she longed for" (290). To be one's own safety, however, may be to accept the privations of ascent.

In perceptive analyses of the ending of *Tar Baby*, both James Coleman and Eleanor Traylor highlight its inconclusiveness, its inability to solve what they each see as the problem of living in the twentieth century without abandoning folk culture and the problem of American disconnection. In both readings, the physical separation of Son and Jadine, particularly given their locations on Isle de Chevaliers and in Paris, signify a reiteration rather than a resolution of the novel's most important issues. Certainly no unity as imaged in a settled relationship between Son and Jadine emerges. On the other hand, both characters have moved beyond their beginning premises. Each has reexperienced his idealized home ground in the company of the other; each has then reevaluated that home. Son finds that Jadine's pictures of Eloe reveal disturbing elements to which he has been blind. Similarly, Jadine finds that New York City cannot shield her from the distrust of her sexuality or the fear of the night women.

In order to continue growing so that communication can be reestablished, perhaps each needs to reexperience another formerly comfortable setting. Thérèse may consider Son a blind rider and Isle de Chevaliers his natural home, but Son has not yet decided. Coleman comments that the novel's final description of Son as moving, like Br'er Rabbit, "lickety-split" is too positive in tone for the events described (70–71). This interpretation accents only one part of a doubled description: "Then he ran. Lickety-split. Lickety-split. Looking neither to the left nor the right. Lickety-split. Lickety-split. Lickety-lickety-lickety-split" (306).

"Looking neither to the left nor the right" rephrases what Son has earlier noticed about African-American men in New York City, who "were looking neither to the right nor the left" (215). Son may not have fused folk and urban identities, but they exist in parallel within him, and he certainly desires their unity. The men's focus originally seems to Son a means of not looking at the pain of African-American women's collective experience. The reversal of right and left in the final description, then, suggests a significant modification rather than an unqualified incorporation of the twentieth century.

Jadine also seems in process. She may be fleeing Son, but she is also resolving to confront necessary issues: "[l]et loose the dogs, tangle with the woman in yellow—with her and with all the night women" (290). Jadine seeks a confrontation with the authentic self and with the African ancestor on the necessary ground. In *Their Eyes*, Tea Cake chooses the territory for Janie's immersion, and a good deal of their interaction may be seen as Janie's substitution of Tea Cake's views for her own (Awkward, " 'The inaudible voice of it all' "). In *Tar Baby*, Jadine chooses the necessary territory for her confrontations, and it is urban. As Son may join the riders and abandon the present, so Jadine may marry Ryk and abandon her tribal past. Her determination to tangle, however, suggests a different aim and a possible victory. If Thérèse is correct and Jadine has "forgotten her ancient properties," then *Tar Baby* shows through Margaret that, given the proper circumstances, women can remember. If *Tar Baby* presents no victories, no maps through Isle de Chevaliers or Paris, neither does it declare the fields lost.

Twice in this century, the issue of a woman's attempt to disengage from historical identity has become an important focus of African-American women's novels. In neither the Harlem Renaissance novels by women nor in their works of the 1980s does any analogue of the melancholy narrator of *The Autobiography of an Ex-Coloured Man* speak of years of alienation yet continue to pass. Emotional and sensual deprivation in *Quicksand,* ennui in *Plum Bun,* material success complicated by others' recognition of one's self-denial in *Tar Baby* and *Praisesong for the Widow,* starvation in *Linden Hills*—these images convey the catastrophes of trying to live outside of or apart from one's tribal history. For black female characters, the extended attempt to separate from historical connection entails isolation and self-denial so extreme that it can prove fatal.

6

EVERY MOTHER A DAUGHTER

TWENTIETH-CENTURY AFRICAN-AMERICAN women's novels sing the necessity of historical knowledge and understanding for tenable female identities in both major and minor keys. The tradition includes both damaging (frequently killing) refusals to acknowledge history and successful quests for historically based identities. Successful quests always entail some pain, for emotionally learning and interpreting an oppressive history must include feelings of shame, fear, and disgust as well as celebration. *Kindred* shows Dana undergoing great physical and emotional suffering as she reexperiences the female tribal past. Her greatest anxiety during the first several trips centers on her inability to return to her present at will. What if she gets stranded in history? In fact, because Butler uses Dana's fear for her life as the mechanism of return, Dana cannot remain trapped and powerless in the historical past. Paule Marshall, Gayl Jones, Alice Walker, and Toni Morrison all confirm their heroines' similar apprehensions about becoming mired in the past.

Marshall's *The Chosen Place, the Timeless People*; Jones's *Corregidora*; Walker's *Meridian*; and Morrison's *Beloved* all recognize that one can still drown on the Middle Passage. That is, the pain of acknowledging the historical past and its influences on the present may immobilize a heroine rather than energizing her. In order not to be overwhelmed and determined by an oppressive past, individual women must be able to live in the present and conceive of a future. Characters without an already solid sense of self may lack the perspective to comprehend historical experience as a part, rather than the whole of, their identities. While early twentieth-century African-American women's novels concentrate on denial/acceptance and their immediate consequences, these more recent novels focus on heroines mired in history, experiencing the pain of slavery and its aftermath without being able to move on.

Although they image various forms of such paralysis, the novels all show the main female characters eventually escaping into creative mobility. Exploring the social and personal conditions that enable women to assimilate the past, they examine the heroines' complicated relationships with communities of varying sizes and constitutions. One of these novels, *Beloved*, is a slave narrative, so the personal past of the heroine is the historical past for contemporary readers. *The Chosen Place, the Timeless People* and *Meridian* depict contemporary heroines in times or places that accent political struggle: respectively, a Caribbean island struggling with post-slavery/post-colonial economics and the American South during the 1960s and 1970s. *Corregidora* bridges these two groups, its heroine Ursa growing up under the controlling influence of Gram and Great Gram, survivors of Brazilian slavery who emigrate to Louisiana about 1906. The relationship to family, both immediate and ancestral, becomes a central aspect of the heroines' recovery from paralysis.

Many of these novels thus adumbrate a theme of crucial importance in nineteenth-century black women's writings and continuing resonance since—motherhood. Hazel Carby has suggested that, in literature, Harriet Jacobs and others have used their status as mothers with children to protect in order to claim more power and agency than nineteenth-century women were otherwise accorded. The lives of black women responsible for children, however, remained incredibly difficult, and a long line of novels details the costs that, although the specifics vary according to time and place, remain constant in their extremity. The costs of becoming a mother are laid out in *Quicksand*; the costs of mothering are detailed in *Their Eyes Were Watching God* (through Nanny), *The Street*, *Sula*, *This Child's Gonna Live*, *Meridian*, and *Beloved*. Recently, however, several writers—Marshall, Alice Walker, Naylor, and Morrison—have shifted viewpoint and now focus on the adult heroine as simultaneously adult and child in search of parenting.

Marshall's *Praisesong* lays out the pattern in boldest relief because of its grounding in ritual and archetype rather than in a realist aesthetic. Marshall's works differ from the other novelists' by focusing on parents rather than specifically on mothers. *Praisesong* constructs a pattern of fetal and infantile imagery to describe its heroine. This imagery accents the rebirth that transforms Avey Johnson into Avatara, but the family relationships that lie in the novel's past as well as Avey's present confirm her status as a child. Her oldest daughter, Sis, for example, takes on many adult responsibilities after her two sisters are born, and her nickname bespeaks her relationship, not only with her siblings, but with Avey. Tracing the imagery of childhood when it does not characterize Avey and is thus removed from the issue of rebirth of the self may, however, give a better indication of its thematic importance. One of Avey's two companions on the cruise, Thomasina, who seems significantly psychologically healthier than either Clarice or Avey, looks "with a child's open-mouth disbelief" (2) when Avey announces her decision to leave the cruise. Wealthy, Thomasina had been married to a husband who "treat[ed] her as if she were all the children they had never had" (27). On vacation the year before, Thomasina had mortified Avey by abandoning the cruise crowd to join a dance in a Colombian carnival; she shows the same spontaneity and susceptibility to dance that Avatara must so painfully reacquire. Conversely, what kills Jay is the forced denial of so many of his childlike traits that he obliterates them all and criticizes their persistence in others; the loss of his nickname signifies his transmutation into the living-dead (wholly and simply adult) Jerome. The imagery of childhood, then, does not signify a lack of maturity, or, in fact, a lack at all.

In order to be whole, women—and, Marshall implies, men also—

must learn to experience themselves simultaneously as children and as adults, which is not difficult if Western ideas of linear time are discarded. In *Praisesong*, this simultaneity is accomplished when Avey observes the nation dances for the Old Parents: "It was the essence of something rather than the thing itself she was witnessing. Those present—the old ones—understood this. All that was left were a few names of what they called nations. . . . The bare bones. The burnt-out ends" (240). Rather than being dismayed by the cultural destruction to which the nation dances testify, Avey focuses on cultural perseverance and loyalty: "And they clung to them with a tenacity she suddenly loved in them and longed for in herself" (240). The continued presence of the Old Parents in one's life is a choice. It means that one can never be simply an adult, a mother of children; one is also simultaneously a daughter.[1]

Many heroines in recent black women's fiction must find some nurturing aspect of the past to help contain history's destructive and obliterating effects. Whereas *Praisesong* images this longing for context as a desire for the Old Parents, *Corregidora*, *Meridian*, and *Beloved* more specifically concentrate on the desire for or relationship with a mother. *Corregidora* contains many of the same elements found in *Praisesong*, including the female griot, but the explicit inclusion of lesbian relationships reconstructs essential issues such as women's relationships to each other.

Within the framework of examining oral means of preserving knowledge of oppressive histories, *Corregidora* indicates the necessity of the mother's support and experience to the growth of a fully functional daughter. Ursa's Gram and Great Gram dedicate themselves, as well as Ursa and her mother, to keeping the accurate record of slavery alive. Self-appointed griots, they hypnotically chant the stories of their experiences with their Portuguese master (Corregidora) to Ursa from the time of her birth: "*They burned all the documents, Ursa, but they didn't burn what they put in their minds. We got to burn out what they put in our minds, like you burn out a wound. Except we got to keep what we need to bear witness. That scar that's left to bear witness. We got to keep it as visible as our blood*" (72). In their world, "bearing witness" becomes literal—their function, Ursa's mother's function, Ursa's function, lies in producing daughters to chant the story anew and ensure its survival. When Ursa undergoes an emergency hysterectomy and is thus forcibly denied the possibility of taking her place in the generative scheme, she must find a new self-definition and a new relationship to the past.

To break out of being a cipher in history, Ursa must redefine the inseparable aspects of the griot's role: audience, content, and form. From the novel's opening, her occupation as blues singer suggests her resolution, her eventual understanding of how to reshape her tradition without betraying it. Initially, however, Ursa's conscious and unconscious commitment to having a child to bear witness overpowers every other thought. After the hysterectomy, she answers a prospective suitor's, "What do you want?" with, "What all us Corregidora women want. Have been taught to want. To make generations" (22). She dodges his repeated question with, "More than yourself?" (22). Unable to formulate a desire for herself, she substitutes her would-be lover's desire. Her upbringing has encouraged her to think of men as tools to secure pregnancy, and such manipulation cannot be quickly unlearned. Ursa's subsequent sexual frigidity shows her profound isolation, a desolation caused by both her inability to fulfill her original role and the devouring nature of the role's requirements.

In Gram's and Great Gram's mouths, history has become a vampire depriving present generations of sexual and emotional intensity and intimacy. The griot repeats unvaryingly the exact chronicle of Gram's and Great Gram's victimization, which becomes dogma: Corregidora sexually exploited Great Gram, beginning when she was thirteen, both for his own pleasure and for profit, and then he did the same with their daughter, Ursa's Gram. The narrative exclusively concerns the slave experience; there are no stories of leaving Corregidora or of living in the United States. Once and once only does Ursa question, "You telling the truth?" (14) about Great Gram's account of being forced to sleep with both Corregidora and his wife. In response, Great Gram slaps the five-year-old Ursa. The form of the stories is invariant, even to the exact repetition of words. This constant repetition makes the stories echo in Ursa's adult consciousness; their power to obliterate personality shows most clearly when Ursa later asks her mother for information: "Mama kept talking until wasn't her that was talking, but Great Gram. I stared at her because she wasn't Mama now, she was Great

Gram talking" (124). This is no ancestral empowerment, no horse carrying the power of a *loa*, but a straightforward displacement/ possession, for the story that emerges has no power of nurturance. With survival, mere survival of the story as its aim, this conception of the griot replaces continuity with repetition. The audience for the story is no longer tribal, but only familial, and only partially familial at that—no males are allowed to belong to the Corregidora family.

The rigid form and content of these failed griots' message simultaneously falsify history and their own lives, each having been oversimplified. As Keith Byerman has observed in *Fingering the Jagged Grain*, Gram and Great Gram's allegory insists on a dualistic universe, neatly divided into good and bad (178–80). Through their insistence on themselves as completely passive and therefore completely innocent victims, Gram and Great Gram are led into denying their own sexuality. After Corregidora, they have no lovers. In turn, they implicitly teach the daughter that her sexuality exists solely for the production of a new griot rather than for pleasure. Ursa has one bit of information with which to complicate this rigid narrative. She knows that after emancipation, Great Gram stayed with Corregidora until she did something that made him want to kill her. Then Great Gram ran away for an indeterminate period, finally returning for her eighteen-year-old daughter (Gram), who also remained with Corregidora though she was technically free. The facts suggest some emotional or psychic bond between Corregidora, Great Gram, and Gram which the standard narrative does not admit.[2] In order to fill out the narrative to a more satisfying whole, the child Ursa asks questions about, for example, whether Gram had brothers. Great Gram frightens her into silence; later she asks her mother, who can't give a definitive answer but thinks that there might have been some boys whom Corregidora sold. Finally, however, in order to heal, Ursa requires not just a more complete version of Great Gram's and Gram's experiences but her mother's story as well. Ursa knows that her mother has a private memory that she refuses to yield to Great Gram and Gram, but she does not know the content of that memory. When she is in her late thirties and her mother in her late fifties, she asks for and receives her mother's private memories. With this knowledge, she can begin to grow toward psychic wholeness.

Ursa's mother's story undercuts the hegemony of Great Gram's and Gram's narrative in several ways. First, it carries irrefutable evidence of Gram's frustrated sexuality. (Gram attempts to attract Ursa's father, Martin. Having failed, she accuses him of attempting to exploit her.) In this new narrative, Martin asks the question that Ursa's mother had wanted to ask, that Tadpole later asks Ursa in a slightly different form (13), that the Invisible Man asks in his dream prologue: "How much was hate for Corregidora and how much was love?" (131). Gram's denied sexual nature, past and present, is asserted. Second, the memory shows that the older women worked to subvert Ursa's parents' relationship by repeating sotto voce the story of Corregidora's hounding and killing a black man who dared to be interested in Great Gram. Males are intruders and exploiters; Corregidora women's sexuality exists only for making generations; intruders will be killed. The memory thus makes untenable the griots' presentation of themselves as passive victims by showing them to be active victimizers also. Third, Ursa's mother bravely reveals her sexual dysfunction, her inability to enjoy sex in a house containing Gram and Great Gram, and her inability to leave the house. She thus relieves some of Ursa's isolation. Ursa can perceive her own dysfunction, not just as a product of particular individual experience (her hysterectomy), but of social conditioning with roots in slavery. Lastly, Ursa's mother's memory enlarges the definition of history. No longer does the authoritative narrative stop with the end of Brazilian slavery. A truncated history is, no less than a too-selective story, a false history; unless history continually grows to include subsequent generations' experiences, it is invalid and Procrustean.

Ursa redefines the interrelated aspects of being a griot—the role itself, the content and form, and the audience. Each redefinition meets resistance, and the necessary struggles are waged on the terrain of socially defined gender and sexuality. Although Ursa's mother eventually supports her daughter by sharing her private memory, she initially resists Ursa's singing so strenuously that Ursa moves away. Gram's blues records notwithstanding, Ursa's mother feels that only gospel singing is moral. Perhaps to avoid condemning Gram and to maintain some consistency, she explains that listening to blues is all right because it is not "the devil coming out of your own mouth" (146). The gospel/blues split re-creates the dichotomy between good and evil inherent in Great Gram's and Gram's narrative; similarly, Ursa's mother accepts the passivity of listening while rejecting the activity of creation. Ursa's question, "What's a life always spoken, and only spoken?" (103), at once addresses the death-in-life of reliving rather than living and her need for a different artistic form.

The blues offer Ursa that more capacious form. The mixture of pleasure and pain, which defines a blues sensibility, distinguishes Ursa's forms from Great Gram's and Gram's recitations. Ursa has felt the emotional falsity of the stories: "*Sometimes I wonder about their desire, you know. Grandmama's and Great Gram's. Corregidora was theirs more than hers. Mama could only know, but they could feel. They were with him. What did they feel? You know how they talk about hate and desire. Two humps on the same camel? Yes*" (102). Ursa uses the same knowledge of desire's mixed nature in her art: "What do they say about pleasure mixed in the pain? That's the way it always was with him [Mutt]. The pleasure somehow greater than the pain" (50). Throughout the novel, Ursa tries to learn what Great Gram did to Corregidora that made him try to kill her and yet desire her unbearably. When she finally discovers the sexual technique, biting her partner's penis just before orgasm, she finds an emblem for pain in the presence of pleasure, vulnerability in the midst of power. Here Ursa discovers vulnerability in the male, whom she has always generically defined as, if not all-powerful, much more powerful than she. Seeing this simultaneously powerful and powerless position, she at last admits that she fears her own vulnerability in emotional and sexual intimacy; the admission is essential for any reestablishment of her relationship with Mutt. Three times he admits his own vulnerability, "I don't want a kind of woman that hurt you," and she evades with, "Then you don't want me." When he shakes her, she finally replies with her own vulnerability, "I don't want a kind of man that'll hurt me neither" (185). Ursa's gentle bite concretizes what, in her blues, remains metaphoric; it represents the movement from an intuitive and somewhat abstract understanding to the immediate lived experience. When she discovers the missing part of Great Gram's history, she thus moves toward wholeness by accepting a sexual relationship with the man she loves.

This recovery of history and self is a slow process, requiring more than twenty years of exploration. Gram's and Great Gram's too-narrow definition of the griot limited her function to a recital of the literally accurate (with a claim that it constituted the whole truth). In blues, Ursa feels free to transmute the details of specific situations in order to communicate their emotional content, to use metaphor and symbol to express pain. Her songs reflect her own psychic concerns and constraints while at the same time voicing a mixture of pleasure and pain that appeals to her audience. When her husband Mutt first hears her, she is singing an original composition about a train that enters an endless tunnel, which suddenly tightens around the train like a fist. The imagery suggests sex, a reversal of power relationships, and surprising violence; the transformation of the vaginal symbol into the fist indicates a refusal of female passivity but no possibility for activity except violent rejection. Another of Ursa's compositions, this one about a bird-woman who takes men on long journeys from which they never return, reiterates the fear that sexual relationships obliterate one partner's character. When Ursa remembers Mutt's question, "What do the blues do for you?" she answers, "It helps me to explain what I can't explain" (56). The audience of the blues cafe hears expressions and explanations of loneliness, longing, pleasure, and pain.

The issue of who properly constitutes this audience is the prime mover of the novel's action. In 1947, Ursa's husband Mutt—after she insists on continuing to sing, not just for him, but in public, in the cafe, where he sees that other men desire her—quarrels violently with her. During this quarrel, she suffers the fall which necessitates her hysterectomy. Clearly, Ursa rejects Mutt's attempt to limit her artistic performance to the private sphere, the audience of one. At the same time, she tends to pick one male member of her audience and sing directly to him; her performance is interactive to a certain extent, but as with all virtuoso performance, the control and power reside with the performer. Establishing personal, more egalitarian ties remains difficult for Ursa. She has been taught to think of herself as separated from others. First, of course, her function as a witness and her destined production of more witnesses distinguish her. Her family's Brazilian background and the particular horror of Corregidora's rape and incest further isolate her. Because this separation protects Ursa from certain vulnerabilities, she resists giving it up. Thus, she dislikes hearing the cafe owner Tadpole's anecdote about his grandfather's rearing and then marrying his grandmother, Mutt's feeling that he's known her from way back, the waitress Sal's remark, "Since I first laid eyes on you I thought you was one of my long-lost relatives" (70). Ursa resists acknowledging similarities to others because recognition implies emotional contact. Ursa gradually widens her idea of kin, moving from the narrowest concept of her Great Gram (only Corregidora women) to a more inclusive definition that encompasses women and men, people of somewhat different experience but with similar histories and personalities.

Corregidora makes clear that Ursa's process of redefinition remains unfinished despite the ending, in which she reconciles with Mutt. The simultaneous acceptance of this male lover (as opposed to "husband" or "sexual partner") and her own vulnerability probably signal an end to Ursa's sexual dysfunction, but accepting her own heterosexuality leaves untouched the issue of dealing with others' differing desires. This unfinished aspect—the sense of a process with an unknown endpoint, as opposed to one with an indefinite timetable but a fixed destination—makes *Corregidora* consist not only of blues but of jazz. Women's experience of each other in *Corregidora* overflows the neat paradigm of daughter claiming mother and mother empowering daughter. A major component of the overflow is the necessity to acknowledge lesbianism and admit the full complexity of a lesbian personally known.

Byerman interprets lesbianism in this novel in an entirely different way. Curiously, since the rest of his excellent book explores folklore's insistence on the irreducible multiplicity of meaning in signs and practices, and on African-American folklore's preservation of these, his argument here rests on assigning a single meaning to an important phrase (what he elsewhere designates as "logocentrism") and a reinstitution of dualism:

> Lesbianism becomes here, as in "The Women," a form of narcissistic evasion. In the case of Cat Lawson, Ursa's friend, it serves as a way of not having to "feel like a fool in my own bed" (*Corregidora*, 64). Because another woman knows this feeling, the bed can become a

place of refuge. But in this sense the relationship is marked by absence and negation rather than by creative assertion. It is a space of not-men rather than of women. This point is reinforced in the character of Jeffry [sic], Cat's obsessive and domineering lover, or in other words, an ersatz man. (179)

Byerman assumes that when Cat says that she disengaged herself from her husband because she did not want "to feel like a fool in my own bed," Ursa's understanding of that feeling's origin is literally correct. Ursa feels that she does know that feeling of being a fool; she has experienced it when she has felt desire and her husband has denied her pleasure. Although Ursa understands the feeling, its origins in her experience may be quite different from those in Cat's. Cat's husband may have been unable rather than unwilling to give her sexual pleasure; perhaps the pain of remaining unsatisfied comes from desiring a woman rather than a man. Although Byerman's "in the case of Cat Lawson" indicates that she might be a special case, the following "because another woman knows this feeling" clarifies his view that the novel presents lesbianism as originating in women's defenses against further disappointment by men. He is correct about the character of Jeffy, who bullies verbally and physically, but in the initial scene, Jeffy is only fourteen years old. Her age alone makes it improbable that, even if she has had sexual experience with men, she has lived with one long enough to feel a fool in her own bed.

In addition, Byerman's separation of desire into opposing categories of heterosexuality and homosexuality—"a space of not-men rather than of women"—exemplifies the dualism that he identifies elsewhere as the discourse of oppression, the discourse that folkloric forms (like the blues) deconstruct. Ursa's experience tells her, furthermore, that she is not completely separated, distinct from Cat, though she would like to be. At one point, she echoes a phrase that Cat has used in rebuking Jeffy ("I'll give you a fist to fuck"), which simultaneously signifies that Cat remains a part of her experience and that lesbian and heterosexual expressions of anger overlap.

Like Merle in *The Chosen Place, the Timeless People*, Ursa originally associates lesbianism with racist oppression, unequal power between a demanding white woman and a powerless black one. (As a thirteen-year-old slave, Great Gram was forced to sleep not only with Corregidora but with his wife.) In addition, a lesbian relationship could not produce the child necessary to bear witness, her sole familial obligation.

Ursa's initial contact with lesbianism, which might give her an alternative definition, occurs when she is a teenager, and she can make no sense of it. She is trying to console her pregnant friend May Alice: "[S]he kept hugging me and crying, and hugging me, and saying why couldn't I have been Harold and then nothing would have happened. I didn't know what she was talking about then" (141). May Alice's desired substitution of her female friend for her male lover denies the polar opposition of heterosexuality and homosexuality, showing the same woman as being able to experience both desires. As May Alice correctly points out, however, Ursa's upbringing has made her "unwomanly," a kind of permanent virgin, her degree of repression thus unfitting her to understand what May Alice says.

Ursa's next contact with lesbianism comes at a time and in a way that reiterates its association with exploitation. Recovering from her hysterectomy, Ursa has accepted an invitation from Cat to stay in her home so as not to exploit a willing male suitor, Tadpole McCormick. When Ursa invites Cat's other guest, the adolescent Jeffy, to share a bed rather than sleep on the floor, she awakens to unwanted sexual attentions. Ursa realizes that Cat's authority to rebuke Jeffy stems from their emotional and sexual relationship. Despite Cat's generosity in caring for her, despite Cat's correct perception that Ursa will be unable to avoid exploiting Tadpole, whom she does not love, if she is dependent on him for care and shelter, Ursa leaves Cat's house without a word. Both women feel hurt, but Cat initiates a discussion with Ursa after legally witnessing her marriage to Tadpole. Ursa denies judging her, but "[Cat] was waiting for an embrace that I refused to give, then she stood up" (66). Ursa does not see her again although the novel ends twenty-two years later.

Because the novel is first-person retrospective, Ursa herself indirectly tells the reader, in the penultimate chapter, of her ambivalences and failure to confront her relationships with women fully. This retrospection in the 1947 chapter ascribes her "evilness" with

Cat and Jeffy to fears that had nothing to do with their personalities or sexualities: "It wasn't until years later that I realized it might have been because of my own fears, the things I'd thought about in the hospital, my own worries about what being with a man would be like again, and whether I really had the nerve to try. But then I just felt evil" (48). Her self-awareness thus suggests her nascent ability to accept Cat.

Aware that she has made a poor response to Cat's friendship, Ursa nevertheless allows other issues to interfere with a possible reconciliation in 1969; she is now in her late forties and Cat in her eighties. The obnoxious Jeffy, now the thirty-six-year-old Miss Jeffrene, remains obnoxious. She informs Ursa that Cat has had an accident and needs Ursa, and she indicates that she knew there was never any sexual tension between Cat and Ursa. Simultaneously, she taunts Ursa with being afraid, makes crude double entendres, insists that Ursa enjoyed her sexual assault, and offers herself as a sexual partner whenever Ursa is ready. Although Ursa feels a strong urge to seek out Cat and knows that Cat and Jeffrene are somewhat estranged, she reacts as though somehow Cat is implicated in Jeffrene's aggression:

> "Maybe you can go see her? Maybe you can help her get her ass together?"
>
> She said it like she meant it, but still it strangled any impulse I'd had to go see Catherine. And after that day, whenever I saw Jeffrene, I'd cross the street. (178)

Avoiding Catherine is confused with avoiding Jeffrene though the women's personalities have little in common. Jeffy's attempt to impose her sexual agenda on Ursa undoubtedly calls up all of the memories of Corregidora's depravity, all her female forebears' loss of choice in sexual desire. Nonetheless, Ursa cannot yet respond to the particulars of Catherine's personality, those particulars of experience which are crucial to the blues and to accurate history. Her simultaneous urges toward and away from Catherine are the remaining microcosm of the earlier, encompassing paralysis. Victory is real but partial, not a static state but a process of living.

Meridian: MOTHERS AND MARTYRS TO HISTORY

Meridian shifts the terrain on which the struggle for wholeness is waged from the sexual desire of *Corregidora* to a broader complex of interactive relationships with family, friends, and the wider black community. It is not only that Meridian experiences no satisfactory sexual relationships with men (women do not seem to occur to her as possible sexual partners) but that she appears to dismiss the idea as irrelevant. Indeed, the components of Meridian's potential fulfillment never crystallize because the novel is concerned instead with laying out the immediate obstacles to it, over which Meridian eventually triumphs. Both novel and title character strive toward a new mode of political commitment that allows the individual to survive and the community to progress. This mode must differentiate itself from the conformist ideology of the Saxon-R.Baron-Con U Civil Rights workers, facilely affirming their willingness to kill. Such a mode violates Meridian's temperament though later she vacillates between feeling able to kill in self-defense and her earlier refusal to do so. She fears that the music of the tribe, its soul, would, as a result of accepting violence, be changed beyond recognition. Meridian's action in the opening chapter, however—the confrontation that allows black children to visit a freak show—bespeaks an individual committed to acts of resistance, whether or not supported by a movement. Meridian seeks a new mode that would require neither the literal death of the individual through the oppressor's violence (or simple exhaustion) nor the figurative death through his/her violation of internal integrity (as killing would violate hers): "The only new thing now . . . would be the refusal of Christ to accept crucifixion. King . . . should have refused. Malcolm, too, should have refused. All those characters in all those novels that require death to end the book should refuse. All saints should walk away. Do their bit, then—just walk away. See Europe, visit Hawaii, become agronomists or raise Dalmations [sic]" (151). The rather flippant list of alternatives demonstrates Meridian's inability to take her initial insight seriously; doing so would require a different understanding of what will happen in the community if the prospective saint refuses martyrdom.

Originally, Meridian perceives blacks' political progress in a way similar to Byerman's paradigm of progress in Gaines's *The Autobiography of Miss Jane Pittman*: the community nurtures an individual leader, responds to his call even when its nature differs from its preconceptions, and then absorbs his inevitable death into the inspiring stories used as part of the nurturance for the next leader (88). Meridian's recurring dream of being a character in a novel, one whose "existence presented an insoluble problem, one that would be solved only by her death at the end" (117), prophesies her death under this mode. The dream's displacement from real life to the artistic realm signifies the responsibilities of artistic forms in perpetuating particular real-life patterns.

In this case, literary presentation lags behind the realities for, near the end, Meridian finds in a church service that the community as a whole has superceded the individual as the catalyst for change: " 'Look,' they were saying . . . 'If you will let us weave your story and your son's life and death into what we already know—into the songs, the sermons, the 'brother and sister'—we will soon be so angry we cannot help but move. . . . the church . . . the music, the form of worship that has always sustained us, the kind of ritual you share with us, these are the ways of transformation that we know. We want to take this with us as far as we can' " (199–200).

This knowledge frees her to discover and pursue her own role as an artist: "When they [the revolutionaries] stop to wash off the blood and find their throats too choked with the smell of murdered flesh to sing, I will come forward and sing from memory songs they will need once more to hear. For it is the song of the people, transformed by the experiences of each generation, that holds them together, and if any part of it is lost the people suffer and are without soul. If I can only do that, my role will not have been a useless one after all" (201).

The old conception, because it overstates the passivity of the community, also over-valorizes the individual. Preserving tribal memory through art will be Meridian's major contribution. Although this realization comes near the novel's end, it chronologically precedes the confrontation that Truman witnesses at the novel's beginning. Meridian moves back and forth between the two ideas— that direct individual actions, like killings, may be the one thing necessary and that preserving the songs must be her profession. This tension is never resolved because, in Walker's presentation, both are necessary. No person, however, is obligated to do one or the other her entire life. Individual activities, like organizing marches, refusing personal insult, and preserving tribal memories now appear as various roles rather than as identities. Perceiving the activist role as both escapable and recapturable changes the fundamental experience of the role, releases the player from inevitable martyrdom.[3]

Meridian's initial explanation to Truman as to why she pursues the activist role shows her still in thrall to a corrupt ideal of self-sacrifice, the heritage of martyred black motherhood: "They're grateful people. . . . They *appreciate* it when someone volunteers to suffer" (25). Gratitude and the obligation(s) that it confers—these are Meridian's mother's themes.[4] Having stolen her life, her children can at least, Mrs. Hill opines, be grateful; her attitude psychically maims Meridian, who almost dies from the psychosomatic effects. If Meridian continued to sacrifice herself beyond her strength, she would simply re-create her mother's life though the "beneficiaries" would be the community and its children rather than her own biological babies.

In *Meridian*, the individual experience of black motherhood within the context of historical black motherhood obliterates the souls of women and damages their children in an ever more serious cycle of destruction. Many critics have commented on this striking theme since Barbara Christian drew attention to it in *Black Women Novelists*. Gloria Wade-Gayles, for example, considers this resistance to motherhood as the sole defining element of black women's worthiness to be *Meridian*'s most original point (11). Christian explores contradictory social definitions of motherhood's paramount value and of black children as worthless, merely evidence of black women's promiscuity (220). Examining this issue further, Susan Willis proposes that, under these circumstances, mothers' impulses toward murder of their children or suicide "are the emotional articulation of social realities" (122). In addition, *Meridian* "is less an indication of future possibilities and more a critique of the way heterosexual relationships have individualized a woman's relationship to *her* children, making them *her* property" (123). *Meridian* simultaneously critiques traditional definitions of motherhood and implies more widely shared responsibility for children. In almost their only act of self-assertion, Saxon students riot when the college administration refuses to allow them to claim the Wild Child as one of their own. In focusing on the novel's opening scene—Meridian leading a "children's crusade" past a tank to desegregate a freak show—critics like Christian and Willis point to a politicized ideal of communal responsibility for children as central to Walker's vision in *Meridian*.

Accurate in itself, this critical focus has obscured another equally crucial component of the novel: the necessity for this rather abstract relationship of community and children to be manifested in an individual mother surrogate who provides emotional nurturance that the traditional role both demands and prevents. *Meridian* consistently focuses on both issues, on oppressive social structures and on the individual's capacity to resist them. Throughout, the novel emphasizes the power of individual example to rally opposition to injustice. The bereaved father testifying in church to the worth of his dead son's life, the minister who consciously imitates Martin Luther King, Jr.'s voice, Truman's inheritance of Meridian's role—all of these make a claim for the individual's power and worth. Both the harm done by oppressive institutions and the effectiveness of specific strategies of resistance are measured by their consequences for particular individuals. *Meridian* does not adopt a purely "quantitative" approach toward social change; that is, while continually emphasizing the need for social change, it values the rescue of each individual life, not only for its potential contributions toward social change, but in itself. With individuality such a strong underlying value, then, *Meridian* pushes beyond an abstract commitment of adults to the community's children and insists on one-to-one mothering nurturance for survival.

As demonstrated through Meridian and her mother, the social realities of black motherhood brutally oppress mothers, who in turn brutally oppress their children. Walker, to some extent, equivocates on whether Mrs. Hill is unfit for motherhood because of personal eccentricity or because the role itself is impossible. The initial description implies that the problem is individual: "Her mother was not a woman who should have had children. She was capable of thought and growth and action only if unfettered by the needs of dependents, or the demands, requirements of a husband. Her spirit was of such fragility that the slightest impact on it caused a shattering beyond restoration" (49). The rest of the novel, however, indicates that the social definition of motherhood for a black woman requires the sacrifice of that spirit. The generational histories of Meridian's female forebears is replete with women who literally worked themselves to death so that their children could have decent lives. As Meridian realizes, they had no choice if their children were to survive. Mrs. Hill's generation, however, had some choice, and their choices have betrayed both themselves and their children, particularly their daughters.

With the exception of the son whom Meridian gives away—his fate remains unknown—no named child in *Meridian* survives. (Critic Karen Stein remarks the many images of death that surround adult women, and both Christian and Willis comment directly on murdered and aborted children.) The Wild Child, Truman and Lynne's daughter Camara, the boy who drowns in an unprotected ditch, the infant killed by the thirteen-year-old mother—these horrible deaths presage the death of the entire community. In order to avoid killing children, the community must stop killing their mothers' souls. Once dead themselves, these zombie mothers trap others in the same quicksand. Mrs. Hill is furious that no one told her the truth about the demands of motherhood (50), yet she denies Nelda and Meridian the sexual information necessary to prevent them from becoming mothers (60). Girls and women who are struggling to maintain themselves are run to earth when they become pregnant; the metaphor becomes literal in the Wild Child's fate.

Burdened by an infant's unbearable demands when she is herself only seventeen, Meridian wants to kill him. To avoid that monstrosity, she thinks of another possibility (no less monstrous to Walker), killing herself. Having given up her child so that he can live and so that she can go to college, she suffers agonies of guilt at being an unworthy successor to the self-sacrificing women who have made her own life possible:

> Meridian knew that enslaved women had been made miserable by the sale of their children, that they had laid down their lives, gladly, for their children, that the daughters of these enslaved women had thought their greatest blessing from "Freedom" was that it meant they could keep their own children. And what had Meridian Hill done with *her* precious child? She had given him away. She thought of her mother as being worthy of this maternal history, and of herself as belonging to an unworthy minority, for which there was no precedent and of which she was, as far as she knew, the only member. (91)

In her own mind, she is not only a bad mother but a bad daughter who has stolen her own mother's life. Yet on some level, she knows that her responses have been more than individual failures, that the role itself is untenable: "Away from her mother, Meridian thought of her as Black Motherhood personified, and of that great institution she was in terrible awe, comprehending as she did the horror, the narrowing of perspective, for mother and for child, it had invariably meant" (96–99). Failure under impossible circumstances is still failure. Were it not for Miss Winter, Meridian would have died a failure.

Critics have commented on the extensive and complex connections of women in this novel, particularly the shared vulnerability of becoming pregnant and the Saxon heritage of Louvinie (Willis 114). Almost alone, however, John Callahan draws attention to Miss Winter's role in healing Meridian (233–34). When Meridian lies delirious, dying of her guilt, "Instinctively, as if Meridian were her own child, Miss Winter answered, close to her ear on the pillow, 'I forgive you' " (125). With the explicit forgiveness of this woman whom she mistakes for her mother, Meridian is just sufficiently healed to agree to live. This partial healing begins Meridian's struggle to establish her identity, provides her with a starting point. In *Meridian*, support from other women—for example, the support of Delores and Nelda for Meridian's decision to go to college—cannot compensate for the loss of a mother's love.

Callahan approaches Meridian's sickness-unto-death as part of a deliberate confrontation with obstacles to her self-realization, a position that diminishes Walker's presentation of martyrdom as a temptation for women. Yes, Meridian follows the traditional patterns of the saint-in-progress, even acquiring a halo visible to Anne-Marion; that very pattern, however, is the subject of both Walker's and Meridian's critique. Further, Meridian cannot know that Miss Winter will be available during her crisis; her recovery seems more a function of coincidence than of her own willed choice. Interpreting Meridian's crisis as part of a planned strategy implies the ability of a conscious intellectuality to control emotional development. Walker seems to me much more interested in showing the difficulty of bringing these issues to consciousness and the helplessness of the isolated individual intellect.

Walker deliberately heightens the critique of motherhood by accenting similarities between the very temporary, if crucial, mother-surrogate, Miss Winter, and the biological mother, Mrs. Hill. Hailing from the Hills' hometown, the childless Miss Winter continues the teaching career that Mrs. Hill abandons for marriage. Meridian alters her surrogate mother's identity in somewhat the same way that she "steals" her mother's self. Meridian attempts to perform the same high school speech that Miss Winter had been assigned years before but breaks down because she comes to understand the falsity of the speech's political content during her recitation. As Callahan notes, while Mrs. Hill berates Meridian, Miss Winter looks on and eventually comments that the adolescent Meridian understands what took Miss Winter considerably longer to recognize. Her generosity in this instance typifies her response for, unlike Mrs. Hill, she does not insist that the next generation follow her path without deviation. Meridian's later matriculation threatens Miss Winter's unique status as the only Saxon graduate from this town, a petty ego prop that Miss Winter surmounts admirably. Ironically, only the childless woman can mother effectively because only she is allowed to preserve sufficient energy to preserve integrity.

Miss Winter's importance to *Meridian* extends past the two brief scenes in which she nurtures the heroine, however. Although Meridian sees the change in the community that allows her to give up her martyrdom, Miss Winter provides the nearest individual role model. "A misfit at Saxon College . . . one of only three black teachers" (120), as organist, Miss Winter plays the European hymns required of her by Saxon. In her classes, however, she teaches materials that are subversive in this context, jazz and blues. Her "ladylike" exterior of matched suits and accessories conforms to the Saxon requirements just enough to maintain her teaching position, but "her fights with the president and the college dean could be heard halfway across campus" (120). Miss Winter's actions thus prefigure Meridian's in two important ways. Like Meridian leading the children to see the bogus exhibition of Marilene O'Shay, Miss Winter supports black students' confrontation with Euro-American forms and simultaneously fulfills Meridian's final understanding of her own role—as griot, she preserves the tribe's songs.

The critical emphasis on these somewhat abstract relationships of the individual to the group should not obscure *Meridian*'s insistence on each girl/woman's need for emotional nurturance from a surrogate mother. The novel begins with Meridian's leading a group of children but does not end there. Further, Walker summarizes the off-stage fights between Miss Winter and the conservative Saxon administration, but she dramatizes Miss Winter's rescue of Meridian. Motherhood comprehends both political responsibility for the well-being of the community's children en masse and the personal responsibility to respond fully and emotionally to particular children in need. Throughout *Meridian*, those who deal largely in abstract concepts are depicted as shallow or at least mistaken: the revolutionary ideologues blithely confirming their commitment to killing, Lynne and Truman insisting on standard arguments that overlook potential voters' valid preoccupation with immediate concrete circumstances. Meridian has honored these immediate concerns and in doing so has been more politically effective than those committed primarily to abstracts. A believer in communal responsibility for children (an abstract) and sensitive to individuals, Meridian nevertheless cannot synthesize these two parts of her character to sustain particular children.

Walker highlights Meridian's continuing internal schism with sequential chapters late in the novel, "Treasure" and "Pilgrimage." The comic "Treasure" reiterates many of the themes surrounding motherhood. When the elderly Margaret Treasure takes Rims Mott as her first lover, her vicious sister Lucille and Mott convince her that she is pregnant. Despite her shame and guilt, she does not want to marry Mott and thus make him heir to her plantation—and parent to their chimerical child. Supporting her decision to remain single, Meridian and Truman act as nurturant parents, eventually getting her to a doctor who can relieve her fear of pregnancy. Margaret's need of mothering is clear. After sexual pleasure, she "lay on the hot ground like a lost child" (210); when Meridian and Truman escort her to the doctor's office, they "supported her every step of the way, holding her fat arms firmly up" (210), like parents helping a toddler walk. Relieved of her guilt and the burdens of a fancied motherhood, Margaret again takes up adult responsibilities and registers to vote—the registration that was Meridian and Truman's original aim. Parental nurturance makes possible both individual perseverance and political gain. This light-hearted incident is, nevertheless, a reprise of Meridian's and Mrs. Hill's combined experiences: women's guilt over sexual pleasure, their fear of motherhood, and the social context's delight in their entrapment.

"Pilgrimage," juxtaposes a uniquely grim episode with "Treasure." Visiting an imprisoned thirteen-year-old who has killed her own child, Meridian responds to the query about who she and Truman are with, "People who ask people to vote" (212). The prisoner laughs scornfully and, indeed, the answer inadequately describes Meridian. The self-definition makes their presence completely inappropriate, the prisoner being much too young to register under any circumstances. "People who ask people to vote" bespeaks a limitation more like those of Lynne and Truman than like Meridian's usual mode. In every other instance, Meridian has been able to respond to individuals' concrete needs and to hold the abstraction in abeyance until an appropriate time. She can respond freely to Margaret Treasure's need for maternal nurturance but not to that of the unnamed child. Obviously, in this situation, no response on Meridian's part could restore the child to health as Miss Treasure is restored. In a statement at once angry dismissal and plea, the child says, "If you all can't give me back my heart . . . go the fuck away" (212). With Truman, Meridian goes away. Her resultant poem, no matter how intensely felt, cannot take the place of an emotional interchange with the child. Usually so responsive to needy individuals, Meridian has not yet resolved the guilt of her own motherhood and daughterhood; thus, she cannot re-create Miss Winter's role in her life with any child. Like Ursa's, Meridian's pilgrimage remains unfinished.

Although *Meridian* honors the individual, Walker at no point in this novel presents individuals' experiences as transcending social construction. True, Miss Winter and her influence at Saxon show that both single individual and tribal memory can survive terrific oppression. The tribe itself, however, cannot persevere without a fundamental restructuring to change the definitions and conditions of motherhood. The occasionally successful intervention of a Miss Winter simply cannot alter the conditions under which soul-withered mothers blast their children's lives. In order to be liberating rather than oppressive, motherhood must be fluid or malleable rather than a Procrustean set of requirements. The definitions of motherhood which developed in the slave community are a valuable part of the African-American heritage, a testament to the strength of the black family and resistance to the oppressor. Under different social conditions, however, *Meridian* shows these definitions themselves to be oppressive.

BELOVED MOTHERS, BELOVED DAUGHTERS

In Toni Morrison's *Beloved*, a constraining definition of motherhood is a major component of the overwhelming historical past in which Sethe is mired. An extremely rich book, *Beloved* contains myriad themes—relationships between black men and women, the differing oppressions of more-brutal and less-brutal slave masters, the effects of printed materials on African-Americans of the nineteenth century, the characters and motivations of white abolitionists, and the nature of black spiritualities. This argument does not seek to explicate the entirety of the novel but, instead, to highlight a central theme. Morrison shows black women's construction of motherhood under slavery; then Sethe's paralysis because she is hampered by the limitations of this idea in the very different conditions of freedom; and finally, *Beloved* shows the joining of the past and the future to mother Sethe and offer a liberating vision of motherhood.

Beloved delineates African-American women under slavery who refuse to mother children not conceived in mutual desire and who fiercely defend those who are. Sethe's mother, for instance, "threw away," without naming them, all her children resulting from rape on the Middle Passage and the plantation. Similarly, when Ella bears a child fathered by one of a father-son pair who confine and rape her for years, she refuses to nurse it, and it dies soundlessly after five days. As Nan, shipmate and friend to Sethe's mother informs her, Sethe lives because she results from a union in which her mother "put her arms around" a black man, because the possibility of a child is chosen rather than imposed. After Sethe kills her daughter rather than allowing her to be reenslaved, she puts only "Beloved" on the tombstone, not the child's given name.[5] In this novel, then, the very existence of any African-American person testifies to mother love and acceptance.

Although the decision not to mother could be simple and unequivocal, slavery constantly circumscribed or outright denied the decision to mother one's children. In affirmation of the flesh so important to her spirituality, Sethe's "mother-in-law" (slave marriages were not legally valid), Baby Suggs, bore eight children. Of these, only one is permitted to stay with her, and after Halle buys her freedom, she loses him too. Of the first seven, several were sold so early that she could learn very little of their personalities and now could not recognize them. Besides, two may have escaped slavery and looking for them thirty years later could imperil their safety.

Even if a woman is permitted to keep her children with her, her ability to mother may be severely limited. On the plantations, where many slaves experienced their only mothering, black women's nurturance—from the physical (nursing milk) to the metaphysical (energy and patience)—is used up primarily in working fields and tending white children. Even in the relatively benign atmosphere of Sweet Home, slavery stunts its black children, quite literally. Raised on a plantation, isolated at Sweet Home with only the childless and therefore ignorant Mrs. Garner for aid, Sethe does not know the basics of child-rearing, such as when to begin feeding an infant solid food. Her third child, Beloved, crawls much earlier than her first and second because the baby has, in freedom, met with a more knowledgeable caretaker, Baby Suggs. Mothering is thus shown to be dependent on a web of women's knowledge and communication that slavery shreds.

Any practice of mother love, however, relies on contact, on having children remain with their mothers. The major means of protecting children from slavery is to value them and to communicate this value to them, as Nan emphasizes Sethe's mother's choice to preserve Sethe. When Sethe sees Schoolteacher coming into Baby Suggs's yard to reenslave her and her children, she acts in the only way that she can to ensure that her children will be with her: she attempts to kill them all, then herself. They will then all join Sethe's Ma'am, on the other side of death. As Sethe herself later thinks about the possibility of another pregnancy, "Unless carefree, motherlove was a killer" (132).

In the twilight area of an illegal freedom, Sethe has immediately, upon being summoned back to slavery, acted on a slave definition of mothering: presence is all. Morrison reiterates strongly that, although this definition is problematic, no one who has not lived with the contradictions of slave motherhood is entitled to judge Sethe—not the African-American male, represented by Paul D (with his callous two-feet/four-feet distinction, calling to mind School-teacher's attribution of animal traits to Sethe); not the community as a whole (which could have prevented the tragedy and out of wounded vanity did not warn Baby Suggs); not even the victims (Ella rejects her starved child's right to haunt her, and Beloved's all-encompassing claims are gradually rejected). Sethe's choice made sense to her at that time and place; it is still defensible. Indeed, her extreme action and its consequent publicity prevent the enslavement of her three remaining children.

Nineteen years later, Sethe remains imprisoned for her deed, not physically but mentally unable to create an ongoing life for herself. The past is constantly with her, memories of Sweet Home troubling any attempt at rest. In fact, the past quite literally haunts her, for the spirit of the murdered daughter lives in the house with Sethe. The ghost claims her attention, punishes her, yet Sethe accepts it. There is, of course, no physical necessity for her to do so. His second day in the house, Paul D gets rid of the ghost in a ten-minute scuffle; for this, he earns both Sethe's and her daughter Denver's disapproval. Still defining motherhood as keeping her children with her, Sethe cannot reject the ghost's presence.

This definition, necessary under slavery, operates in freedom to prevent the creation of tenable families and the growth of individual mothers as well as individual children. At the opening of the novel, Sethe lives in a present that is completely disrupted by the intrusion of the past; at this point, the past endlessly repeats itself, the ghost never growing older than the already crawling child who died.[6] Because the past lives in the house in answer to Sethe's desire, Paul D's exorcism can only be temporary. Beloved therefore returns in the flesh of a young woman. When Beloved leaves of her own will at the end of the novel, she does so out of a misunderstanding of Sethe's actions. Sethe goes to the gate to attack the man she thinks is Schoolteacher, come yet again to take her children; Beloved perceives her mother as leaving her again, moving on. And yet Beloved is correct; Sethe's response—homicide rather than suicide—belongs to freedom, not to slavery. Once her internal context becomes freedom in consonance with external reality, she will of necessity move away from Beloved, who did not live in freedom. Once Beloved is gone, Sethe is able to revise her idea of motherhood and, implicitly, her self-definition so that "her best thing" is no longer her children but, as Paul D suggests, herself.

Morrison does not, of course, simplistically recommend jettisoning history. As all of her earlier novels show, such an attempt is doomed and dooming. Here, contact with the past is a driving need for Paul D. Unable to establish a stable relationship with a woman, not knowing what he seeks, he finds Sethe and wants to build a life with her. Paul D has secreted his many painful memories in a metaphorical tobacco tin where his heart used to be. Sex with Beloved—unwilling on Paul D's part, coercive on Beloved's—opens the tobacco tin that "nothing in *this* world could pry . . . open" (113, my emphasis). Clearly, Paul D has distanced himself from history in an unhealthy way and requires visceral contact in order to reintegrate his experiences and personality. Sethe, on the other hand, has submerged herself in history.

Sethe's tolerance of the ghost, based on keeping her children with her to nurture, debilitates both her and her other three children. In fact, the system becomes self-contradictory. Sethe's sons, Buglar and Howard, are old enough to remember her attempt on their lives and fear her somewhat. They live as part of the family, however, until the ghost persecutes them beyond endurance. Buglar leaves when the ghost smashes a mirror; Howard, when the ghost's footprints in his cake deny him his birthday celebration. In other actions, the ghost is childishly spiteful (smashing jam jars) or sadistic (maiming the dog), but in both of these crucial actions, she explicitly returns the household to slavery conditions; under slavery, black people could maintain no public self-image and frequently could not celebrate birthdays because the dates had not been recorded. Unlike slaves, however, Buglar and Howard can and do move on. Thus, Sethe's rigid idea of motherhood truncates her relationship with two of her living children.

It also impoverishes her relationship with her surviving daughter,

Denver. After a casual question associating Denver with Sethe's guilt strikes Denver deaf for two years and ends her schooling, she does not leave the yard without her mother for a decade. In this claustrophobic environment, especially after her grandmother, Baby Suggs, dies, Denver has no emotional interests except Sethe. Naturally, she resents Paul D's presence, and, the first to recognize Beloved's identity, she initially welcomes the ghost's embodiment because it provides company. Sethe's possessiveness engenders Denver's, and both are carried to parodic extreme in Beloved. When Stamp Paid tries to repair the damage he has done by telling Paul D about Sethe's murder of Beloved, he hears confused voices ringing through 124 Bluestone Road: "He thought he heard a conflagration of hasty voices—loud, urgent, all speaking at once so he could not make out what they were talking about or to whom. The speech wasn't nonsensical, exactly, nor was it tongues. But something was wrong with the order of the words and he couldn't describe or cipher it to save his life. All he could make out was the word *mine*" (172, original emphasis).

This ominous claim, *"mine,"* reflects all three women's claims on each other. Denver is initially jealous of Beloved's interest in Sethe because she wants the girl to fill the void left by Paul D's interference in her exclusive relationship with her mother. Beloved indicates to Paul D that her own love for Sethe is different from Sethe's love for her because Sethe loves others as well. Thus, only in Sethe's case is the claim of "mine" reciprocal: "And when I tell you you mine, I also mean I'm yours" (203). Neither the dependent Denver nor Beloved has ever nurtured another, and reciprocal caring is forever beyond Beloved because she died still an infant. Beloved cannot endure in the present forever, Morrison implies; the flesh that she has assumed is put together poorly so that she loses a tooth now and again or cannot hold up the neck that Sethe had cut. In order to make Sethe hers, she must move Sethe from the present into the past by killing her. Frozen in an unchangeable past imaged as an all-demanding infant whom she cannot deny, Sethe could not survive without outside intervention.

Indeed, the ghost physically attacks Sethe in the clearing where Baby Suggs once preached. Denver interferes and, in her first disagreement with Beloved, privately charges her with the attempt.

Unsuccessful with the direct approach, Beloved begins to manipulate Sethe. In the rapture of discovering Beloved's identity, what
she sees as the permanent return of her child, Sethe spends more
and more time with her, even fantasizing that Howard and Buglar
now may return. Fired from her job for her sudden unreliability,
Sethe stops eating properly, then stops eating at all because the
house has no food. Obsessed with, nearly possessed by her history,
Sethe reacts to the present as though it were the past. When
Denver's employer, Mr. Bodwin, arrives to escort her to work,
Sethe sees his general physical similarity to Schoolteacher, concludes
that Schoolteacher has returned, and attempts to kill him. Beloved's
indirect strategy, empowered by Sethe's desire to keep her children
always with her, has nearly worked.

Sethe's necessary emergence from the past is orchestrated by two
forces, Denver and a crucial if somewhat tardy visit by the women
of the community. Beneath Sethe's passionate commitment to
motherhood lies an equally passionate desire to be mothered, to be
a daughter to her mother.[7] Her contact with Beloved brings this
desire to consciousness twice.

In answer to specific questions from Beloved, Sethe remembers
suddenly Nan's story of Sethe's origins and her mother's love.
Interestingly, she remembers the substance of the monologue but
not its words: "Nan was the one she knew best . . . And who used
different words. Words Sethe understood then but could neither
recall nor repeat now. She believed that must be why she remembered so little before Sweet Home. . . . What Nan told her she had
forgotten, along with the language she told it in. The same language
her ma'am spoke, and which would never come back. But the
message—that was and had been there all along" (62). The details
of the original tribal life and language of the mother-daughter bond
are gone beyond recall, but they are not necessary to the continuity,
to the memory of belonging and having been loved.

In the second instance, Sethe rejoices in the discovery of Beloved's
identity and immediately associates their mother-daughter tie with
the longed-for contact with her own mother: "My plan was to take
us all to the other side where my own ma'am is. They stopped me
from getting us there, but they didn't stop you from getting here.
Ha ha. You came right on back like a good girl, like a daughter

which is what I wanted to be and would have been if my ma'am had been able to get out of the rice long enough before they hanged her and let me be one" (203). This unsatisfied hunger in Sethe conditions her own extremely possessive definition of motherhood.

Sethe's two daughters address this need, one to possess and one to sustain her. Because Beloved has no sense of reciprocity and her need for Sethe is limitless, she becomes a parody of Sethe's own possessiveness:

> Then it seemed to Denver the thing was done: Beloved bending over Sethe looked the mother, Sethe the teething child, for other than those times when Beloved needed her, Sethe confined herself to a corner chair. The bigger Beloved got, the smaller Sethe became; the brighter Beloved's eyes, the more those eyes that used never to look away became slits of sleeplessness. Sethe no longer combed her hair or splashed her face with water. She sat in the chair licking her lips like a chastised child while Beloved ate up her life, took it, swelled up with it, grew taller on it. And the older woman yielded it up without a murmur. (250)

The passage clearly delineates the vampirish nature of all-possessive love, its self-aggrandizement and lack of care for the ostensibly loved object. Sethe's simultaneous need to be with her lost daughter and her need to be mothered—the sorest points of her difficult history—make her vulnerable to the relentless ghost.

In this emergency, Denver calls on her latent capabilities and becomes a nurturing mother to Sethe. The preparation for this transformation, which occurs soon after Beloved's arrival, reiterates the need for mother-daughter and grandmother-granddaughter communication of person and tribal history. In retelling the tale of her own birth, Denver clearly becomes a figurative mother: "So she anticipated the questions by giving blood to the scraps her mother and grandmother had told her—and a heartbeat. The monologue became, in fact, a duet as they lay down together, Denver nursing Beloved's interest like a lover whose pleasure was to overfeed the loved" (79). The confusion of maternal and romantic imagery, in addition to the unhealthy implications of "overfeed," reveals Denver's vulnerabilities as well as her potential.

In becoming the creative teller of her own story rather than a passive listener, Denver feels her potential to become a mother while simultaneously affirming her status as daughter. Her ambivalence about this story demonstrates the potential of Sethe's motherhood to become the destroying "dedication" of *Meridian*'s Mrs. Hill: "She loved it because it was all about herself; but she hated it too because it made her feel like a bill was owing somewhere and she, Denver, had to pay it. But who she owed or what to pay it with eluded her" (77). In this telling, however, she has a new vision and consequently an important insight: "Denver began to see what she was saying and not just to hear it: there is this nineteen-year-old slave girl—a year older than herself—walking through the dark woods to get to her children." (77). In the midst of the conflict between her narcissism and her feeling of obligation, Denver realizes for the first time that the heroine-Sethe—the mother of three children, with the birth of a fourth imminent—is close to her own age. Denver's identification does not shift from herself-as-infant to character-Sethe, but its wavering shows her potential for assuming responsibility when necessary.

Denver's eventual dual mother/daughter identity and the necessity of being mothered in order to be a good daughter resolve an apparent paradox. In her first foray out of the yard, Denver goes to the woman who taught in her school, Mrs. Jones. Mrs. Jones has both raised several of her own children and, in answer to the favors that her light skin has brought her, nurtured the most despised children in her community. Mrs. Jones's verbal caress, "Oh, baby," paradoxically initiates Denver's maturity: "[Denver] did not know it then, but it was the word 'baby,' said softly and with such kindness, that inaugurated her life in the world as a woman" (248). Baby Suggs's name likewise incorporates her identities as daughter, mother, and wife, a point reiterated when Denver notes another of her relational identities by referring to her as "Grandma Baby" (96). Only by remembering one's history as a loved daughter (or experiencing such care as an adult as in Sethe's case) and excavating history for empowering female models can one become a complete woman.

To mother Sethe efficaciously and prevent Beloved from starving her, Denver must be able to leave the yard in which she has spent most of her life. To do so, she must replace Sethe's idea of mothering with another, less restrictive definition. When she needs the idea, she hears the voice of her grandmother, Baby Suggs, now dead for several years:

> Baby Suggs laughed, clear as anything. "You mean I never told you nothing about Carolina? About your daddy? You don't remember nothing about how come I walk the way I do and about your mother's feet, not to speak of her back? I never told you all that? Is that why you can't walk down the steps? My Jesus my."
> But you said there was no defense.
> "There ain't."
> Then what do I do?
> "Know it, and go on out the yard. Go on." (244)

Not wanting Sethe to have had a history earlier than her own existence (another manifestation of possessiveness), Denver had never wanted to listen to these stories; now they propel her into adulthood. Emphasizing preparedness rather than protection, Baby Suggs's method of mothering promotes, through historical examples, the same self-valuing and self-reliance as her preaching. History is thus to be kept available, useful to the present, but not dominant. Denver has grim occasion to act on Baby Suggs's ideas of motherhood, for the destructive Beloved-Sethe dyad is beyond her influence; she can earn food for her mother, but she cannot keep her safe from Beloved's psychic depredations.

The house is thus deadlocked, the battle between Beloved and Denver for Sethe's life evenly balanced. Into this stalemate come the women of the community. Sethe's household has been officially isolated since she refused to repudiate her murder of Beloved; unofficially, the isolation began when Baby Suggs gave a party to celebrate the freedom of Sethe and the children, twenty-eight days after their arrival. The community loves Baby Suggs, enjoys the party, but considers it somehow "too much." The community withdraws in surly fashion, and their failure to warn Baby Suggs of the white men's approach leads directly to Sethe's murder of her child. To some extent an allegory of destructive class divisions within the African-American community, this incident begins the isolation from much of the everyday present which makes the ghost's initial, unfleshed presence a possibility.

The community's presence and participation liberate Sethe, but not by the physical and quasi-spiritual means that it had planned. Having long ago judged Sethe as lacking, thirty women nevertheless rally when they hear that a ghostly daughter has returned to whip her. These women tolerate a certain degree of historical persistence in the present but reject the past's attempt to enslave the present; as Ella thinks, "She didn't mind a little communication between the two worlds, but this was an invasion" (257). When the group arrives at 124 Bluestone, they see, instead of Sethe and Beloved, their own earlier selves frolicking at Baby Suggs's party, a reminder of their partial responsibility for Beloved's death. Probably each of them has committed some deed analogous to what has isolated Sethe, and they collectively disavow the extremity of Sethe's punishment. Ella, for example, remembers starving her child conceived in rape, and "the idea of that pup coming back to whip her too set her jaw working" (259). The product of those individual jaws working, a holler picked up and amplified by the noisy crowd, frees Sethe by joining her with her ancient heritage.

Ella's call and the female crowd's response restores the primacy of African and African-American women's knowledge despite the obliterative overlay of European cognitive structures. Traditional European male structures depend on the word and assume a correspondence between language and that represented by it, a concept flatly stated in Genesis: "In the beginning was the word, and the word was God." *Beloved* explicitly refutes this crucial European text. When the women holler, "They stopped praying and took a step back to the beginning. In the beginning there were no words. In the beginning was the sound, and they all knew what that sound sounded like" (259). Given the constraints of nineteenth-century life for African-American women, this group must be composed of mothers; "the beginning" thus revoices not only God's creation of the world in Genesis but women's creation of other life, the sounds accompanying birth. This sound, then, is tied to Nan and Sethe's Ma'am's lost language, as it is to the chain gang songs created by the call of Hi Man and the response of Paul D and his companions as they struggle under ghastly oppression: "They sang it out and beat it up, garbling the words so they could not be understood; tricking the words so their syllables yielded up other meanings"

(108). Nan and Sethe's Ma'am presumably use an African language; the group of women here create a language from the sounds that women know. The chain gang, on the other hand, subverts the European word, converts it to a dialect expressive of African-American experience. Denver preserves Sethe's life until the female community marshals the resources to fight an alien system of representation. Herein lies the answer to Paul D's query as to whether the manhood of Sweet Home's black men lay in the white slavemaster's say-so—"Was he naming what he saw or creating what he did not?" (220)—and to Sethe's bitter memory of Schoolteacher's training his nephew to write down her human and animal traits in different columns. The word does not define. The word is neither alpha nor omega, only an imposition.[8] Beyond the word lies the tribal memory, thus the core of communal and individual identity, which is always in flux. Released from the tyranny of static definition, Sethe can exchange one conception of motherhood for another that is more responsive to social conditions of freedom.

Denver has anticipated Sethe here, both in using Baby Suggs's suggestions and in realizing her own value as the result of being nurtured as a treasured daughter. When Nelson Lord tells Denver to take care of herself, "It was a new thought, having a self to look out for and preserve . . . she heard it as though it were what language was made for" (252). Paul D offers Sethe this same sustenance after Beloved's departure: "You your best thing, Sethe. You are" (273). Sethe, having experienced considerably more brutality than Denver and considerably less mothering, entertains the idea without being able to embrace it immediately; the penultimate chapter ends with her response, "Me? Me?" (273).

Although Morrison's heroine is not the artist emergent of Walker's *Meridian* or the blues artist of Jones's *Corregidora*, *Beloved* concerns the roles of African-American artists, both male and female. Morrison shows the communal process of creation at work through storytelling. Stories exist to preserve historical memory, to embellish historical facts so that the meanings rather than the details persist. Telling the story of one's experience both relieves the teller and sustains the listener, who frequently retells and embellishes the story for another audience, as Denver tells Beloved the tale of her birth. Thus, Sethe feels relieved when she can tell her murdered daughter the whole story of her death though, of course, Beloved knows the events already. Sethe stutters until she meets her loving husband Halle; she bites her tongue when Schoolteacher's nephews sexually abuse her. In telling stories to Beloved and Paul D, she gains her voice, another voice to add to the female community's holler, when necessary. Stories change as the teller's understanding changes, and collectively, these stories constitute tribal historical knowledge. When Paul D wants to commit himself emotionally to Sethe, "He wants to put his story next to hers" (273); together the survivors of Sweet Home decide the meanings of their experiences and construct the meanings of their futures.

Denver's creative process in embellishing Sethe's version of the escape and traumatic birth is analogous to what Morrison describes as the genesis of *Beloved*. After doing considerable research on slavery, Morrison happened on a story about a fugitive slave who had killed one of her own children; instead of doing further research, she imagined the story of *Beloved*. In similar fashion, Sherley Anne Williams's "Author's note" to *Dessa Rose* reveals that Williams found two quite separate accounts of a pregnant slave leading a revolt from a coffle and a white woman who was rumored to have sheltered slaves. By bringing them together, she created *Dessa Rose*. If storytelling is conceived of as telling the tale to relieve a particular teller and to sustain a particular audience, then clearly different stories are required at different times. The last chapter of *Beloved*, with its twice-repeated "It was not a story to pass on" may be somewhat less puzzling in this light. Sethe, Paul D, Denver, and the rest of the community forget Beloved "like a bad dream. . . . Remembering seemed unwise" (274). But first, "They made up their tales, shaped and decorated them, those that saw her that day on the porch" (274). For them, the creation and telling of stories has been a needed exorcism; submersion in this part of history nearly killed Sethe. Another generation—ours—needs immersion in this precise piece of history, and so Morrison has told it. The final turn on the refrain, "This is not a story to pass on," demonstrates the inherent flexibility of language; it says simultaneously that the story should not be told and that the story will not die. Perhaps this is not a story to be told but a story to be retold. *Beloved* can be only one version, and its form is fixed in print. The essence of storytelling is not replication through the accurate repetition of passing on but transformative development according to the griot's and the audience's changing needs. In this time and place, Morrison implies, every African-American mother needs historical strength imaged as a mother, even when it must be her daughter.

Afterword
On Getting the Whole Story

THE TWENTIETH-CENTURY TRADITION of African-American women's novels includes enormous variety in its presentations of black women's heritages and identities. The novels cover a wide expanse of time and geographic location while simultaneously exploring a range of age and class in their heroines. Through female characters in their teens and their sixties, the tradition encompasses slavery in Brazil and the United States; it ranges from the freedom of rural American Reconstruction to the post-colonial Caribbean to the urban, corporate United States of the 1980s. The range of the tradition grows from an insistence that claiming heritage cannot be merely an abstract intellectual absorption of general facts about the diaspora. Instead, it must be grounded in particulars—a local, familial, and emotional process that is distinct for each heroine.

This concern with history's effects on female identity links works from the Harlem Renaissance to the 1980s. *Kindred* makes literal the necessary confrontation with history by showing a contemporary heroine time traveling to experience slavery. Like other heroines of this tradition, she encounters specifically female history: on the one hand, definitions of the female body as sexualized property during slavery or colonialism, vulnerability to racist stereotypes of black femininity and sexuality, primary responsibility for nurturance of children under impossible circumstances; on the other, the examples of coping, of economic and spiritual survival.

The costs of acknowledging historical oppression of this magnitude are figured in *Kindred* by Dana's loss of her left arm. The costs of not acknowledging it are the subject of early novels by Nella Larsen and Jessie Fauset and revoicings in the 1970s by Gloria Naylor and Toni Morrison. While Larsen's *Quicksand* shows the conditions that make passing—for either white or black—a necessity, Larsen's *Passing* and Fauset's *Plum Bun* concentrate on passing itself. Those who choose to pass by denying their history have extremely fragile self-definitions. They are vulnerable both to exposure and to an internal, corroding sense of their alienation from what they consciously or unconsciously value. The later novels image separation from the nurturant community in other ways, with class as a primary element. Through their portraits of the dismal fates of those who separate themselves from their pasts, both their own and that of their communities, these writers establish the necessity of coming to terms with history as a premise.

Other writers explore a variety of means of identifying and exploring formative elements of historical events, among them contact with an ancestral figure, folklore, and travel. This confrontation has both liberating and confining possibilities for the individual. If the heroine becomes overwhelmed by the horrors of the past, she may be, in effect, trapped in history, dysfunctional in her present. Contemporary novels such as Gayl Jones's *Corregidora* and Toni Morrison's *Beloved* show this problem in two different forms. *Corregidora* shows its heroine's entrapment in history as the cause of her personal stasis; *Beloved* deals with a Reconstruction heroine caught in her own personal past—the contemporary reader's historical past. As the earlier novels tended to show failures, later novels frequently show partial, painfully won victories. If the heroine can identify sources of strength within her ancestors and within herself, she can emerge from the confrontation with a tough, realistic definition of self-in-a-chosen-community.

Several critics, Christian and Willis among them, have pointed out this concern with community as an identifying marker of African-American women's novels. Afrocentric conceptions enlarge the European understandings of community, which is seen as the extended family or people living in the immediate area, to include ancestral spirits; they extend community through time as well as space. Although community is necessary to survival, neither the immediate nor the larger historical community is simply nurturant. The visible community includes examples of betrayal, viciousness, and jealousy, whether it is the slaves in *Kindred*, the two island classes of *The Chosen Place, the Timeless People*, or the free and fugitive slave mix of *Beloved*. Just as the immediate community sometimes fails its members, so the history of the tribe sometimes entraps. The sheer horror of oppression can overwhelm, as can the historically generated definitions of women's social roles which are so inappropriate to the present day.

For women, the construction of a self-in-community raises particularly difficult problems. A community in constant peril may absorb all available energy, leaving the self defined only as a giver, not as a receiver. In literary history, motherhood is often the relationship through which this danger is articulated. Educated, skilled, intellectually aware of her plight, *Quicksand's* Helga Crane does not leave the rural south and her certain impending death because she cannot leave her children. *Corregidora, Linden Hills,* and *Beloved* critique different aspects of the role of motherhood. *Corregidora* shows that "motherhood" becomes synonymous with "womanhood" so that Ursa loses her identity with her womb. *Linden Hills* shows generations of women in the Nedeed family destroyed by the various Luthers' imposition of just such a definition. As *The Bluest Eye* explored the damage of internalized racist definitions, so *Beloved* delves deep into the process by which internalized, rigid definitions of motherhood threaten a woman's life. Motherhood per se does not damage Avey Johnson in *Praisesong for the Widow* although unexpected pregnancy and the responsibility for children destroy the Johnsons' connections to their heritage. Although the role of motherhood is seen as a vampire, the children in these novels sometimes nurture their mothers, particularly Marion in *Praisesong for the Widow* and Denver in *Beloved*.

A second expression of the theme shows the integrity of the female self as it is threatened by nurturant responsibilities to the community as a whole rather than by motherhood. In *The Chosen Place, the Timeless People,* for instance, Merle temporarily leaves communal responsibilities in Bournehills for a compelling individual need—reestablishing contact with her child. *Kindred* shows the sharpest conflict between individual female and communal needs; to remain useful to the slave community, Dana must be willing to submit to the master's rape. *Meridian* participates in both representations by showing that the wider community can be all-consuming and that the family is inevitably so. Not surprisingly, both *The*

Chosen Place and *Meridian* end with the heroines outward bound, on solitary quests for a different self-definition.

Of the novels centering on childless women, many feature artists whose vocation allows the novelists to depict a nurturant community function without the constraining demands of the role of mother. (Although there may be exceptions—Morrison's Pauline Breedlove is a thwarted artist, and Marshall's depiction of Avatara as griot might qualify—African-American women's novels have not generally depicted women as simultaneously mothers and artists, Alice Walker's "In Search of Our Mother's Gardens" notwithstanding.) The specific artistic expression varies considerably. In *Kindred*, Butler uses a print artist, a writer; Fauset, a graphic artist in *Plum Bun*; Hurston, a storyteller in *Their Eyes Were Watching God*; Marshall, a dancer in *Brown Girl, Brownstones*; Jones, a blues singer in *Corregidora*. (Part of the ominous prognosis for *Tar Baby*'s Jadine lies in Morrison's shift from depicting an active if suppressed creativity, in Pauline Breedlove and Sula, to Jadine's passive role as fashion model; *Linden Hills* shows the same movement toward increasing passivity in its three generations of Nedeed mothers.) Even in those novels without a designated artist, art remains important; Meridian Hill, for instance, considers her role to be the preservation of tribal art for a less violent time.

The role of art in this tradition unifies the seemingly disparate themes of motherhood and orality. Mother love physically and emotionally nurtures individuals; oral art analogously sustains the tribe. The written works of literate daughters incorporate the oral ancestral voices of tribal mothers. These novels exist to be read, and their very existence gives an example of their shared thematic insistence on continuity and change: they incorporate both historical knowledge and mode (orality) while changing their message and mode sufficiently to offer stories accessible and useful in the present.

Figurations of black female creativity concentrate, though not exclusively, on orality because oral narratives communicate histories, both of the tribe and of its constituting individuals. The female character's ability to construct and tell her own story, in a version that she can bear to speak and to finish, is frequently the measure of her wholeness. Often a heroine's mature narrative requires missing information or perspective that can be supplied by a fuller version of her mother's or mother surrogate's story. The extent of history's authority over a particular woman's life (Janie's dilemma) also puzzles Ursa in *Corregidora*. Here her mother's story gives her added information that allows her to intuit the missing parts of Gram and Great Gram's stories. This fuller, more honest history then empowers her to risk a more honest version of her own story.

The intricate connections, sometimes determinative, between artistic patterns and lived experience appear often in this tradition. In *Plum Bun*, Angela Murray bases her early commitments on the sentimental novel's romance plot; Gram and Great-Gram in *Corregidora* and Nanny in *Their Eyes* unconsciously seek to force the heroines to re-create ancestral patterns in their lives. In *Meridian*, the antagonist of prescriptive historically based narrative is imaged in both individual and social terms; Mrs. Hill's stories set standards of motherhood that are impossible for Meridian, and Meridian dreams three times of herself as the heroine of a novel that can only end with her death. At the same time, novels like *The Chosen Place, the Timeless People* insist on the necessity to preserve historical realities through communal rituals.

Historical narratives do not offer detailed patterns to live by but, instead, strategies appropriate to particular circumstances. Clearly, having a range of strategies to choose from enhances the individual's abilities to survive and prosper. Particular historical narratives cannot serve as blueprints for present action, however. In this tradition, writers portray attempts to force stories to be directly prescriptive as oppressive (Nanny, Gram, and Great Gram). At the same time, they show the temptation to accept these prescriptions as maneuvers to evade the necessary pain of constructing one's own story.

Whether a narrative is enslaving or liberating depends to some extent on how it is constructed, whether its form and content have rigidified into dogma or whether teller and audience can reshape and reinterpret. *Their Eyes Were Watching God* reiterates the nurturant possibilities of participatory storytelling on several levels. Janie preserves the ancestral narrative (Nanny's story) but contextualizes it to refuse its prescriptions; symbolically, she acknowledges history, uses it as part of her own story, but refuses to let it dictate the plot. For dyads—Tea Cake and Janie, Janie and Pheoby—collaborative construction reconciles and inspires; on the collective level—Eatonville's lying contests, the Belle Glades community after Tea Cake's death—it both reconciles and celebrates.

The responsibility to tell and retell discovered stories characterizes these works. Again, *Kindred* offers the paradigm. Although Dana's last words in the novel are "If we told anyone about this, anyone at all, they wouldn't think we are so sane" (264), the novel's viewpoint is first-person retrospective—generally first-person plural retrospective, in line with its emphasis on broadening definitions of tribe. Like Avatara Johnson, Janie, and Denver, Dana becomes a griot.

African-American women's novels, then, with their detailed examinations of storytelling and the storytellers' responsibilities, have a particular implication for the academy. In a literal sense, most teachers of literature must accept the role of griot. Surveys, theme courses, and studies in the development of a genre claim to tell an authoritative narrative of cultural development. Disclaimers, such as "this is a sampling," will have little effect on students; they will construct their narratives primarily from what is offered. Until very recently, the "plot" of the historical tale as presented by literature departments was covertly oppressive through its omission of narratives by minorities; its construction was often overtly oppressive, shutting off all collaboration in favor of a supremely authoritative teller, the professor. This extremely limited narrative occluded the tribal histories of all but a small, powerful band, and even it was falsified by being out of context. Students from the excluded groups lost not only pride in tribal achievement but access to written tribal strategies of resistance. In the last twenty years, feminist pedagogies of sharing power in the classroom and rediscovered texts by excluded groups now challenge this model. Many teachers use both Ursa's and Janie's solutions for reshaping historical narratives to the needs of the present—additional content, recontextualizing. The continuing "canon wars" illustrate, however, academic resistance to adaptation of the historical narrative.

Whether they hail from political left, right, or center, critics of American education agree that our students know almost no American history. Certainly, then, they know little of American histories. They know only bits of the universalist, melting-pot version of the country; and they know even fewer stories consciously inflected by race, ethnicity, and gender. Like other meta-narratives in these postmodernist times, the dream of the monomyth is now dead, but deluded academic Frankensteins may still try to reinvigorate its corpse. The academy must continue to explore specific traditions for some time before generalizations on the scale of "the American novel" will again be tenable. "Difference" may be in fashion or out; the specific vocabulary of exploration matters little. What does matter is that the records of historical voices be played, listened to, and incorporated into new songs. Like too many others, I never heard my grandparents' songs of themselves. The task of the literary academy in our time is to ransack the archives and the attics, to listen in the nursing homes and the streets, and to restore finally these voices to the human chorus.

NOTES

CHAPTER 1

1. For a theory concerning the relationships of these presences, see Hortense Spillers, "*Chosen Place, Timeless People:* Some Figurations on the New World," *Conjuring: Black Women, Fiction, and Literary Tradition*, eds. Marjorie Price and Hortense Spillers (Bloomington: Indiana University Press, 1985), 151–75.

CHAPTER 2

1. Susan Willis has recognized Octavia Butler's 1979 *Kindred* as a metaphor for experience of the past though her notice is limited to the briefest of mentions.

2. For a summary of feminist critiques of the androcentric model of self-in-isolation, the subsequent need to go beyond women-centered psychologists' postulates of self-in-relation dyads, and the possibilities of self-in-community, see Gillespie and Kubitschek, "Who Cares? Women-Centered Psychology in *Sula*."

3. The only two white women in *Kindred*, Kevin's sister Carol and Rufus's mother Margaret, are one-dimensional characters who never move toward identification of a self, either in isolation or in community. (Carol, indeed, never appears in the novel; the reader hears her story in a one-page, second-hand summary from her brother.) Instead, they accept definitions of the self-reliant on patriarchal marriages and property ownership. Both women clearly reject chances to form supportive alliances with other women in order to form or preserve destructive ties with men.

Carol's story, told very briefly by Kevin, introduces the theme of white women who choose to separate from African-American women, of capitulation to racial bigotry as the price of emotional and economic security under patriarchy. Carol's apparently close high school friendship with an African-American girl includes plans to attend college together. Because Carol and her friend are fat, they experience rejection from their peers. When Carol becomes a dental technician, she stops looking for peers and marries her first dentist-employer, gradually absorbing his racial bigotry, which she at first mocked. When Kevin and Dana marry, Carol forbids them to enter her house.

Through Margaret Weylin, *Kindred* shows the historical sources of Carol's decision. As Sarah heatedly recalls, Margaret badgers Tom Weylin to sell Sarah's three sons to buy "new furniture, new china dishes, fancy things you see in that house now. What she had was good enough for Miss Hannah, and Miss Hannah was a real lady. Quality. But it wasn't good enough for white-trash Margaret" (95). Margaret's motivations remain somewhat unclear here, but Sarah's emphasis on "new" may imply either a desire for an identity clearly different from Hannah's or an attempt to live up to the class standard that Hannah has set. (Ironically, given her treatment of Sarah, her personality collapses entirely when she loses sickly twins soon after birth.)

Margaret Weylin's dealings with black women are mediated through relationships with men, either her jealousy of her husband's choice of rape victim, or her thwarted desire for another white man who has chosen a black lover, Kevin. As desperate as Carol is for emotional commitment, she nevertheless cuts herself off from any possible source of emotional sustenance other than that provided by her son. Using the pretext of Christian objection to Dana's sleeping with Kevin, Margaret attempts to drive Dana from her house, an echo of Carol's rejection. Carol and Margaret acquiesce to, and actually promote, the separation of women which is required by patriarchy.

4. Yvonne Singh-O'Faolain, a graduate student in Africana Studies at Cornell University, first drew my attention to this pattern.

5. Deconstructionist critics might argue that scraps of the past, particularly if they exist as scraps of text, are a part of actual experience. *Kindred*'s response to the conflation of reading and living as the same kind of experience is implied by the changes in Dana as she first reads about the role of a slave, then playacts it, and finally experiences a lashing.

CHAPTER 3

1. This "context" always mitigates particular events in *Their Eyes Were Watching God*. In an article that justly chastises several critics, including me, for our identification of Janie's silence as her acceptance of being beaten, Michael Awkward argues that Tea Cake has important sexist traits in addition to violence toward women. He focuses on Tea Cake's "Ah need no assistance to help me feed mah woman. From now on, you gointuh eat whutever mah money can buy yuh and wear de same. When Ah ain't got nothin', you don't get nothin' " (191) to argue that "[i]t is difficult to interpret these lines as anything other than unabashed sexism" (83). In isolation, Tea Cake's statement certainly sounds sexist. Janie has just revealed, however, her fears that she will be pauperized and abandoned by a younger husband as Annie Tyler was earlier. In this context, Tea Cake's assertion testifies to his willingness to set Janie's mind at rest: no matter what happens between them, Janie will retain her bankroll. On her return to Eatonville after his death, Janie has the same financial security that she had when she left.

CHAPTER 5

1. The African-American novel between 1939 (the end of the Renaissance) and 1970 did, of course, sometimes address the middle class. With the exception

of most of James Baldwin's works, though, it treats the subject indirectly. Ellison's *Invisible Man*, for example, does not highlight class per se, and the narrative follows a single individual's attempt to construct a coherent self. The novels of the 1970s and 1980s discussed in this chapter investigate the whole structure of the middle class as well as an individual's psychic development as part of, or as outside, that class.

2. Hazel Carby's *Reconstructing Womanhood* redefines the traditional understanding of the mulatta from an appeal to a white audience to this idea of a figure subversive of racist ideologies of separatism.

3. Cheryl Wall makes a point somewhat analogous to this in discussing the middle-class black female characters other than Clare in *Passing*: "Each of these characters, like Clare, relies on a husband for material possessions, security, identity. Each reflects and is a reflection of her husband's class status. Clare's is merely an extreme version of a situation all share" (107). One of these women, Gertrude Martin, who is married to a white man, is aware of her mixed heritage, and her situation might seem to contradict my assertion of the impossibility of synthesizing segregated histories. Her fear of having a dark child, however, bespeaks a submersion of her black heritage and the hope that, although she cannot pass, her children may.

4. In line with her emphasis on individual personality, Lay compares Henry James's *Portrait of a Lady* with *Quicksand*. In accord with my emphasis on social conditions, I would suggest that a Euro-American analogue closer in both time of publication and theme would be Edith Wharton's 1905 *The House of Mirth*.

5. Peter's relationship with Helga resembles that of Meadowes and Proctor Lewis in Ernest Gaines's "Three Men." There, Meadowes's paternalism aims to infantilize Proctor permanently.

6. The bitterness of Helga's reaction to Anderson's intended kindness may come from his diction. In asking Helga to stay at Naxos, Anderson has said, "You musn't desert us, Miss Crane" (21). The immediate shift to discussion of her family may make the term "desert" appear to be an unintended accusation.

7. In its presentation of Cholly's rape of his daughter Pecola as an act of love, Toni Morrison's *The Bluest Eye* explains: "Love is never any better than the lover. Wicked people love wickedly, violent people love violently, weak people love weakly, stupid people love stupidly, but the love of a free man is never safe" (159). Although a large number of white nineteenth-century literary artists posit love of one variety or another—Harriet Beecher Stowe's Christian love, Charles Dickens's familial love, George Eliot's and others' romantic love—in keeping with the traditions of Toomer, Chesnutt, and Jacobs, Morrison never presents love as an abstract in which individuals participate. Cholly's reaction does not, then, corrupt or distort love. Instead, the very experience of the feelings designated "love," as well as their expression, is socially determined. The emotional context can never exist outside the social context; in fact, emotional context is antecedent to social context. Love cannot in itself transcend social problems; rather than offering alternatives to society by participating in a flawed manner in a Platonic ideal, love always reflects the social context.

8. Anthony's surname, Cross, is assumed; his father's name was Hall. The pseudonym probably alludes to the Langston Hughes poem "Cross" published in *The Weary Blues* (1926).

9. Despite Euro-American biases, particularly against the oral tradition, Catherine C. Ward's "Gloria Naylor's *Linden Hills:* A Modern *Inferno,*" *Contemporary Literature* 28, no. 1 (1987): 67–81, is a useful compilation of Dantean correspondences.

10. Oddly, in an article that ascribes complete agency—and thus blameworthy responsibility for their fates—to all the novel's women, Ward mentions Willa's discovery of her face as though it were an accident rather than a quite deliberate construction.

11. Sherley Anne Williams's *Dessa Rose* offers an incisive commentary on African-American motherhood and white women's relationship to it. In order for the friendship between the African-American Dessa and the white Ruth to develop, Dessa must realize that white women are subject to the same male sexual violence as black women; Ruth must, on the other hand, reject the infantalization on which her status as upper-class white woman rests. That childishness includes a fascination with gee-gaws to enhance beauty, the resolution to remain ignorant of the slaves who provide the labor to buy these ornaments, and above all, the reliance on black women to be the eternally patient Mother who is designated "Mammy." Dessa and Ruth quarrel bitterly when Ruth refers to Mammy, meaning Dorcas, a slave who mothered her for many years. Insisting that Mammy means Dessa's own mother, Dessa points out that Ruth cannot even remember Dorcas's real name and does not know if Dorcas had children. Dorcas is dead by the time of the quarrel, but even so, giving up her fantasy of being Dorcas's child is difficult for Ruth because it forces a mature recognition that Dorcas's life was not bounded by Ruth's concerns and desires. The transformation of "Mammy" into "Dorcas" in Ruth's mind suggests a new willingness to perceive black women as individuals and as mothers of families unconnected to "the big house."

CHAPTER 6

1. If this experience of being simultaneously child and adult appears in contemporary Euro-American culture at all, it is present in psychology, the transactional analysis popularized by *Games People Play.* The different figurings in Euro-American and African-American culture bespeak their fundamental divergences. Transactional analysis shows child and adult voices within the same person. Because the adult must learn to listen and care for this still-present child within himself or herself, the concept becomes solipsistic. The African-American idea, on the other hand, situates the child and the adult in a *tribal* context: child because her ancestors persist, adult because of her own experience, mother because her children also persist.

2. The usual word for describing such entanglement, "complicity," seems inappropriate here, both in its psychoanalytic usage and its extra-psychoana-

lytic, quasi-legal implications of blame. At some point, Great Gram and Gram acquire at least a limited agency, which allows them to leave Corregidora; their narration denies any such agency and stops when they leave the former master.

3. Susan Willis, in *Specifying*, argues that "Meridian has chosen to relinquish personal and sexual relationships, which in this society cannot help but be the means and form of a woman's oppression, as a way of advancing her own struggle—and that of her loved ones—toward their liberation" (124). Freezing Meridian in one phase of an ongoing development, this interpretation overlooks the fluidity of the conception that allows Meridian to avoid martyrdom. At the end of the novel, having passed the necessity of "bearing the conflict in her soul" to Truman and perhaps thence to Anne-Marion, Meridian reclaims ordinary life—as she says earlier, visiting Hawaii or raising Dalmatians.

John Callahan, on the other hand, presumes not only an ongoing political commitment on Meridian's part but a continued dedication to the direct action that has characterized her life since her rejection by the "revolutionaries." This position also posits a manifestation of Meridian's identity as its core integrity.

4. As part of her exploration of the damage done to women's identities and personal growth by this concept of serving others as their sole duty, Carol Gilligan has noted that what masquerades as freely given service in fact becomes an insatiable demand for eternal gratitude from the recipients.

5. Sethe does, early on, consider trying to move away from the ghost. Baby Suggs discourages her, however, saying that every available house will have a similarly disruptive presence because violent history has overwhelmed them all. Baby Suggs's fatalism results in Sethe's living with a harassing guilt, for surely her feelings of responsibility would be less if she were confronted with any other reminder of the violent past. At the same time, Sethe cannot simply escape from her action (that is, the ghost might follow her); she must re-imagine her present self and duties, her relationship to the past, in order to lay the ghost.

6. Sethe's action here recalls Pilate's defiant assertion over Hagar's coffin, "And she was loved." Racism can, Morrison has shown in *The Bluest Eye*, damage African-American women past valuing themselves or their daughters. More frequently, however, the mothers and grandmothers of girls rise to their defense by assuring them that they deserve and receive love.

7. The intensity of Sethe's desire is similar to Miranda's in Gloria Naylor's *Mama Day*. That Miranda receives her solace via dream contact with Sapphira, an incarnation of the Great Mother, while Sethe receives hers awake, from a living daughter, testifies to the differences between the two visions. In Naylor's presentation, the mythic realm offers powerful sustenance to the unconscious seeker; in Morrison's depiction, balm comes or, sometimes, does not come from the immediate members of one's family—which one has helped to shape—and community.

8. Margaret Homans argues in "Her Very Own Howl" that several women's novels of the 1970s "have accepted the necessity for representation, while

undercutting the premises of representation in the act of depicting various anxieties about its implications for women," thus achieving "an 'ambiguously non-hegemonic' structure" (205). In her view, these novels combine the appropriative strategies typical of American feminist thinking and the strategies of rejecting language-as-logos characteristic of French feminism.

What emerges, however, is not triumphant. In Morrison's *Sula*, for example, Nel's final cry "exemplifies the paradox of separatism in language: what finally expresses her woman-identified self is of necessity nonrepresentational" (193). Further, "Nel's referentless cry closes the novel with an image of women's language that radically questions the compatibility of genuine female self-expression (to say nothing of literal or lyrical discourse)" (194). Morrison's *Beloved* seems in these terms far more optimistic. If the women's sounds are not directly representational of female selves, they express a collective memory of a primally nurturant and protective force that is simultaneously invoked and incarnated to protect an individual woman, Sethe.

WORKS CITED

Awkward, Michael. " 'The inaudible voice of it all': Silence, Voice, and Action in *Their Eyes Were Watching God.*" In *Studies in Black American Literature.* Vol. III. Eds. Joe Weixlmann and Houston A. Baker, Jr. Greenwood, Fla.: Penkevill, 1988. Pp. 57–110.

————. *Inspiriting Influences.* Gender and Culture Series. Eds. Carolyn C. Heilbrun and Nancy K. Miller. New York: Columbia University Press, 1989.

Bakerman, Jane S. "Failures of Love: Female Initiation in the Novels of Toni Morrison." *American Literature* 52, no. 4 (1981): 541–63.

Bethel, Lorraine. "This 'Infinity of Conscious Pain': Zora Neale Hurston and the Black Female Literary Tradition." In *But Some of Us Are Brave.* Ed. Gloria T. Hull et al. Old Westbury, N.Y.: Feminist Press, 1982.

Blake, Susan L. *Afro-American Fiction Writers After 1955. DLB* 33. Eds. Thadious M. Davis and Trudier Harris. Detroit: Gale, 1984. Pp. 187–99.

Brown, Lloyd. "The Rhythms of Power in Paule Marshall's Fiction." *Novel* 7 (1974): 159–67.

Butler, Octavia. *Kindred.* Garden City, N.Y.: Doubleday, 1979.

Byerman, Keith. *Fingering the Jagged Grain: Tradition and Form in Recent Black Fiction.* Athens: University of Georgia Press, 1985.

Callahan, John. *In the African-American Grain.* Urbana: University of Illinois Press, 1988.

Campbell, Joseph. *The Hero with a Thousand Faces.* 1949. Reprint. Bollingen Series XVII. Princeton: Princeton University Press, 1968.

Carby, Hazel. *Reconstructing Womanhood.* New York: Oxford, 1987.

Chase, Richard. *The American Novel and Its Tradition.* Garden City, N.J.: Doubleday, 1957.

Chodorow, Nancy. *The Reproduction of Mothering: Psychoanalysis and the Sociology of Gender.* Berkeley: University of California Press, 1978.

Christ, Carol. *Diving Deep and Surfacing: Women Writers on Spiritual Quest.* Boston: Beacon Press, 1980.

Christian, Barbara. *Black Women Novelists.* Westport, Conn.: Greenwood, 1980.

————. "The Concept of Class in the Novels of Toni Morrison." *Black Feminist Criticism.* New York: Pergamon, 1985. Pp. 71–80.

————. Introduction. In *Bake-Face and Other Tales.* By Opal Palmer Adisa. Berkeley: Kelsey St. Press, 1986.

Coleman, James. "The Quest for Wholeness in Toni Morrison's *Tar Baby.*" *Black American Literature Forum* 20, nos. 1–2 (1986): 63–74.

Collier, Eugenia. "The Closing of the Circle: Movement from Division to Wholeness in Paule Marshall's Fiction." In *Black Women Writers, 1950–1980*. Ed. Mari Evans. Garden City, N.Y.: Doubleday, 1984. Pp. 295–315.

Collins, Patricia Hill. "The Social Construction of Black Feminist Thought." *Signs* 14, no. 4 (1989): 745–73.

Crossley, Robert. Introduction. In *Kindred*. By Octavia Butler. Boston: Beacon Press, 1988.

Cudjoe, Selwyn R. "Jamaica Kincaid and the Modernist Project: An Interview." *Callaloo* 12, no. 2 (1989): 396–81.

Dearborn, Mary. V. *Pocahontas's Daughters: Gender and Ethnicity in American Culture*. New York: Oxford, 1986.

Du Bois, W. E. B. *The Souls of Black Folk*. 2nd ed. Chicago: McClurg, 1903.

Ellison, Ralph. *Invisible Man*. New York: Random House, 1952.

———. "Richard Wright's Blues." In *Shadow and Act*. 1953. Rpt. New York: Signet, 1966. Pp. 89–104.

Ensslen, Klaus. "Collective Experience and Individual Responsibility: Alice Walker's *The Third Life of Grange Copeland*." In *The Afro-American Novel Since 1960*. Eds. Peter Bruck and Wolfgang Karrer. Amsterdam: Grüner, 1982. Pp. 189–218.

Erickson, Peter B. "Images of Nurturance in Toni Morrison's *Tar Baby*." *CLA Journal* 28 (1984): 11–32.

Fauset, Jessie. *Plum Bun: A Novel Without a Moral*. 1928. Reprint. London: Pandora, 1985.

Feeney, Joseph, S. J. "Black Childhood as Ironic: A Nursery Rhyme Transformed in Jessie Fauset's Novel *Plum Bun*." *Minority Voices* 4, no. 2 (1980): 65–69.

Ferguson, Otis. "You Can't Hear Their Voices." *The New Republic*, 13 October 1937, 276.

Friday, Nancy. *My Mother, My Self*. New York: Dell, 1977.

Friend, Beverly. "Time Travel as Feminist Didactic in Works by Phyllis Eisenstein, Marlys Millhiser, and Octavia Butler." *Extrapolation* 23, no. 1 (1982): 50–55.

Gates, Henry Louis, Jr. *The Signifying Monkey: A Theory of Afro-American Literary Criticism*. New York: Oxford University Press, 1988.

Genovese, Eugene D. *Roll, Jordan, Roll*. 1974. Reprint. New York: Vintage, 1976.

Gilbert, Sandra, and Susan Gubar. *The Madwoman in the Attic: The Woman Writer and the Nineteenth-Century Literary Imagination*. New Haven: Yale University Press, 1979.

Giles, James R. "The Significance of Time in Zora Neale Hurston's *Their Eyes Were Watching God*." *Negro American Literature Forum* 6 (1972): 52–53, 60.

Gillespie, Diane, and Missy Dehn Kubitschek. "Who Cares? Women-Centered Psychology in *Sula*," *Black American Literature Forum* 24 (1990): 21–48.

Gilligan, Carol. *In a Different Voice*. Cambridge, Mass.: Harvard University Press, 1982.

Hemenway, Robert. *Zora Neale Hurston: A Literary Biography*. Urbana: University of Illinois Press, 1977.

Hite, Molly. "Romance, Marginality, Matrilineage: Alice Walker's *The Color Purple* and Zora Neale Hurston's *Their Eyes Were Watching God*." *Novel* 22, no. 3 (1989): 257–73.

Homans, Margaret. "Her Very Own Howl." *Signs* 9, no. 2 (1983): 186–205.

Howard, Lillie P. "A Lack Somewhere: Nella Larsen's *Quicksand* and the Harlem Renaissance." In *The Harlem Renaissance Re-Examined*. Ed. Victor A. Kramer. Georgia State Literature Studies 2. New York: AMS, 1987. Pp. 223–33.

Hurston, Zora Neale. *Their Eyes Were Watching God*. Urbana: University of Illinois Press, 1978.

Jones, Gayl. *Corregidora*. 1975. Reprint. Boston: Beacon Press 1986.

Jones, Leroi. *Blues People: Negro Music in White America*. New York: Morrow, 1963.

Jordan, June. "Notes Toward a Black Balancing of Love and Hatred." *Civil Wars*. Boston: Beacon Press, 1981.

Kalb, John D. "The Anthropological Narrator of *Their Eyes Were Watching God*." *Studies in American Fiction* 16 (1988): 169–80.

Kapai, Leela. "Dominant Themes and Technique in Paule Marshall's Fiction." *CLA Journal* 16 (1972): 49–59.

Kilson, Marion. "The Transformation of Eatonville's Ethnographer." *Phylon* 33 (1972): 112–19.

Larsen, Nella. *Quicksand* and *Passing*. 1928, 1929. Reprint. Ed. Deborah McDowell. Modern Women Writers Series. New Brunswick, N.J.: Rutgers University Press, 1986.

Lay, Mary M. "Parallels: Henry James's *The Portrait of a Lady* and Nella Larsen's *Quicksand*." *CLA Journal* 20, no. 4 (1977): 475–86.

Lee, Dorothy H. "The Quest for Self: Triumph and Failure in the Works of Toni Morrison. In *Black Women Writers, 1950–1980*. Ed. Mari Evans. Garden City, N.Y.: Doubleday, 1984. Pp. 346–60.

McCluskey, John Jr. "And Called Every Generation Blessed: Theme, Setting, and Ritual in the Works of Paule Marshall." In *Black Women Writers, 1950–1980*. Ed. Mari Evans. Garden City, N.Y.: Doubleday, 1984. Pp. 316–34.

McCredie, Wendy J. "Authority and Authorization in *Their Eyes Were Watching God*." *Black American Literature Forum* 16 (1982): 25–28.

McDowell, Deborah. "New Directions for Black Feminist Criticism." In *The New Feminist Criticism*. Ed. Elaine Showalter. New York: Pantheon, 1985. Pp. 186–99.

———, ed. Introduction. In *Quicksand* and *Passing*. By Nella Larsen. Modern Women Writers Series. New Brunswick, N.J.: Rutgers University Press, 1986.

McKay, Nellie. "An Interview with Toni Morrison." *Contemporary Literature* 24 (1983): 413–29.

Marshall, Paule. *Brown Girl, Brownstones*. 1959. Reprint. Old Westbury, N.Y.: Feminist Press, 1981.

———. *The Chosen Place, the Timeless People.* 1969. Reprint. New York: Random House, 1984.

———. "From the Poets in the Kitchen." *Reena and Other Stories.* Old Westbury, N.Y.: Feminist Press, 1983. Pp. 1–12.

———. *Praisesong for the Widow.* 1983. Reprint New York: Dutton, 1984.

Morrison, Toni. *Beloved.* New York: Knopf, 1987.

———. *The Bluest Eye.* New York: Washington Square, 1970.

———. *Song of Solomon.* New York: New American Library, 1977.

———. *Tar Baby.* New York: Knopf, 1981.

Naylor, Gloria. "Famous First Words." *New York Times Book Review,* 2 June 1985, 52.

———. *Linden Hills.* New York: Tichnor and Fields, 1985.

———. *Mama Day.* New York: Tichnor and Fields, 1988.

———, and Toni Morrison. "A Conversation." *The Southern Review* 21 (1985): 567–93.

O'Neale, Sondra. "Race, Sex, and Self: Aspects of *Bildung* in Select Novels by Black American Women Novelists." *Melus* 9, no. 4 (1982): 25–37.

Pratt, Annis. *Archetypal Patterns in Women's Fiction.* Madison: University of Wisconsin Press, 1981.

Raglan, Fitzroy Richard Somerset. *The Hero.* 1935. Reprint. New York: New American Library, 1979.

Schneider, Deborah. "A Search for Selfhood: Paule Marshall's *Brown Girl, Brownstones.*" In *The Afro-American Novel Since 1960.* Eds. Peter Bruck and Wolfgang Karrer. Amsterdam: Gruner, 1982. Pp. 53–73.

Schultz, Elizabeth A. "The Insistence upon Community in the Contemporary Afro-American Novel." *College English* 41, no.2 (1979): 170–84.

Scruggs, Charles. "The Nature of Desire in Toni Morrison's *Song of Solomon.*" *Arizona Quarterly* 38, no. 4 (1982): 311–35.

Showalter, Elaine, ed. *The New Feminist Criticism.* New York: Pantheon, 1985.

Singh, Amritjit. *The Novels of the Harlem Renaissance.* University Park, Pa.: Pennsylvania State University Press, 1976.

Smith, Barbara. "Toward a Black Feminist Criticism." In *The New Feminist Criticism.* Ed. Elaine Showalter. New York: Pantheon, 1985. Pp. 168–85.

Spillers, Hortense. "*Chosen Place, Timeless People:* Some Figurations on the New World." In *Conjuring: Black Women, Fiction, and Literary Tradition.* Eds. Marjorie Pryse and Hortense Spillers. Bloomington: Indiana University Press, 1985. Pp. 151–75.

Stein, Karen. "*Meridian:* Alice Walker's Critique of Revolution." *Black American Literature Forum* 20, nos. 1–2 (1986): 129–41.

Stepto, Robert B. *From Behind the Veil.* Urbana: University of Illinois Press, 1979.

Stetson, Erlene. "Silence: Access and Aspiration." In *Between Women: Biographers, Novelists, Critics, Teachers, and Artists Write about Their Work on Women.*

Eds. Carol Ascher, Louise DeSalvo, and Sara Ruddick. Boston: Beacon Press, 1984. Pp. 237–51.

Sylvander, Carolyn Wedin. *Jessie Redmon Fauset*. Troy, N.Y.: Whitson, 1981.

Thornton, Hortense. "Sexism as Quagmire: Nella Larsen's *Quicksand.*" *CLA Journal* 16 (1973): 285–301.

Traylor, Eleanor W. "The Fabulous World of Toni Morrison's *Tar Baby.*" In *Confirmation: An Anthology of African American Women*. Eds. Amiri Baraka and Amini Baraka. New York: Morrow, 1983. Pp. 333–52.

Turner, Darwin. *In a Minor Chord*. Carbondale: Southern Illinois University Press, 1971.

Wade-Gayles, Gloria. *No Crystal Stair: Visions of Race and Sex in Black Women's Fiction*. New York: Pilgrim, 1984.

———. "The Truths of Our Mothers' Lives: Mother-Daughter Relationships in Black Women's Fiction." *Sage* 1, no. 2 (1984): 8–12.

Walker, Alice. "In Search of Our Mothers' Gardens." *In Search of Our Mothers' Gardens*. New York: Harcourt Brace Jovanovich, 1983. Pp. 231–43.

———. "Looking for Zora." *In Search of Our Mothers' Gardens*. New York: Harcourt Brace Jovanovich, 1983. Pp. 93–116.

———. *Meridian*. 1976. New York: Washington Square, 1977.

———. *The Third Life of Grange Copeland*. New York: Harcourt Brace Jovanovich, 1970.

———. "Zora Neale Hurston: A Cautionary Tale and a Partisan View." Introduction. In *Zora Neale Hurston: A Literary Biography*. By Robert Hemenway. Urbana: University of Illinois Press, 1977. Reprinted in *In Search of Our Mothers' Gardens*. New York: Harcourt Brace Jovanovich, 1983. Pp. 83–92.

Wall, Cheryl. "Passing for What? Aspects of Identity in Nella Larsen's Novels." *Black American Literature Forum* 20, no. 2 (1986): 97–112.

Ward, Catherine C. "Gloria Naylor's *Linden Hills*: A Modern *Inferno.*" *Contemporary Literature* 28, no. 1 (1987): 67–81.

Washington, Mary Helen. "I Sign My Mother's Name: Alice Walker, Dorothy West, Paule Marshall." In *Mothering the Mind: Twelve Studies of Writers and Their Silent Partners*. Ed. Ruth Perry. New York: Holmes & Meier, 1984. Pp. 142–63.

———. "Zora Neale Hurston: A Woman Half in Shadow." Introduction. In *I Love Myself When I Am Laughing: A Zora Neale Hurston Reader*. Ed. Alice Walker. Old Westbury, N.Y.: Feminist Press, 1979. Pp. 7–25.

Werner, Craig. *Black American Women Novelists*. Englewood Cliffs, N.J.: Salem Press, 1989.

Williams, Sherley Anne. *Dessa Rose*. New York: Morrow, 1986.

———. "Roots of Privilege: New Black Fiction." *Ms.*, June 1985, 69–72.

Willis, Susan. *Specifying*. Madison: University of Wisconsin Press, 1987.

Wright, Richard. "Between Laughter and Tears." *New Masses*, 5 October 1937, 22, 25.

INDEX

Stereotypes of women: Angel-of-the-household, 105; Cult of Woman-hood, 105; racial divergence in, 2; in literature, 10; of black women, 5, 95, 97, 134, 178. *See also* Racism, internalized images from

Stetson, Erlene, 3, 4

Stories, mothers', 77, 80–81, 84, 88, 148, 181, 182

Storytelling, 21, 53, 54, 61, 64, 67, 71, 80–85, 88–89, 121, 137, 157, 171, 175–77, 181, 182; communal, 62, 63, 70, 175; female, 66; and quest, 63, 71, 74–76. *See also* Oral narrative; Stories, mothers'

Stowe, Harriet Beecher, 187*n7*

The Street (Petry), 7, 101, 145

Suicide, 39–40, 41, 42, 76, 82–83, 84, 88, 93, 113, 117, 123, 158, 168

Sylvander, Carolyn, 105, 110

This Child's Gonna Live (Wright), 145

Thornton, Hortense, 95

Toomer, Jean, 92, 187*n7*

Trabelin' On: Journey to an Afro-Baptist Faith (Sobel), 12

Traylor, Eleanor, 136, 141

Tribe, definition of, 50–51, 152, 183, 188*n1*. *See also* Community

"The Truant" (McKay), 101

Turner, Darwin, 53

Universalism, 13, 17, 53, 183

Violence, physical, racist, 18, 27, 33, 35, 37, 72, 108, 176. *See also* Lynching; Rape

Vodun, 18, 88

Wade-Gayles, Gloria, 4, 21, 158; "The Truths of Our Mothers' Lives," 3

Walker, Alice, 4, 10, 21, 47, 53, 116, 143, 144, 145, 160, 175; **Essays:** "In Search of Our Mother's Gardens," 2–3, 116, 181; "Looking for Zora,"

53; **Characters:** Anne-Marion, 161, 189*n3;* Camara, 160; Delores, 161; Grange Copeland, 95–96; Mrs. Hill, 158, 159, 160, 172; Lynne, 163; Margaret Treasure, 163–64; Meridian Hill, 140, 155–65, 181, 189*n3;* Nelda, 160, 161; Truman Held, 157, 163, 164, 189*n3;* Wild Child, 158, 160; Miss Winter, 161, 164; **Novels:** *The Color Purple,* 47; *Meridian,* 23, 145, 146 155–65, 172, 175, 180, 181, 189*n3; The Third Life of Grange Copeland,* 6, 95; **Themes:** art, 156–57, 162; children, 158, 159, 162, 164; community, 156; identity, 158; individuality, 149, 156; motherhood as destructive role, 158–61, 163, 164; martyr-dom, 156, 158, 161, 189*n3;* mother's crucial importance, 146, 159, 162–63; politics, 156; sexuality, 163, 164

Wall, Cheryl, 95, 99, 103, 187*n3*

Ward, Catherine, 115, 188*n9–10*

Washington, Mary Helen, 2, 21, 53; "I Sign My Mother's Name," 1, 3

Werner, Craig, 53

West, Dorothy, 1; *The Living is Easy,* 2

Wheatley, Phillis, 3

Williams, Sherley Anne, 92; *Dessa Rose,* 4, 50, 139, 176, 188*n11;* "Roots of Privilege," 91

Willis, Susan, 5, 158, 159, 160, 161, 179, 185*n1,* 189*n3*

Women: black, 141; white, 94, 96; relationships between black and white, 139, 153, 185*n3,* 188*n8;* roles, historical, 28, 35, 40, 52, 107, 158, 180. *See also* Mothers, and daughters; Stereotypes

Women's culture, 12

Wright, Richard, 53; *Black Boy,* 91

Writing, theme of: in *Kindred,* 46–51, 52, 181; in *Linden Hills,* 111, 115–17, 122–25